TAILGATING, SACKS, AND SALARY CAPS

How the NFL Became the Most Successful Sports League in History

MARK YOST

KAPLAN) PUBLISHING

This publication is designed to provide accurate and authoritative information in regard to the subject matter covered. It is sold with the understanding
that the publisher is not engaged in rendering legal, accounting, or other
professional service. If legal advice or other expert assistance is required, the
services of a competent professional should be sought.

President, Kaplan Publishing: Roy Lipner
Vice President and Publisher: Maureen McMahon
Acquisitions Editor: Michael Cunningham
Development Editor: Trey Thoelcke
Senior Managing Editor: Jack Kiburz
Production Editor: Karen Goodfriend
Typesetter: Janet Schroeder
Cover Designer: Jody Billert

Library of Congress Cataloging-in-Publication Data

Yost, Mark.
  Tailgating, sacks, and salary caps / Mark Yost.
     p. cm.
  Includes index.
  ISBN-13: 978-1-4195-2600-8
  ISBN-10: 1-4195-2600-6
  1. National Football League—History. 2. Football—Economic aspects—
United States. I. Title.
  GV955.5.N35Y67 2006
  796.332'64—dc22

                                        2006014413

Kaplan Publishing books are available at special quantity discounts to use for
sales promotions, employee premiums, or educational purposes. Please call
our Special Sales Department to order or for more information at 800-621-
9621, ext. 4444, e-mail kaplanpubsales@kaplan.com, or write to Kaplan Publishing, 30 South Wacker Drive, Suite 2500, Chicago, IL 60606-7481.

DEDICATION

To "The Snake";

None of this would have happened without him.

CONTENTS

Foreword   vi
Acknowledgments   viii
Introduction   x

1. "In the Best Interest of the League": The NFL Builds Its Future on Its Past   1

2. Anything but "Free": Playing for the NFL   21

3. Any Given Sunday: How Bert Bell Built the NFL's Even Playing Field   49

4. A Perfect Team: Television and the NFL   65

5. The NFL Goes Prime Time: Monday Night Football and Mainstream Audiences   83

6. Sports Bars, Satellites, and Fantasy Football: New Media, New Markets   101

7. NFL Merchandising: The Empire's New Clothes   121

8. The Super Bowl: Who Really Wins?   139

9. Stadium Fever: Who Plays and Who Pays?   167

10. Down to the Wire: Inside the 2006 Negotiations   203

11. Super Teams, Savvy Owners, and the Future of the NFL   221

Resources   245
Index   247

FOREWORD

As a former player, president of the old AFL Players Association, and an unabashed free enterpriser, I have always been bothered by those who criticize that the NFL is somehow a "socialistic" system because it shares revenues among the league's 32 teams. In reality, nothing could be further from the truth.

Saying that it is is akin to calling Taco Bell or McDonald's a "collective" because individual franchises don't compete against one another. Rather, they work together, share best practices, and compete with other restaurant chains in a competitive marketplace.

That's the exact same business model that guided the American Football League from its inception and the NFL since the early 1960s—when Pete Rozelle, the greatest football commissioner in history, convinced owners that by working together they would most prosper.

Looking at today's NFL, it's abundantly clear that this business model has worked. In 2006 the league will take in revenues of more than $5 billion. It recently renewed the biggest television contracts in all of sports. NFL stadiums are sold out every week. The Super Bowl—another Rozelle creation—has transcended the NFL and become a sporting event like no other.

How has the NFL accomplished all this? By competing with other sports franchises—not itself—and winning in a free marketplace of ideas. The NFL, by offering a superior product, has bested its competition—the NBA, NHL, Major League Baseball, and NASCAR—and has succeeded like no other. That's not collectivism; it's capitalism.

This spirit of cooperation is not new to the NFL. It began in 1935 when Philadelphia Eagles owner Bert Bell proposed the reverse-order draft, a system that still works to this day. The idea was expanded upon in 1962 when the NFL signed its first national television broadcasting contract.

It's important to note that the NFL would never have had a national broadcast contract if New York Giants owners Jack and Wellington Mara hadn't agreed to give up their lucrative, exclusive local contracts in favor of a national contract that shared revenues equally with other teams. And even though Wellington Mara passed away in November 2005 after a valiant fight with cancer, his spirit lived on during the March 2006 labor and revenue-sharing negotiations.

Faced with its first potential labor strike in more than 20 years, the NFL owners and players ultimately looked to their own history and realized that cooperation and compromise were the best path. This cooperation was masterfully negotiated by NFL commissioner Paul Tagliabue, NFL Players Association executive director Gene Upshaw, and a handful of visionary owners that included—not coincidentally—Wellington Mara's son, John Mara. In the end, the players and owners brokered a deal that works well for everyone.

The players will have a bigger share of the NFL revenue than ever before, as well as enhanced health care and financial planning benefits. These are the elements that make this league the envy of every other.

Mark Yost has captured all of this—the history, the economics, the personalities, the NFL. I invite you to sit back, read, and learn why the NFL has become the greatest sports league in history. It's a truly fascinating and well-written story.

Jack Kemp
May 2006

ACKNOWLEDGMENTS

I first have to thank all the folks at Kaplan Publishing, who took a chance that a pretty good newspaper reporter could also write a pretty decent book. Thanks, Michael Cunningham, for letting me prove that I could. And special thanks to Lorna Gentry, the content editor who was able to step back, look at a year's labor, and move some pieces around. Her efforts made a pretty good book into a great book.

I want to thank the staff at the NFL offices in New York, without whom this book wouldn't have been possible. I particularly want to thank Susan Rothman for her insights into NFL merchandise, especially the league's focus on female fans. Thanks are due also to Greg Aiello and his media staff, who were always professional, courteous, and helpful. Across the league, I want to thank Arthur Blank, Dick Sullivan, and Sandra Van Meek of the Atlanta Falcons; Bridget Huzicka and Reid Sigmon of the Cleveland Browns; Pat Bowlen and Jim Saccomano of the Denver Broncos; Bob Harlan, John James, and Steve Klegon of the Green Bay Packers; Bob McNair, Jamey Rootes, and fellow Brooklynite Tony Wylie of the Houston Texans; Matt Birk of the Minnesota Vikings; Bob Kraft and Stacey James of the New England Patriots; John Mara, Ernie Accorsi, and Pat Hanlon of the New York Giants; Joe Banner and Bonnie Grant of the Philadelphia Eagles; Seda Atam, Larry Michael, and Karl Swanson of the Washington Redskins; and Matt Waechter of the Pro Football Hall of Fame in Canton, Ohio.

Thanks very much to Randy Williams (Sr. and Jr.) for letting me inside the world of Redskins fanatics (and Tommy Bird and Chris McDaid, two die-hard Eagles fans, for going with me on that trip and suffering through another tough loss).

Special thanks to Jonathan Wood of Expat Flying Services of Chicago, Illinois.

Bob Boyles, author of *Fifty Years of College Football*, was a great help, as was Chuck Zona, salesperson extraordinaire who offered his insights into the NFL's merchandising business. Syndicated columnist Ladd Biro helped me understand the ever-growing world of fantasy football. Sean Brown, Paul Happe, Ben Koster, Jon McDaid, and Jim Styczinski all gave a human face to the often anonymous world of online fantasy football.

Thanks to salary cap guru Al Lackner at *www.askthecommish.com* for helping me understand the NFL draft and everything else related to player salaries, as well as uber-agent Tom Condon. Thanks to Rama Yelkur and Chuck Tomkovik of the University of Wisconsin for their outstanding work on Super Bowl advertising. And thanks to University of Wisconsin economist Kevin Bahr for his excellent study of two small-market teams—the Green Bay Packers and the Milwaukee Brewers—and his analysis of the NFL and MLB salary and revenue structures.

I wouldn't have been able to unravel the economics of stadium financing without the help of some brilliant sports economists. Special thanks to St. Cloud State economics chair King Banaian (pretty smart for a Red Sox fan); Neil deMause, who was not only smart enough to write *Field of Schemes* but to settle in Midwood, Brooklyn; Phil Porter, the economist the NFL loves to hate; Art Rolnick of the Minneapolis Federal Reserve; and Allen Sanderson of the University of Chicago.

And, of course, I couldn't have done any of this without the love and support of my wonderful family, all of whom put up with far too much, far too often, for far too long. That would be my loving and supportive wife, Boo Boo, the true and forever love of my life; and my son, George, whose reward for all those nights dad was on the road was the greatest collection of NFL credentials an eight-year-old could ever have.

INTRODUCTION

If anyone wants to understand why the National Football League is such a phenomenal success, they need look no further than the 2005 playoffs. In one of the league's most exciting postseason games, the Pittsburgh Steelers (13–5) traveled to Indianapolis to play the Colts (14–3). Up until the 13th week of the season, many thought the Colts would be only the second team in NFL history to post a perfect record. But it was not to be.

Pittsburgh dominated from the start of the game, ending the third quarter with a 21–3 lead. But future Hall of Fame quarterback Peyton Manning led the Colts back, scoring 15 points in the fourth quarter. When the Steelers sacked Manning on the two-yard line with just over a minute left to play, it looked like it was all over for the Colts. But on the very next play, Steelers star running back Jerome Bettis fumbled, and the Colts picked up the ball. The only thing that kept the Colts from running it back for a touchdown, taking the lead, and completely shifting the tide of the game was a shoestring tackle by Steelers quarterback Ben Roethlisberger.

Undeterred, Manning led a masterful drive downfield. With about 20 seconds left in regulation, he turned the ball over to kicker Mike Vanderjagt, who had missed only two field goals all season and was perfect inside Indy's RCA Dome. But his 46-yard field goal attempt went wide right, ending any hope Manning had of shedding his postseason jinx. The win sent the Steelers on to play the Denver Broncos in the AFC Championship game and, eventually, to victory in Super Bowl XL in Detroit.

While most fans will remember the Bettis fumble, the tackle, the drive, and the missed field goal, the entire Colts-Steelers game produced instant highlight reel material; it was an amazing game. But what I found most remarkable about it—and all of the 2005 playoff games—is that the featured teams came from some of the NFL's smallest markets. Indeed, the four teams that advanced to the AFC and NFC Championship games were from the decidedly nonmajor metropolitan areas of Charlotte, Denver, Pittsburgh, and Seattle. The Steelers and the Seahawks, the two Super Bowl XL combatants, represent the 21st and 14th largest markets in America. This balanced competitive play on the field—in partnership with balanced economics off the field—has made the NFL the envy of every other league.

THE NFL'S 70-YEAR-OLD FORMULA FOR SUCCESS

The financial and competitive success of the NFL is no secret, and that success is tied directly to the league's revenue sharing and salary cap. This formula has helped the NFL operate with little labor unrest over the past 20 years—unlike the other three major U.S. sports leagues. The NFL's salary cap places an annual ceiling on player payrolls. While players' salaries are still the single biggest cost for every franchise, the cap keeps them manageable. The cap also works well with the league's reverse-order draft system to ensure that teams from some of the country's smallest markets—like Green Bay, Wisconsin—can compete against teams from the country's largest markets—for example, the New York Giants. As NFL commissioner Bert Bell noted when the draft system was proposed back in 1935, even the best teams couldn't fill their stadium week after week if fans knew the outcome of the game before the kickoff. Competitive play—the idea that any team can beat any other on "any given Sunday"—is what fills the stands.

The NFL maintains competitive balance off the field through its shared revenue agreement. In the early 1960s, revolutionary commissioner Pete Rozelle convinced big-market teams like the New York Giants that the best interest of the league lay in sharing their television revenues with the Green Bay Packers and other small-market teams. Since then, the NFL has expanded its successful revenue-sharing model to encompass all national contracts with the league.

As a result of its reverse-draft and shared-revenue model, the NFL is arguably the most financially successful sports franchise in the world. During the 2005 season, in addition to taking in more than $5 billion in revenue, the league renegotiated its television rights contracts with the four major networks, setting records that many on Madison Avenue thought impossible to eclipse. The NFL's financial strength and stability puts it in an enviable position—one it achieved through bold leadership and strong internal cooperation. Here are just a few of the NFL's important milestones since its 1966 merger agreement with the AFL:

- In 1970, the league signed a four-year television contract under which CBS televised all NFC games and NBC all AFC games. *Monday Night Football* was born and brought the NFL to a broad, prime-time audience.
- In 1973, the league announced that the Super Bowl was a sell-out and that the game would be televised.
- In 1978, a Louis Harris sports survey revealed that 70 percent of the nation's sports fans followed football, compared to 54 percent who followed baseball.
- In 1980, NFL regular season attendance hit 13 million, the 3rd record year in a row and the highest in the NFL's 61-year history. Stadiums reported over 92 percent of total capacity, and television stations covering the games posted record ratings.
- In the late 1980s and 1990s, a nationwide stadium building boom resulted in dramatic surges in revenues for the league

and its franchises, including the dramatic financial boon of skyboxes and associated luxury perks.

The league has continued to lead the way in expanding into new media, including cable and satellite television, satellite radio, and the Internet, helping the league further build its brand by digitizing fantasy football, a new media subset in a world all its own. But in early 2006, the NFL's financial juggernaut was at risk of coming to a screeching halt due to a dispute that divided the league along generational lines, pitting some of its oldest families against some of its newest—and most entrepreneurial—team owners.

Within the NFL, a small group of team owners had mastered the art of making money that didn't have to be tossed into the league's shared revenues. Nonshared revenues included funds from stadium-naming rights, local sponsorships, local radio and television deals, and pregame and postgame clubs. The growing local revenue stream led to a rift among NFL owners. On one side of the divide were the league's new breed of owner/entrepreneurs, including the Redskins' Daniel Snyder, the Dallas Cowboys' Jerry Jones, and Miami Dolphins owner Wayne Huizenga. These relative newcomers were pitted against older NFL families, such as the Rooneys, who own the Pittsburgh Steelers, and the Maras, who own the New York Giants.

NFL commissioner Paul Tagliabue formed a committee to look into the revenue-sharing model, but the issue proved more contentious than anyone thought. The league had hoped to have a new revenue-sharing formula worked out early in the 2005 season, but the issue dragged on. Not until the league was on the verge of entering the 2006 season without a new labor contract did the owners and the NFL Players Association, the union that represents the players, hammer out a deal—after being locked in a Dallas hotel ballroom for two days in March.

And while it took them right up until the 11th hour to reach a new labor and revenue-sharing agreement, today's NFL owners reaffirmed that the one-for-all, good-of-the-league spirit that has been key to the NFL's financial and competitive success since 1935 is still alive and well. Indeed, even the league's most entrepreneurial owners agreed that it was better for them to give up some of their locally generated revenue than to enter the 2006 season without a new labor agreement. "We were willing to make some sacrifices to get this thing done," said Dallas Cowboys owner Jones, perhaps the most vocal opponent of revenue sharing.

Snyder, the brash young owner of the Washington Redskins and Jones' ally among the high-revenue owners, was even more conciliatory. "It's really a win-win situation," he said after two tough days of negotiations in early March 2006.

"The whole idea was that no one was totally dissatisfied," said Al Davis, the outspoken, independent owner of the Oakland Raiders who once sued the league to prove that he had the right to move his team. "We had to have labor peace."

Under the labor and revenue-sharing system that was modified in March 2006, every NFL owner starts out with about $100 million a year each from national television and radio contracts, sponsorships, and shared ticket revenue from each game. Teams also receive equal portions from a 12 percent royalty on NFL merchandise. In total, about $3 billion of the league's $5.2 billion revenue stream is shared equally among teams. As a result, the Houston Texans, the team with the worst record in 2005, are benefiting from the merchandise sales of the Super Bowl XL champion Pittsburgh Steelers.

The NFL owners also agreed to extend the collective bargaining agreement (CBA) with the players by 6 years, ensuring labor peace through the 2011 season. The new contract raises the salary cap to $102 million in 2006, up from $94.5 million in 2005, and to $109 million in 2007. As a result, players will get more of the league's total revenues than ever. Finally, the owners also tweaked their revenue model to adjust for disparities. The 15 highest-revenue teams will contribute $850 million to $900 million over the next 6 years to a fund from which the lower-revenue teams can draw to help boost their revenues. In addition to settling the simmering revenue-sharing dispute among owners, the new CBA averted the possibility of a 2007 season without a salary cap and a players' strike in 2008. In short, the NFL, when push came to shove, stuck to the model that has served it so well for the past 70 years.

WHY I WROTE THIS BOOK

As a journalist, I've been covering the business of sports for over 20 years, and I knew without question that the years 2005 and 2006 represented a critical time for the NFL. The business and economic issues the league had to resolve offered a comprehensive look at the league—where it came from, how it got here, and what was at stake for the future. And this book lays it all out for you, whether you've followed the league for the past 40 years or are a new football fan.

In this book, I take a look at the NFL's humble roots and its turbulent early years, when more teams failed than survived. Here, you'll see how the NFL dueled with other upstart professional football leagues and fought hard to replace baseball as America's pastime. In fact, you'll learn how the NFL has eclipsed every other sport on the planet, thanks not just to its semisocialistic revenue-sharing agreement but also due to its tailor-made-for-television game format. I'll also give you an inside look at how the NFL operations are guided more by the rules of business than by those of the sport of football. When you read the words of NFL and team executives in this book, you might be struck by the fact that they sound like they could be CEOs of Best Buy, Home Depot, or any other highly successful, market savvy, sophisticated, customer-oriented *Fortune* 500 company.

As I researched the material for this book, I was most interested in the new breed of NFL owner and the impact of that group on the league's long-standing operational model. What I discovered—and what you'll learn within the next 11 chapters—is that the people who run the NFL and its teams fully understand the value of building a brand and providing a unique fan experience that extends far beyond any single season. This book gives you an inside look at all the business elements that make the NFL a success, including merchandising, luxury suites, tailgating, and—the most important revenue stream of all—television. I think you'll be interested in what I learned about how the league manages local and national advertising and why advertisers such as General Motors and Visa considered spending $2.5 million for a 30-second spot during Super Bowl XL a good use of their precious advertising budget. You'll also hear what sports economists have to say about stadium subsidies, tax breaks, and other "gifts" to the world's most successful sports league and its billionaire team owners. Although economists continually warn that stadium subsidies are far from the best use of increasingly scarce tax dollars, taxpayers just keep on giving to the NFL.

To find out what might lie ahead for the NFL and its teams, I've also taken a close look at some of the most successful franchises, which are run by the league's most entrepreneurial owners. My research ran the gamut, from interviewing Houston Texans owner Bob McNair, who built his wealth in the oil and gas business, to learning more about Daniel Snyder, the Washington Redskins owner who made his money in marketing and advertising and who many see as the poster boy for the 21st-century spoiled rich kid. Love 'em or hate 'em, you can't argue with what these owners are doing with their franchises as they help reform the NFL today and set the mark for how all league franchises will be run.

When you've finished this book, I think you'll thoroughly understand how the NFL developed a business model that is the envy of all other professional sports leagues. More importantly, you can stand back with me and shake your head at how a group of billionaire owners, operating sports franchises made up of millionaire players, nearly ruined it all during the winter of 2005–2006 in a tiff over a few decimal points within a multi-billion-dollar deal.

CHAPTER ONE

"IN THE BEST INTEREST OF THE LEAGUE"

THE NFL BUILDS ITS FUTURE ON ITS PAST

At the start of the 2005 season, the NFL was the envy of every other league on the planet. League revenues totaled about $5.2 billion, up from $3.6 billion in 2000. The NFL had turned its declining merchandising business into a $3.4 billion annual cash cow. And the league had just inked four new national television contracts worth a record $3.75 billion a year. But over the course of the year, the NFL faced two of the biggest financial challenges in the history of the league: It had to forge a new collective bargaining agreement with the players and, at the same time, come up with a new revenue-sharing formula that would satisfy all of the league's team owners.

To understand the gulf that had to be bridged between the owners, consider two of the key protagonists in the debate over revenue sharing. On one side was Buffalo Bills owner Ralph Wilson. One of the NFL's oldest owners, he celebrated 45 years in professional football in 2005. He is the only original American Football League owner still in his original host city. While Wilson himself has been very successful, the Bills are a different story. In

2005, the team was ranked 25th in value among the NFL's 32 teams. In terms of revenue, it was ranked 22nd.

On the other end of the spectrum was Washington Redskins owner Daniel Snyder. Considered the epitome of the new breed of entrepreneurial NFL owners, Snyder bought the Redskins in July 1999 for $800 million, the highest price ever paid for a professional sports franchise. When he bought the team, the Redskins annual revenue was $10 million less than that of the highest-grossing team in the league, the Dallas Cowboys. In just five years, Snyder had increased the team's revenue by $100 million and eclipsed the Cowboy's as the NFL's highest-revenue team.

While Wilson and other smaller, less financially successful NFL franchises claimed they couldn't compete with Snyder and a host of other high-revenue teams in the league, those teams dismissed the concern. In essence, the large-market teams seemed to be saying, "You don't have to compete with my revenues, so don't ask me to share them with you." This was the stalemate that faced NFL owners as the clock ticked down toward the start of the 2006 season in early March.

Furthermore, the NFL Players Association, the union that represents the players, told the owners in no uncertain terms that, if they didn't settle their revenue-sharing differences, there would be no new collective bargaining agreement. As the deadline neared, the NFL was about to enter a free agency trading period that would allow certain players to renegotiate their contracts with any franchise in the league. Because the NFL places a cap on the amount of money any franchise can spend on salaries, some teams were forced to consider cutting veteran players. With time running out and the start of free agency already delayed twice, the owners huddled in a hotel ballroom in Dallas for one last try. The $64,000 question on the eve of free agency was this: Would the owners and players come to some sort of resolution and continue with the economic model that had served them so well for 70 years, or were their differences truly irreconcilable? In short, the NFL was facing the real possibility of economic uncertainty and labor strife—its first such period in decades.

Since 1935, the NFL has maintained an economic and competitive model that distributes talent and revenues throughout the league. The foundation of this model is the league's reverse-order draft, which guarantees that big- and small-market teams alike have an equal opportunity to draft the best college players. Economic parity among the teams was guaranteed in 1962 when legendary NFL commissioner Pete Rozelle, with the help of New York Giants owners Jack and Wellington Mara and others, would get big-market teams to scrap their lucrative local television contracts in favor of a national deal, which spread the riches of televised professional football among all members of the league. Thirty years later, a salary cap and a rigid system that controlled where and when players can be traded further helped to equalize talent among franchises.

By operating within this quasisocialistic system, the NFL guarantees fans the high-caliber competition that has kept stadium seats filled and television viewers enthralled. In short, by sharing talent and wealth among all its members, the NFL has succeeded wildly and become one of the most profitable sports leagues in the world. If the model collapsed as a result of the 2006 negotiations, therefore, the league was at risk of losing the very foundation of that success.

Then on March 8, with just minutes to spare, the NFL hammered out a new, six-year collective bargaining agreement that will take the league through 2011. Furthermore, the owners reworked their revenue-sharing compact to help redistribute some of the profits from the Dan Snyders of the league to the Ralph Wilsons of the league. In short: The NFL owners—sometimes stubborn, sometimes egotistical—stared into the abyss and stepped back. Ultimately, they all realized that it was better to share some of their wealth, maintaining an economic system that has enriched them all well beyond what any one owner could ever accomplish on his own.

"This agreement is not about one side's winning or losing," said Gene Upshaw, executive director of the NFL Players Association. "Ultimately, it is about what is best for the players, the owners, and the fans of the National Football League." Upshaw continued, "As caretakers of the game, we have acted in the manner the founders intended. While they could not possibly have predicted the economic growth and revenue streams, they clearly saw the structure. Wellington Mara would be proud and pleased today."

Indeed, Mara's name was invoked a lot leading up to and throughout the 2006 labor and revenue negotiations. Up until his death on October 25, 2005, after a battle with cancer, Mara was considered by many to be the conscience of the league, the voice of wisdom who constantly reminded even the most aggressive and entrepreneurial owners that what was good for the league was, ultimately, good for them. Many a time, he would quietly rise during cantankerous owners' meetings, and the roomful of CEOs, corporate titans, and ruthless businessmen would fall silent, ready to listen raptly to what the wise old man had to say. "We need the ghost of St. Wellington to appear with some of the forefathers," Colts owner Jim Irsay said, when it looked as though the owners wouldn't be able to reach a deal in March 2006.

When the NFL owners did reach the agreement that would ultimately keep the revenue model in place, it was poignant and fitting that Mara's son, New York Giants president and chief executive officer John Mara, was a key player in the resolution. "I think it is in the best interest of the league," John Mara said of the deal, using words that could have easily been spoken by his father more than 40 years ago.

Few organizations have succeeded longer—or better—than the National Football League. Understanding the forces that brought the NFL to the brink of organizational and economic collapse and the long and painfully protracted negotiations that saved the league in March 2006 tells us much about the future direction of the NFL—and professional sports as we know them today. But first—some pregame highlights.

THE DISPUTE OVER STADIUM REVENUES

The biggest issue that the NFL owners faced going into the 2006 labor and revenue negotiations was unshared stadium revenues. Throughout most of its history, the NFL has had two types of revenue: shared and unshared.

The league shares equally the revenues from national television rights, licensing fees for official NFL merchandise, and 40 percent of all regular ticket sales, which are considered "away" team ticket sales. Unshared revenue is everything else, mostly generated at the stadium on game day. It includes the 60 percent of "home" ticket sales, concessions, parking, and team store merchandise sales. Another important source of unshared revenues is club- and suite-level ticket sales, if the team is paying off stadium debt.

Premium seating generates enormous revenues for new and remodeled stadiums, and was, the Ralph Wilsons of the league claimed, upsetting the historic balance of team finances. In effect, these owners claimed, stadium revenues were creating not a league of parity, but a league of haves and have-nots.

New Stadiums, New Revenues

The NFL revenue-sharing model has been the foundation of the league's success. Rather than allowing the sport to be dominated by a handful of "super teams," as baseball often is, shared revenues give all teams an opportunity to bid for the best players, keep their facilities modern and up to date, and make a little money on the side. As avid NFL fans know, this model also means that almost any team—no matter how large or small the market—might be the next Super Bowl champion.

But the seeds of uproar within the NFL revenue-sharing system were sown in the mid-1990s, when teams went on a stadium-building boom. Over the decade leading up to the 2006 negotiations, more than 20 of the NFL's 32 franchises had either built new stadiums or renovated historic ones, like the Chicago Bears' Soldier Field and the Green Bay Packers' Lambeau Field. Before this construction boom began, stadium revenues accounted for just over 10 percent of the average NFL team's total revenues. In 2006, that figure was closer to 25 percent and rising fast.

The primary source of this growing and disparate revenue stream is premium seating—box seats, private suites, and exclusive stadium clubs. Because none of this high-dollar revenue was shared with the rest of the league, it primarily went to enhancing a team's profitability. Generally, the more club and suite seats a team sells, the higher its annual revenue. In short, stadium revenues became highly profitable for big-market team owners but extremely destabilizing for the league's level playing field.

Just as these new stadiums were changing the economic stability of the NFL, they also were changing the experience of attending a live football game. NFL stadiums began to cater increasingly to affluent fans. Such fans—who are remarkably plentiful—don't think twice about paying $2,000 for a personal seat license (PSL), a one-time fee that gives them the privilege to buy a season ticket that includes an entree to premium seating. Many exclusive stadium clubs are replete with comfy, over-stuffed, leather easy chairs; top-shelf Cognac; cigar bars; and dozens of flat-panel, plasma-screen TVs.

Snyder and the Redskins are the masters of the economics of NFL premium seating. Even at $7,500 a season (with a two-ticket minimum), membership in the Redskins exclusive Touchdown Club at FedEx Field is sold out, the tickets snapped up by a veritable "who's who" of Capitol Hill. Frequent guests in Snyder's owner's box include former Federal Reserve chairman Alan Greenspan and his wife, NBC news correspondent Andrea Mitchell, congressman and NFL quarterback Jack Kemp, and other Washington power players. In Charlotte, bankers rather than politicians hobnob on the club level of Bank of America Stadium before Carolina Panthers games. At Denver's Invesco Field at Mile High, oil, gas, and real estate executives gather before Broncos games in the club level sponsored by United Airlines.

The economics of NFL premium seating boiled over in 2005. And, in fact, there was some truth to team-owner claims that the rise of unshared, stadium-generated revenue was creating an NFL revenue hierarchy. For a prime example of the difference a new stadium can make in team revenues, just look at the Green Bay Packers. The team was ninth in the league in revenue in 1997, had fallen to 16th by 1999, and was projected to be 25th by 2003 if the Packers didn't do something to stop their slide. So the league's only publicly held team completed a $300 million renovation of Lambeau Field, paid for partly by issuing stock, partly through the sale of PSLs, and partly by the taxpayers. The renovation added, among other things, 3,000 club seats, priced at $200 a game, which sold out instantly and earned the team $8 million in new revenue.

The new club seats and luxury suites are part of Lambeau Field's Atrium, a five-story, 360,000-square-foot glass box tacked onto the end of the stadium that is revolutionizing NFL stadium economics. The Atrium has made Lambeau Field a year-round destination, and not just for Packers fanatics. The team specifically designed the Atrium so that the suite and club levels could be configured in the off-season to host corporate meetings, seminars, and wedding receptions for up to 1,000 people.

"We now have 1,600 special events a year," said Steve Klegon, the Packers director of business development. "We have at least one wedding reception every Saturday." Green Bay's stadium renovation has helped place the Packers in the upper half of the

NFL in terms of annual revenue. "The Atrium is the smartest business decision we ever made," Klegon said.

So smart that other NFL teams are looking to copy it. The Atlanta Falcons, who are setting the bar for growing revenues in an out-of-date, not-built-for-NFL facility, the Georgia Dome, are thinking about adding an atrium-style complex. It would include year-round restaurants, sports bars, and other entertainment venues—possibly even a hotel. The Houston Texans, one of the top-revenue teams in the league, also are thinking about copying the Packers' Atrium. The model would work particularly well for the Texans, because Reliant Stadium is just one of four facilities in Reliant Park, a complex of arenas and stadiums that draws fans year round, including the two million people who attend the Houston Livestock Show and Rodeo every year.

With the revenue hierarchy taking shape and a rush among some team owners to maximize these unshared stadium revenues, the NFL had no option but to address the issue during the 2006 negotiations.

Entrepreneurial Owners Make Waves

These changes in stadium operations and offerings frequently bear the touch of a new breed of entrepreneurial NFL owner that also had begun to reshape the league and unsettle its economic parity in other dramatic ways.

The Dallas Cowboys, for example, play in one of the oldest facilities in the NFL, but that doesn't keep team owner Jerry Jones from ranking consistently in the top five in the league in annual revenues. (It also helps the Cowboys' revenue equation that Texas Stadium has nearly 400 suites, more than double the number at most other NFL stadiums—old or new.) Jones is a master when it comes to inking local marketing and advertising deals. Indeed, he distinguishes himself through his ability to turn anything and everything into a marketing event, generating revenue that he doesn't have to share with the rest of the league. For example, Jones was one of the first NFL owners to figure out that there were no league rules against double dipping when it came to NFL sponsorships. If Pepsi paid to be the official beverage of the NFL—a fee that's shared equally among the NFL's 32 teams—Jones would sell the pouring rights at Texas Stadium to Dr. Pepper. Today, such multimarketing deals are standard at most NFL stadiums, but much of it was started in Texas Stadium by Jerry Jones.

Dan Snyder, a marketing whiz who made billions selling advertising in doctors' offices, has turned the Redskins' FedEx Field into a facility that is almost as good at producing money as the nearby Bureau of Engraving. As mentioned earlier, the stadium's premium seating licenses generate hundreds of millions of dollars annually. But Snyder's entrepreneurship hasn't stopped with PSLs. According to SEC filings related to Snyder's bid for Six Flags, since buying the team in 1999, he has expanded Redskins sponsorship revenues from $4 million to $48 million. Snyder accomplished that, in part, by developing lucrative concession revenues with vendors. The Redskins partnered with major consumer brands like Coca-Cola in deals that increased gross concession receipts without requiring the team to maintain concession equipment. And, to make the fans' concessions purchases faster and easier, the Redskins instituted a "tap and go" payment system using a Redskins-branded debit card. When Snyder purchased the team, per capita food spending at FedEx Field was about $9; as a result of his innovations, by 2005, Snyder had grown that figure to $15—a 66 percent increase. Multiply that $6-per-fan increase by 90,000 fans, at 8 games a year, and you've got some serious coin. Snyder also created a special events business at FedEx Field that generates over $2 million a year.

All of this entrepreneurship has paid off handsomely for Snyder. According to SEC filings, Snyder has "transformed the franchise into the most valuable franchise in U.S. sports . . . increasing annual revenues from $162 million to $300 million." While many snickered when he paid a League-record $800 million for the Redskins, his team went on to become the first NFL franchise in history to be valued at more than $1 billion.

Snyder and Jones are just two of the NFL's new breed of owners. The savvy business maneuvers and successful marketing techniques of these new NFL entrepreneurs help bring enormous new revenues to the league. At the same time, however, their success added fuel to the fire over the need for shared stadium revenues that was building within the league as the 2006 negotiations drew near.

Do Smaller Markets Lose Ground?

Of course, the concern about growing revenues among teams with new stadiums has to be balanced by the little evidence supporting the idea that revenue has any measurable impact on a team's performance on the field. The prime example again is the Washington Redskins. The team finished the 2004 season with a 6–10 record despite a record payroll of $120 million (some $40 million above the salary cap). And the New England Patriots, arguably the NFL's first 21st-century dynasty, were lauded as much for their low-buck payroll as their three Super Bowl championships. Indeed, with salaries controlled by a fairly rigid structure and a salary cap, the added revenue from club levels and suites doesn't go into bulking up the offensive line. Instead, those revenues fatten the team's bottom line, which—for the most part—benefits only the team owners.

These facts didn't keep the NFL team owners who struggle to sign their own equally lucrative local marketing deals—or prefer to just sit back and live off the largesse of the league's revenue-sharing model—from carping the most about an uneven economic playing field. Indeed, owners like Buffalo's Ralph Wilson and Cincinnati's Mike Brown contended that the unshared revenues generated by new and renovated stadiums gave the teams an extra pool of cash that could be used to compensate players above, beyond, and "around" the salary cap limitations. They feared that, by allowing some teams to grow increasingly wealthier than others, the NFL was destroying its level playing field.

Ultimately, Wilson and Brown were the only two to vote against the March 2006 collective bargaining agreement (CBA) extension and revenue-sharing modifications. Each claimed that they were in small markets with few local revenue opportunities and were losing financial ground to owners in bigger markets.

"Now the league is riding a crest of popularity, and I am afraid that some of the new owners who have come in the past 10 or 15 years don't know what some of the clubs went through 25, 30, 45 years ago," Wilson said in a 2005 interview in *Buffalo Business First*. "We have to agree [on] something on revenue sharing, because they are going to put us out of business."

What made Wilson and Brown's pleas galling to Jones, Snyder, and other NFL owners, who believe the league needs some entrepreneurial incentives to remain economically healthy and vibrant, was the fact that both have failed to sell naming rights to their stadiums, which could easily be worth $100 million or more. Brown, whose Cincinnati stadium was financed largely by the good taxpayers of Hamilton County, Ohio, chose to name it after his father, legendary Cleveland Browns coach and Bengals owner Paul Brown. Bills owner Ralph Wilson chose to name the team's Orchard Park, New York, stadium after . . . Ralph Wilson.

These issues aside, however, some NFL owners fretted in 2005 that the league was going the way of Major League Baseball, which is dominated economically by a slew of big-market, wealthy teams like the New York Yankees and Boston Red Sox. "This league was based on people being partners and being together and helping out," said Pittsburgh Steelers owner Dan Rooney. "It's one of the strong points of our league—the competitiveness, the idea of 'on any given Sunday.' It's a matter of fairness."

Other owners, like Bob McNair of the Houston Texans, disagreed. "I don't see a crisis," he said in an October 2005 interview. McNair's opinion carried weight because he was a member of the NFL subcommittee set up by Commissioner Paul Tagliabue to study league economics. While agreeing that stadium revenues have contributed to a "bit of disparity," McNair firmly believed that the issue would fix itself over time. McNair, Patriots owner Robert Kraft, and other members of an NFL panel set up to look at league economics initially argued in favor of preserving the NFL's revenue-sharing model as it was, sharing most, but not all, revenues. The panel agreed that the vitality of the league's economic health depended on incentives for owners to look at entrepreneurial ways to generate their own local revenue and not just live off the shared revenues from the league.

"Whether you are a small market or a large market, you have to manage the business like any other industry, controlling costs, getting value for the money you spend, and being sure you are giving your customers a quality product," Kraft told the *Washington Post*. "If we don't maintain our entrepreneurial spirit, then our league will die."

David Downing, a blogger who often comments on economics, put it this way: "If the teams shared this [growing stadium] revenue, no team would have had the incentive to be the first to invest in premium seating," he said. "If the Green Bay Packers had had to share their premium seat revenue—keeping only 1/32 for themselves—they would have never bothered to try to improve themselves in this way."

As the March 2006 contract negotiations got under way, these were the voices—and issues—the NFL had to respond to in resolving the dispute over unshared revenues within the league.

IN SPITE OF NFL FRANCHISE WEALTH, TAXPAYERS SUBSIDIZE THE STADIUM BOOM

Over the past ten years, the NFL has loaned more than $700 million to teams to help build or renovate stadiums. Still, the majority of the stadium-building boom has been financed by the taxpayers, most of whom will never see the inside of an NFL stadium. Indeed, while the NFL continues to grow revenues and profits, the average taxpayer contribution to NFL stadiums has remained relatively constant at about 65 percent—even though sports economists have been able to show that neither investment pays off for the host cities and, sometimes, not even for the players themselves.

In fact, solid economic evidence shows that investing in a professional arena or stadium is one of the worst expenditures of taxpayer money. The host community never recovers the tax breaks and assistance that teams get. Furthermore, stadiums take valuable tax dollars that could have reaped a much greater return had they been put into other community projects. Despite this evidence, there seems to be no end to taxpayer generosity when it comes to building NFL stadiums. At the start of the 2006 season, the Arizona Cardinals began playing in a new $700 million, state-of-the-art stadium. The team enjoys a field that, among other things, can be rolled out of the stadium during the week to get sunlight and fresh water—all courtesy of the taxpayers of Glendale, Arizona. With public-financed stadiums, taxpayers are willingly handing over ever-shrinking community funds to some incredibly profitable sports franchises.

While the league won't discuss profits, many NFL franchises are doing *very* well. The publicly held Green Bay Packers earned $29.1 million on revenue of $179.2 million in 2004, the latest year for which figures are available. That's a 16 percent margin.

And just look at these estimates of other franchise values:

- *Atlanta Falcons*—$545 million
- *Baltimore Ravens*—$607 million
- *Carolina Panthers*—$609 million
- *Cleveland Browns*—$618 million

IN SPITE OF NFL FRANCHISE WEALTH, TAXPAYERS SUBSIDIZE THE STADIUM BOOM

- *Dallas Cowboys*—More than $750 million (even without a new stadium)
- *Denver Broncos*—$606 million
- *New York Jets*—$635 million
- *Tampa Bay Buccaneers*—$606 million

TOUGH NFL LABOR ISSUES: DO PLAYERS GET A PIECE OF THE ACTION?

As tough as it was to resolve the revenue-sharing issue among the owners; it had to be done in coordination with a new CBA with the NFL Players Association (NFLPA), the union that represents the players. In part, player salaries are a function of the NFL revenue-sharing model. Under the system in place before March 2006, every NFL team started the year by getting nearly $100 million from the league in shared revenue (a figure that goes up with the renegotiation of every TV contract). All told, about $3 billion of the NFL's 2005 annual revenue of $5.2 billion was shared equally in 2005. How much players are paid is directly related to the amount of the shared revenue funds distributed throughout the NFL.

In 2004, the per-team salary cap was about $80 million, or about 65 percent of shared revenues. In 2005, the cap rose to $85 million. If the owners hadn't agreed to a new deal in March 2006, the salary cap would have been only $94.5 million. Not coincidentally, the salary cap is set so that it is always less than the total shared revenues. In other words, not only does every NFL team start the season with about $100 million, but that amount covers the team's labor costs.

The players had watched the stadium-building boom—and the flood of revenues flowing into owners' pockets—as closely as anyone. They made it clear going into the 2006 labor negotiations that they wanted a piece of the action, too. Indeed, one of the major issues the league faced as the contract deadline loomed was whether or not the owners would give the players what they wanted or risk labor unrest.

Another labor issue that historically has roiled NFL collective bargaining negotiations is free agency. This policy began a decade ago and was conceived as a means of guaranteeing that players could move from team to team within the NFL. However, the current form of NFL free agency is really part of a rigid salary structure that sets salaries, categorizes players, and tells both players and teams when and where they can make deals. Under this system, players are anything but free to move about and market their skills. If the league failed to reach a new collective bargaining agreement in 2006, the players coming into the league would only be able to negotiate their contracts for four years instead of six. And if they still hadn't reached a deal by the start of the 2007 season, the salary cap would have gone away altogether. And the NFLPA's Gene Upshaw made it clear to owners that if the cap ever went away, they would never get it back.

Yet another economic issue that came to the table in 2006 was that of so-called "guaranteed money." Unique among major league sports, NFL salaries are not guaranteed. Yes, there are clauses for injury and the like, but if a team simply grows to dislike a player—as the Minnesota Vikings did with bad boy wide receiver Randy Moss at the end of the 2004 season, or as the Philadelphia Eagles did with Terrell Owens in 2005—they can simply let him go and not owe him a penny. This situation was supposed to change with the advent of guaranteed money, which is money paid up front to players in the form of signing and other bonuses.

These bonuses guarantee that the player will receive some percentage of his contracted salary, even if he is later injured or dropped from the team. But not every player gets guaranteed money; most of these bonuses go to untested rookies, not veteran players. In short, NFL teams are using guaranteed money to ensure that they can get the number-one college draft pick. And that has some of the NFL's veteran players—particularly linemen who toil out of the spotlight—upset.

While NFL players universally welcome the benefits of guaranteed money, many feel NFL riches should come with a player's second contract, not his first. They argue that the NFL salary structure should be more like baseball's, where rookie players who have yet to prove themselves are paid a league minimum salary for the first few years. Only after they have proven they can make the steep transition from college football to the pros would they get the big bucks.

The counter to this argument is the fact that NFL players on average have the shortest career of any professional athlete—a little more than four years. Given this harsh reality, some say, NFL players should be able to get as much money as they can, as soon as they can. For while an Alex Smith or an Eli Manning, two recent number-one draft picks, might make the transition from college football to the NFL just fine, they could suffer a career-ending injury during their first or second season and never see a big payday.

No firm resolutions about guaranteed money were reached during the 2006 NFL contract negotiations. Although the issue of guaranteed money didn't hold center stage in this latest round of negotiations, it well could be one of the most contentious issues roiling the NFL in the years ahead.

A SOCIALIST SYSTEM MEETS MARKETING, MERCHANDISING, AND MEDIA

Of course, economic debates among the NFL's players, owners, and commissioners are nothing new. They are grounded largely in the stresses placed on the league's collectivist system by new and increasingly profitable opportunities for individual entrepreneurship.The league formula of "all for one, and one for all" has served the NFL well since 1935, when Philadelphia Eagles owner Bert Bell proposed the reverse-order NFL draft that's still in existence today. In spite of its socialist roots, however, the NFL hasn't shrunk from the pursuit of capitalism's free market benefits. The league's expansion into new markets and new media during the second half of the 20th century built the NFL into the economic juggernaut that it is today.

Most historians peg the emergence of the NFL onto the national sports landscape to the televised coverage of the 1958 title game between the Baltimore Colts and the New York Giants. That game was won by a cool young quarterback named Johnny Unitas, whose square shoulders, clean-cut boy-next-door image, and aggressive style of play epitomized postwar America. Millions watched the game on television, including President Eisenhower. America was enthralled with this new form of television drama, and advertisers took note. Four years later, visionary NFL commissioner Pete Rozelle convinced big-market teams like the New York Giants and Chicago Bears that the best interest of the league lay in negotiating a national television contract and sharing the revenues equally. Through the 1960s and 1970s, NFL football became the most-watched programming on television and produced what is considered by many to be the world's greatest television programming event, the Super Bowl. Today, the Super Bowl is the single most bankable television event for the league, television networks, and advertisers.

When the NFL migrated to prime time in 1970 via *Monday Night Football*, the spectacle's bright lights, creative camera angles, and compelling story lines (along with those muscular, good-looking quarterbacks in tight pants) further expanded the NFL's reach to women. The NFL is still reaping the benefits of that move today, with women making up nearly 50 percent of a typical NFL audience, both at the stadium and at home.

The NFL learned the lessons of *Monday Night Football* well and has embraced the latest new media better and faster than any other professional sports league. Thanks to cable and satellite television, Washington Redskins fans in Morton, Illinois, can follow their team as closely as the fans living in suburban Maryland or Virginia. Moreover, cable and satellite television are helping the NFL to build its brand beyond the United States. While European football leagues and owners lose money every year, the NFL only gets financially stronger as it continues to expand into international markets. In 2005, the NFL played its first regular season game outside of the United States, selling out 100,000-seat Estadio Azteca stadium outside Mexico City. The NFL also has embraced the Internet and wireless communication devices such as cell phones and PDAs, and it has tapped into the exponentially increasing world of fantasy football, capturing younger fantasy players through popular video games like Madden 2006. And the NFL has accomplished all of this while maintaining a tight rein on its image and the products marketed under its brand.

All of this market discipline has paid off for the NFL. While the NFL's collectivist bent might bother some fans in what is arguably still the most capitalist country on the planet, it's hard to argue with success. The NFL posted record attendance for the fourth year in a row in 2005, and every year, the playoffs and Super Bowl deliver some of the highest ratings in the history of television. In fact, Super Bowl XL, played February 6, 2006, in Detroit between the Pittsburgh Steelers and Seattle Seahawks was watched by 141.4 million people. And just when Madison Avenue thought that ad rates for a 30-second spot during the Super Bowl couldn't go any higher, they did. The cost for such a spot during Super Bowl XL was $2.5 million, up from $2.2 million the year before.

Most amazingly, with all of these changes, the NFL has continued to benefit from its traditional economic model—a system that generates immense revenues and profit margins and, at the same time, allows the smallest- and largest-market teams to compete against each other on relatively equal footing.

"We're in the 20th biggest market," said Denver Broncos owner Pat Bowlen. "We do well, but it would be very difficult to be competitive if the NFL didn't share revenue."

"We compete against each other for three hours a week," New England Patriots owner Robert Kraft said in an interview. "Otherwise, we have aligned interests."

In short, the NFL has managed to benefit from the socialist concepts of shared wealth, even as it capitalizes on the opportunities presented by the free-market system. How long the league could maintain this delicate balancing act, however, was in question as the 2006 season began.

CHAPTER TWO

ANYTHING
BUT "FREE"

PLAYING FOR THE NFL

In 2004, Indianapolis Colts quarterback Peyton Manning became the highest-paid player in the NFL. He signed a $99.2 million contract for seven years that included a $34.5 million signing bonus and performance bonuses that could earn him an extra $19 million. And while that may sound like a lot of money for merely playing a nationally televised game of catch for 16 Sundays a year, Manning clearly earned it.

In 2003, he was the NFL's co-MVP, sharing honors with Tennessee Titans quarterback Steve McNair. After going 0–3 in previous playoff appearances, Manning won his first NFL playoff game on January 4, 2004, against the Denver Broncos. Between the Broncos game and a subsequent playoff game against the Kansas City Chiefs, Manning achieved a perfect quarterback rating of 158.3.

The following season, Manning proved he was worth every penny of a contract that paid him more than $14 million a season. In 2004, mostly thanks to Manning, the Colts broke a more than 50-year-old NFL record set by the 1950 Los Angeles Rams for most offense in a single season (see Chapter 5). The Colts finished the season with a 12–4 record and their second consecutive AFC South division title.

Manning also broke a number of the NFL's most impressive personal records:

- Most touchdown passes in a single season: 49 (previously held by Dan Marino with 48 in 1984)
- Highest passer rating in a single season: 121.1 (previously held by Steve Young with 112.8 in 1994)
- Four touchdowns or more in 5 consecutive games
- Five touchdown passes in 4 different games in less than 12 months (previously held by Dan Marino)

During the 2004 season, Manning also became the only NFL player to pass for 4,000 yards in 6 consecutive seasons and for 20 touchdowns in 7 consecutive seasons. He and Marvin Harrison also set the NFL record for quarterback-to-wide receiver completions (664), eclipsing the previous record held by the Buffalo Bills' Jim Kelly and Andre Reed. As a result, Manning was the near-unanimous selection for the 2004 Associated Press NFL Most Valuable Player and was named NFL Offensive Player of the Year and the Pro Bowl MVP.

Peyton Manning was worthy of all these honors and thoroughly deserved his record salary and contract in 2004. Moreover, Manning's astronomical salary was arranged within the parameters of a very rigid, very structured NFL salary system. And while the NFL is often lauded for having both a salary cap and free agency, the fact of the matter is that teams routinely find creative ways to "stretch" the salary cap, and players in the NFL are anything but free to sell their talents to the highest bidder.

The importance of all this, of course, was highlighted in the approach to the 2006 season. With the very real possibility of no new collective bargaining agreement (CBA) or revenue-sharing agreement, many teams had to formulate plans that included cutting very veteran, very competent players, primarily out of salary cap concerns. The Washington Redskins, for example, at about $300 million, are the highest-revenue team in the NFL. But before the new labor and revenue-sharing agreements were reached, they were estimated to be as much as $25 million over the projected 2006 salary cap of $94.5 million. As a result, the team faced some of the toughest choices in the league.

Redskins quarterback Mark Brunell had signed a seven-year, $43 million contract, including a guaranteed $8.6 million signing bonus. His base salary for 2006 was $4 million, the second-highest on the team. Coach Joe Gibbs refused to comment on Brunell's situation when labor negotiations were still under way, but he did say that the team was considering all options to get in under the salary cap. "A lot of teams have a number of scenarios going on, and they're talking to a number of their players to find ways to fulfill their obligations with the salary cap," Gibbs said.

In addition to Brunell, who turned 36 in September 2006, the Redskins were looking at the contracts of offensive linemen Jon Jansen and Randy Thomas as other possible salary cap cuts. Jansen and Thomas are both good examples of the difficult choices teams faced. Jansen, proving that he'd do almost anything for the team, played much of the 2005 season with broken thumbs. Thomas had what was arguably the best season of his career in 2005.

Other NFL teams faced equally tough choices. The Oakland Raiders, projected to be about $20 million over the $94.5 million cap of the old CBA, looked at waiving starting nose tackle Ted Washington, starting guard Ron Stone, and starting quarterback Kerry Collins. Cutting Collins alone would have saved the team $12.9 million in 2006. (However, it's only fair to point out that Collins' eventual dismissal was as much about personal performance as salary cap concerns.)

Washington, 38, a 16-game starter for the Raiders in 2004 and 2005, had been one of the team's most durable and consistent defensive players, but he was scheduled to earn $4.75 million in

salary based on the average of the top 10 salaries at that position, or a 20 percent increase of the previous year's salary (whichever is greater).

- Any team can decide to take back its franchise or transition designation. If that happens, the player becomes an unrestricted free agent, and the team can give the designation to another player.
- Restricted and unrestricted free-agent players have specific dates within which they can negotiate new contracts and signing periods within which they can ink deals. Outside these dates, signing rights can be affected by offers from the player's original club, and—under some circumstances—the original club has the right to match new offers and retain the player.

As even this incredibly simplified explanation makes clear, NFL free agency is anything but free. It is, in fact, a very rigid system that dictates when, where, and how players can be traded or move to another team. Fortunately, the NFL salary structure is a little (though not much) simpler.

UNDERSTANDING SALARY CAPS AND FLOORS

The NFL salary cap was established as part of the 1993 collective bargaining agreement. It is a percentage of the league's shared income, which comes from the national television contracts, merchandise sales, and away-game ticket sales. A percentage of that income, called defined gross revenues (DGR), is allocated for salaries. The percentages agreed upon in the 2001 CBA extension were:

2002	64%
2003	64.25%
2004	64.75%

2005	65.5%
2006	64.5%
2007	Uncapped year

Under the March 2006 CBA, the salary cap was set at $102 million in 2006 and $109 million in 2007. The salary caps in the "out" years of the contract will be negotiated in subsequent years.

While many people know that NFL teams must operate below a salary cap, many don't know that each team also has a salary floor.

That salary floor—the minimum team salary (MTS)—is 56 percent. That means that NFL team owners must spend at least 56 percent of the shared revenues they receive from the league on player salaries. As you can see, the salary cap and floor work together to bracket NFL salaries within a pretty narrow window. In 2005, for example, every team had to pay its players somewhere between 56 percent and 64 percent of shared revenues (about $130 million). That's a window of about $10 million in a multibillion dollar business.

Stretching the Cap

It's also important to note, however, that the NFL salary cap is not as firm as the league and some team owners would like you to think—in fact, the cap is pretty malleable. That's because NFL contracts can be laden with all sorts of special bonuses, such as a "workout bonus" (money paid to the player to show up on certain days in the off-season and for off-season training) and signing bonuses. Historically, teams were allowed to prorate, or amortize, player bonuses over the life of the contract. Stated simply, if a player gets a five-year contract with a $20 million signing bonus, the team only has to account for $4 million of the bonus each year, even though it paid the $20 million up front. This, too, changed somewhat with the 2006 CBA.

NFL SALARY 101

- Every year, players are guaranteed a minimum salary; in 2005, for example, they were guaranteed about $550,000.
- For every year a player is in the NFL, his minimum salary goes up. These numbers change each year with the salary cap, but in 2005, a 10-year veteran was guaranteed approximately $750,000.
- Base salaries are paid in 17 equal checks, 1 each game plus 1 for the bye week. Agents get 3 percent of each check.
- Preseason compensation in 2005 was $775 per week for rookies and $1,100 per week for veterans. Veterans also receive an additional $200 per week for all preseason game weeks.
- Postseason payments per player are paid by the NFL and don't count against individual teams' salary caps. For 2005, here are those payments: wild card $17,000, wild card division winner $19,000, divisional playoffs $19,000, conference championship $37,000, Super Bowl loser $38,000, Super Bowl winner $73,000.
- Practice squad minimum salary is $4,700 per week, including playoff weeks. Prorated over a 17-week season, a practice squad player makes at least $79,900.
- Off-season workouts are paid $110 per day, 4 days a week, during teams' 13- or 14-week off-season workout programs.
- On travel days during the 2005 preseason, regular season, and postseason, a player is reimbursed for meals not provided by his club as follows: breakfast, $17; lunch, $25; and dinner, $43.

"The franchise player rules basically stay as they are with some minor tweaking," NFL commissioner Paul Tagliabue said in explaining the new CBA to the media. According to Tagliabue, the rule structure was modified to help avoid situations where a single player was designated three times by a single club. The new structure makes it possible for players and clubs, Tagliabue said, "to work out multiyear agreements, including signing bonuses, either the first time a player was tagged or the second time a player was tagged."

"Another change," Tagliabue continued, "is that drafted players in rounds two through seven will have a maximum contract length of four years. Some clubs have been signing players to five- and six-year contracts. That had become an issue with the Players Association in this negotiation relative to the concept of free agency after four years. We agreed there would be a maximum contract length of four years for players drafted in rounds two through seven. The first round can still be negotiated with longer deals."

Said Gene Upshaw, executive director of the NFL Players Association, "Moving forward, this new agreement gives us the opportunity to continue our unprecedented success and growth."

One aspect of NFL salaries didn't change with the new CBA: part of each player's salary is accounted for in the current year, and part is accounted for in the future. This rule extends to bonuses, as well; if a player is traded or ends his career because of injury, the team must account for the remainder of the signing bonus the very next year. So if a player has a $20 million signing bonus and only plays for two years, then in the third year, the team would count the remaining $12 million of the $20 million signing bonus against its salary cap for that year. The cap money that counts toward a player who's no longer on the team is called "dead cap space." For instance, in 2005, the Green Bay Packers had about $10 million in dead cap money because they cut Darren Sharper, Joe Jackson, and Jamal Reynolds.

This "floating" cap calculation has created an army of green eyeshade experts throughout the league whose sole job is to make sure that a team stays within the salary cap limits. More importantly, these financial executives almost always consult with the coach, general manager, and team scouts to ensure that a team is getting the biggest bang for its buck. And, just to keep everyone honest, every NFL contract goes through the league offices at 280 Park Avenue, where the league's own salary cap specialists look it over to make sure it complies with league rules.

An Inside Look at One NFL Star's Salary

Tom Condon is perhaps the NFL's premier agent. In addition to Peyton Manning and his younger brother, Eli Manning (quarterback for the New York Giants), Condon also represented Alex Smith, the 2005 number-one draft pick who set the record for guaranteed money for a rookie. (We'll talk more about "guaranteed money" later in this chapter.) These are just 3 of the more than 30 first-round draft picks that Condon has helped guide through the NFL contract maze since 1997.

Peyton Manning has had only two contracts since being named the NFL's number-one draft pick from the University of Tennessee in 1998. His rookie contract was a $48 million, 6-year deal that would void after 3 years, the minimum allowed under the NFL's collective bargaining agreement. Like the record contract he signed in 2004, Manning's rookie contract included performance thresholds that earned him bonuses, such as passing for 1,600 yards in any given season, or an average of 100 yards per game. These, Condon noted, are nothing more than bare minimums that almost guaranteed that Manning would see all the money promised in his $48 million contract.

"When it comes to the minimum threshold, I want it—he wants it—to be the absolute minimum," Condon said.

More importantly, Condon negotiated those minimum performance requirements into Manning's rookie contract, because once Manning reached those minimums, the Colts had the right to buy back the remaining three years of his six-year rookie contract.

"They purchased years four, five, and six for a second signing bonus that was guaranteed," Condon said. That made Manning's total rookie contract bonuses—the first signing bonus as well as the buyback bonus—$20 million. Why? All to allow the Colts to pay Manning the maximum without violating the NFL's salary cap.

Indeed, in years four through six of his rookie contract, Manning earned $30 million. That put huge pressure on the Colt's salary cap, especially in the sixth year of Manning's rookie contract, which paid him $11.5 million but for salary cap purposes was accounted for as $15 million.

"That was a *huge* cap number," Condon said, "easily the largest cap number in the NFL."

"The idea is that, if he is going to achieve at some high level in years that are considered free agency, which are years four through six, then you want him to be compensated as if he were the star player," Condon said. And that's exactly what happened.

The Colts bought back years four through six from Manning when he became eligible to be an NFL free agent. They designated him the team's franchise player and he played through year six of his rookie contract.

When Peyton Manning's rookie contract expired, under the NFL's rules, the team had either to pay him $15 million, the average of the top five quarterbacks in the league, or 20 percent above the salary he earned in the last year of his contract, which was also $15 million. So, if the Colts wanted to keep Peyton Manning in year seven of his NFL career, they had to pay him $18 million. The salary cap that year was about $75 million, so the Colts would have used nearly a quarter of their salary cap for that year on one player.

Reenter Tom Condon.

"That was an enormous percentage of the Colts' salary cap," Condon said. "Furthermore, unlike in years when you're amortizing a signing bonus or guaranteed money, his cap number matched the actual cash he would have received, which was $18 million."

So between July 15, 2004, and the start of training camp, Condon and Manning struck another deal with the Colts to relieve that salary cap pressure. They gave him a signing bonus of $34.5 million and paid him the league-minimum salary of $550,000. As a result, Manning's average salary over the life of his second contract was $14.5 million, making him the highest-paid player in the league. (Green Bay's Brett Favre was the next closest player with an average annual salary of about $10 million.)

"What we did was essentially trade Peyton's $18 million salary for a $35 million salary," Condon said. "But because most of it was given as a signing bonus, the Colts were allowed to amortize that salary over multiple years and lessen the impact on the salary cap."

Adjustments, Incentives, and Escalating Salaries

While all this makes for good reading if you have a master's in economics, wasn't the whole point of a salary cap and free agency to keep salaries in check? The answer is yes, and many believe that the NFL has done a good job of doing just that.

"I think the answer is a clear yes," said Joe Banner, president of the Philadelphia Eagles, who's considered one of the league's salary cap gurus. "You just had a Super Bowl with two teams that, in terms of revenues, are far from the highest," he said in a February 2006 interview, referring to the two teams in Super Bowl XL, the Pittsburgh Steelers and the Seattle Seahawks. "Five of the 12 teams in the playoffs were toward the bottom in revenue.

"There are advantages to being in stronger financial shape," Banner said, "but the advantages aren't so great that it prevents you from being successful." Indeed, Banner points to the Tampa Bay Buccaneers, the Carolina Panthers, and the Green Bay Packers as examples of teams in modest-size markets that have three of the most successful teams in the league. "Those are teams with sustained success both on and off the field," Banner said. "No matter how you measure it—fan interest, television revenues, win–loss record—they're successful."

Al Lackner, a senior editor at *www.askthecommish.com*, one of the better sports economist Web sites, agrees somewhat with Banner.

"The NFL salary cap has worked in a number of areas, but it has not worked to keep salaries in check," said Lackner, whose *Capanomics 101* is required reading if you want to understand the true intricacies of the NFL salary cap.

Lackner notes that the NFL Players Association (NFLPA) has itself pointed out that the NFL's average 2005 salary is 6 percent over the 2004 average and 13 percent above the 2003 average.

"With the salary cap going up from a little over $80 million in 2004 to about $85.5 million in 2005, that 6 percent increase seems to be right in line with the salary hike that the NFLPA cites," he said. "However, when you take a closer look, the median salary—which is probably a better measuring stick, as a significant number of the players on the roster make the league minimum—has gone up 17 percent from 2004 to 2005. More specifically, the median salaries for starters have gone up 27 percent over the same time frame."

In addition to the salary cap, which rises along with the television contract, the free agent market has pushed salaries up as well.

"The salary cap may be the owners' greatest friend in terms of controlling escalating salaries, but free agency has had the opposite effect," Lackner said. "With owners like the Washington Redskins' Daniel Snyder willing to pay top dollar for the players of his choosing, player salaries continue to escalate."

But more importantly, Lackner notes, teams are increasingly finding ways around the cap. For instance, $85.5 million was the *unadjusted* salary cap in 2005. The actual figure is adjusted based upon a player's bonus, which is designated either "likely to be earned" (LTBE) or "not likely to be earned" (NLTBE).

"If a team defined an incentive as LTBE in a player's contract in 2004, then the incentive would have counted against last year's cap," Lackner said. "If the player never, in fact, achieved the required goal to trigger the incentive, then a portion of that incentive counts as a credit against this year's cap."

This is but another example of the NFL's rigidly controlled—and hard to decipher—salary structure. Lackner notes that the NFL instituted LTBE and NLTBE incentives as a means to prevent teams from circumventing the cap. The collective bargaining agreement even has clear language stating what cannot be considered NLTBE. When in doubt, they call in an arbitrator.

"Obviously, teams in cap trouble can benefit immensely when a perfectly obtainable incentive is defined as NLTBE, wherein they can then push some cap relief into the next season," he said.

Other teams have used the designation in the opposite manner, to free up future cap space. In 2005, for instance, the Vikings actually had a salary cap that was well over $100 million, largely thanks to a nearly $16 million cap adjustment.

"Thus, they were allowed to exceed the $85.5 million unadjusted cap and still remain almost $10 million under their adjusted cap," Lackner said. "You can certainly expect the team to approach a number of players during the season about reworking their contracts with ridiculously unobtainable incentives, which will be specified as LTBE regardless. That will allow them to again push a positive cap adjustment onto the 2006 season."

Teams will also design incentives based on team performance, such as points scored, points allowed (on defense), and number of games won. These are usually categorized as NLTBE. It's another way for a team to create cap room.

Is this all fair?

"You certainly can't fault the Vikings—or any other team that uses this strategy—for playing by the rules," Lackner said. "But it will be very difficult for teams in cap trouble to ever catch up."

Many teams cheered the 2006 CBA because it would give them $7.5 million more in 2006 to manipulate the salary cap. And while NFL salaries automatically go up with increases in the national television contract, another factor pushing up salaries is the trend toward guaranteed money.

SHOW ME THE (GUARANTEED) MONEY

If there's an Achilles' heel in the NFL's salary structure, it's the fact that player contracts are not guaranteed. Yes, there are provisions for injuries, even career-ending ones. But if a coach or owner doesn't like a particular player, they can simply tell him to go home, and the team won't owe the player a dime. While that's an extreme example, it happened during the 2005 season with bad-boy wide receiver Terrell Owens and the Philadelphia Eagles. More common, however, are the experiences of Minnesota Vikings center Matt Birk and Green Bay Packers wide receiver Javon Walker.

Birk, a Harvard grad and Pro Bowl lineman, is one of the anchors of the Vikings offensive line. He's often lauded for his leadership, intelligence, and combination of size and athletic ability. But early in the 2005 season, he tore his labrum, a hip muscle. Repairing the muscle would have required Birk's fifth surgery on his midsection, an important part of the body for linemen, who count on core body strength as well as overall size to keep 350-pound rushers at bay.

The Vikings were supposed to pay Birk his $3.25 million base salary in 2005. After that, he had $13.89 million remaining on his eight-year, $31 million contract. But per the NFL's collective bargaining agreement, that money is not guaranteed. Despite his medical condition, Birk took the extraordinary step of offering to play out the season with his injury if the Vikings would guarantee his contract. Guaranteed contracts are becoming increasingly common in NFL teams, but only for their biggest superstars. No offense to Matt Birk, but a center (no matter how many Pro Bowls he's been to) doesn't qualify for guaranteed money. The Vikings told him as much, so Birk opted to have the surgery instead of playing hurt and risking further injury.

"I played injured last year," Birk said of the 2004 season. "And I felt like it shortened my career. If I had played injured, gotten hurt, and was released by the Vikings, I would have been on the free agent market after two years of playing hurt, and I wouldn't have been able to maximize my market value. . . . By playing hurt, you're really hurting yourself," Birk said. "In my situation, I wasn't willing to do that."

Javon Walker's case was even more tragic. A fourth-year receiver, he was to have been paid $515,000 in 2005 and $650,000 in 2006, part of a five-year deal he signed in 2002 for nearly $7.5 million. Moreover, his stock was rising. He went to his first Pro Bowl in February 2005 after catching 89 passes for 1,382 yards and 12 touchdowns during the 2004 season. His agent, Drew Rosenhaus, thought it was the perfect time to renegotiate Walker's contract with the Packers. Walker initially threatened to hold out for more money, but instead he did what many saw as the honorable thing and reported to training camp on time, saying he'd honor his current contract. In the first game of the 2005 season against the Detroit Lions, Walker tore the anterior cruciate ligament in his knee. Walker had been on track to begin cashing in on his growing fame and skill as one of the NFL's most sought-after wide receivers in 2006. All of that was called into question with his injury.

"It hurt my heart when Javon got hurt because I know how hard he worked," said Vikings safety Darren Sharper, who played in Green Bay for three years with Walker. "It's just tough to see one of your friends go down with an injury like that, because you know how bad he wants to be on the field."

Moreover, Walker deserved a new deal, Sharper said. "One season is not enough to be the highest-paid player at your position. You don't have that many yards and that many touchdowns against the players that he did it against and not be one of the top receivers." But that's the way the NFL salary system works. Un-

less you're one of the Mannings or a handful of other top-tier superstars, your pay is not guaranteed. While many players are
insured against injury, without guaranteed pay, the financial impact of an injury on a player's career can be devastating.

Matt Birk said it's a cruel irony that NFL players have a well-
deserved reputation for toughness, but teams don't recognize
that they often play hurt. Moreover, Birk, a former representative
on the National Football League Players Association, feels that
the union doesn't do as much as it could to remedy the situation.
"[The NFLPA] really isn't a voice for the players," Birk said, ex-
pressing an opinion held by a lot of today's NFL players. "The executive board is made up of ten players, and Gene Upshaw sells
his ideas to them, and then they basically rubber stamp everything he wants."

Indeed, many players feel that Upshaw, the former Oakland
Raider lineman who walked the picket lines in the 1980s and
helped form the union, is too cozy with NFL commissioner Paul
Tagliabue. "I have a lot of respect for Gene Upshaw," Birk said,
"but when he calls the NFL, Tagliabue's first response should be
'Oh no, what does this guy want now?' He should be the league's
worst nightmare."

Upshaw and Tagliabue both draw praise for the relatively
calm labor environment in the NFL over the past 20 years. And
Upshaw may have earned back some credibility among players
with his tough stance that resulted in the 2006 CBA and enhanced
revenue sharing. But some of the players think there has been too
much "go along and get along." "It's Gene's job to get every
penny he can and push [the NFL] to the brink of calling off negotiations," Birk said. "I don't think that they push hard enough."

Vets, Rookies, Midcareer Players: Who Gets Guaranteed Money?

The other problem, players say, is that much of the guaranteed money that is starting to become more common in NFL contracts is going to rookie players who've never proven themselves in the NFL. The perfect case in point is Alex Smith, the number-one draft pick in 2005.

The San Francisco 49ers signed the University of Utah quarterback to a six-year, $49.5 million contract, which included $24 million of guaranteed money. Smith's average annual salary of $8.25 million tops the $7.5 million average salary the New York Giants gave to another number-one draft pick, quarterback Eli Manning. Smith's $24 million guarantee is 20 percent higher than the deal given Manning, who had $20 million of his $45 million contract guaranteed by the Giants. Not surprisingly, both deals were negotiated by Tom Condon and his IMG colleague, Ken Kremer.

Like Eli and Peyton Manning, Alex Smith deserved a high salary. He left Utah after his junior season, having led the Utes to their first BCS bowl win, a victory over Pittsburgh in the Fiesta Bowl. Under Smith's leadership, Utah finished the season 12–0. Individually, Smith completed 185 of 280 passes for 2,624 yards and 28 touchdowns with only 4 interceptions. He also rushed for 563 yards and 10 touchdowns and finished 4th in the Heisman Trophy voting.

But here's what bothers veteran players. "It's 50–50 that a player will pan out," Birk said. That's because the learning and talent curve from college football to the NFL is so steep. Instead, Birk and other veteran players think that the money that's being guaranteed to rookie players should be given to veterans who've proven they can play in the NFL. Indeed, while many love the NFL salary structure, including the cap based on shared revenues, they'd like to see the NFL morph toward a salary model similar to baseball's. In major league baseball, most players work their way up through the farm system, earn the league minimum salary in their first few years in the big league, and then cash in with their second contract, after they've proved they can play the game. "Take the up-front money away from the young players and make them work for it and then reward them," Birk said. "Alex Smith has already made more money than I'll make in my career, and no one knows what kind of player he'll be."

"The money might not be going to the right players," Upshaw said, "but at least it's going to players." That attitude annoys Birk and other veteran players. "I understand that the superstars drive the league, but the guys who really get hurt are veterans who may or may not be starters and have to back up two or three positions," Birk said. "The problem is that there is no middle class in the NFL."

He's right. The highest-paid players are either rookie phenoms or veterans who are into their second or third contract. The entry-level league minimum under the 2006 CBA is $275,000 the first year and increases by $10,000 every year through 2011, far from the multimillion-dollar contracts that most people think of when they think of professional athletes.

"The CBA is supposed to be our support, and it's just not there," said Birk, who's one of the highest-paid linemen in the NFL. "They [team owners] love the rookies because the fans love the rookies. And they love the superstars. The rest, they don't care about." Birk speaks from experience: He was a sixth-round draft pick and was paid the league minimum salary of about $110,000 with a $54,000 signing bonus. Before signing his current contract, which would have paid him $31 million over seven years through 2008, he signed a one-year, $1 million contract.

The trend of guaranteed money is also causing veteran players with big contracts to go back into negotiations with their team and ask for more guaranteed money. This is exactly what Birk's Vikings teammate, quarterback Daunte Culpepper, did at the start of the 2005 season. That's because, since signing his incentive-laden, 10-year, $102 million contract in May 2003, more than 18 other NFL players have eclipsed Culpepper financially. His 2003 contract included about $15 million in guaranteed money, which was a respectable figure at the time but has since paled in comparison to some of the more recent NFL contracts.

When Culpepper got his new contract in 2003, it was just one of a handful of $100 million deals, reserved almost exclusively for quarterbacks. In addition to Culpepper, quarterbacks Drew Bledsoe, Brett Favre, and Donovan McNabb also had $100 million deals. The next year, all that started to change. Peyton Manning reset the big-money bar for NFL quarterbacks by signing his seven-year, $98 million contract with the Indianapolis Colts that included $34.5 million in guaranteed money—$14 million more than the previous record set by McNabb. Then quarterback Michael Vick agreed to an eight-year, $130 million contract with the Atlanta Falcons that included a whopping $37 million in guaranteed money. And then New England Patriots quarterback Tom Brady reworked his deal and received $26.5 million in guaranteed salary.

For now, these guaranteed money contracts are a fact of life in the NFL. And with a new CBA giving the players more money than ever, the issue of guaranteed money is likely to receive much attention over the next few years. Get the players away from the TV cameras and the locker room, and it's clearly a hot topic.

Calculating the Costs of Guaranteed Money

So what—besides personal pride and self-esteem—you may ask, keeps these NFL MVPs from taking their guaranteed money and sitting on the couch?

"I call this the Barry Sanders Rule," said Lackner. "Owners try to protect their investments by including language in the contract that calls for a player to return a portion of the signing bonus to the team if the player 'fails or refuses' to practice or play with the team. In certain situations, a team will be repaid some of the signing bonus it paid to a player, or a team will fail to pay part of a signing bonus that was already allocated toward team salary. If this happens, the amount previously included in team salary will be added to the team's salary cap in the next year."

Guaranteed money places a heavy burden on teams. They must scout well and make sure that they're picking players who can make the tough transition from college to professional football. "Guaranteed money demonstrates exactly how important it is for teams that are picking at the top of the draft to get their picks right," Lackner said. "A wrong move—such as the San Diego Chargers' misstep with Ryan Leaf—can set a franchise back for many years."

Lackner is referring to abysmal NFL quarterback Ryan Leaf, the second player picked in the 1998 draft, who was given an $11.25 million signing bonus by the San Diego Chargers. He's considered the textbook example of the disaster guaranteed money can be if a player doesn't pan out. The problem for the Chargers wasn't that he played poorly; to remedy that they merely benched him. The problem was the salary cap. If they would have cut him at the start of the second season, they would have been forced to account for five-sixths of his signing bonus, a financial hit the team couldn't afford to take given the NFL's salary cap rules. "Professional sports—and the NFL in particular—may be the only industry in which an inexperienced, unproven employee can immediately accept a position and make more money than a seasoned, proven, veteran performer," Lackner said.

That, he said, is the equivalent of bringing an inexperienced, just-minted college grad in off the street and putting them in charge of a *Fortune 500* corporation. But that's what is happening in the NFL. And the consequences go well beyond finances.

"When a young, unproven player is given that much money up front, the coaching staff has an enormous amount of pressure from both the fans and ownership, who want to see a quick return on their investment," Lackner said. "When a team is comprised of primarily veterans, they are in more of a win-now mode and not as willing to be patient with the younger players' learning curves."

The perfect example is the Buffalo Bills, who were willing to cut Drew Bledsoe because they wanted to see what young J.P. Losman had to offer. "By week five—and after a 1–3 start—the coaching staff made the decision to move toward journeyman Kelly Holcomb," Lackner said. "This move was at least partially brought about by the locker-room mutterings of such veterans as Eric Moulds, Lawyer Milloy, and Sam Adams."

It's also important to note that, when a single player takes up such a large chunk of a team's salary cap, there is less money to spend elsewhere. "It isn't just that a young, inexperienced player walks in and makes more money than the team's tried-and-true veterans, but they also take money out of the veterans' pockets," Lackner said, reinforcing Birk's point.

Lackner agrees that the relatively short career of the average NFL player makes it almost impossible to rework guaranteed money into the second contract, as Birk and other veteran players would like to see. "The big up-front money is really reserved for only the top 10 or 15 draft picks," Lackner said, "so they represent the exception to the rule. To equalize the hit sustained by the large up-front signing bonuses, teams usually sign these top-rated players to much longer deals (five-plus years). By the time they reach the stage where they are ready for their second contract, many—if not most—of them are already in the twilight of their career."

Lackner notes that many NFL general managers refuse to sign players who are over 30 to long-terms deals with large signing bonuses. "For some positions, most notably running backs, that age barometer is even younger," Lackner said, "which is why we've seen such marquee players as Shaun Alexander and Edgerrin James have trouble getting long-term deals."

Furthermore, Lackner said, the more recent trend for top draft picks has been to tier the signing bonuses. In some cases, bonus payouts are not guaranteed. In others, the bonuses are incentive based. And most contracts contain language that protects the team from player behavior that is determined to be "detrimental to the team."

"Oftentimes, the language is cloudy enough to be open to interpretation," Lackner said. "For example, is showing up to training camp out of shape 'detrimental to the team'? We've already seen the Cleveland Browns try and recoup some of the guaranteed money they've already paid to Kellen Winslow II."

TRAINING PLAYERS TO BE BUSINESS MANAGERS

Because their salaries make them almost instant executives and financial planners, NFL players need more tools than ever before to help manage their finances and plan for their life after football—even with outside help from accountants, brokers, and agents. During 2005, nearly 100 players enrolled in executive education programs at Harvard Business School and the Wharton School at the University of Pennsylvania. The three-day seminars are part of an ongoing joint initiative between the NFL and NFL Players Association to help players prepare for their post-playing careers. Tuition is covered by the NFL's tuition reimbursement program, part of a broader program that will reimburse veteran players up to $15,000 per year for education expenses at an accredited institution. San Diego Chargers quarterback Drew Brees, Green Bay Packers receiver Ahman Green, Philadelphia Eagles linebacker Dhani Jones, and wide receiver Freddie Mitchell are just a few of the players who participated in the programs in 2005.

As part of its custom executive education programs, Harvard Business School has developed a customized workshop targeted to the needs of NFL players interested in owning, operating, or building their own businesses. The Wharton Sports Business Initiative and Wharton Executive Education have collaborated to develop a combination classroom and field-based workshop. It focuses on personal investments as well as entrepreneurial opportunities for players as they transition from their football careers to the real world.

"This is one of many important steps that the union is taking to assist NFL players in their lives off the playing field," said Buffalo Bills cornerback Troy Vincent, who was president of the NFL Players Association in 2005 and participated in the Wharton program.

The NFL also does a better job now than in the past of helping players on the front end of their career. For the past ten seasons, the NFL has conducted an annual Rookie Symposium for incoming players. The four-day seminar, akin to college freshman orientation, tries to help players make the transition from college to professional football and get them ready for summer training camps. The program includes presentations, videos, and workshops about the operation of the NFL and the challenges players will face.

"This helps the rookies get off to a good start with regard to the new lifestyle they are about to enter," NFL vice president of player and employee development Michael Haynes, himself a Pro Football Hall of Fame cornerback, told the Associated Press. "The lessons learned at the Rookie Symposium help players develop personal and professional goals that will sustain them during and beyond their playing careers."

The symposium covers personal finance and conduct, team and league media policy, substance abuse, family issues, NFL security, and life after football. Speakers typically include league executives, representatives from the NFL Players Association, finance professionals, and current and former NFL players.

"We are all held to very high standards," NFL commissioner Paul Tagliabue told the rookies in a video address at the 2005 Rookie Symposium. "We expect you to do your best on and off the field. You need to focus on your personal responsibility 24 hours a day, 365 days a year. It's important to think through every decision and make good choices."

In addition to the lifestyle advice offered by these authority figures, the players also hear from former players who haven't always made the best choices. And while the symposium is usually held at some warm-weather exclusive resort, there is little down time. The message the NFL sends to its newest players is abundantly clear.

"How long you play in the NFL will depend on how well you conduct yourself," Tagliabue told the rookies in 2005. "NFL fans do not support players who make negative public spectacles of themselves. That includes players who do not honor their contracts or violate the law or do not adhere to our substance abuse policies. If you engage in that type of negative conduct, you will suffer severe consequences."

And with baseball players, including the New York Yankees Jason Giambi, in the news in 2005 for illegal steroid use, Tagliabue reminded NFL players, "Our steroids policy, the best in sports, is strict and very effective. We will catch players who try to cheat. We are committed to making sure the playing field is level for all players in the league."

"You're not invisible," Gene Upshaw told the rookies. "You're no longer the kid or the young man that was a star in college. You're now in the National Football League, which raises you to a different level. We expect good citizens, and character does matter in the National Football League. If you think something is wrong, it probably is."

"We want you to be successful, and this week will give you a good road map for getting there," Tagliabue said. "But it is up to you to stay on the road and succeed."

THE NFL PLAYERS ASSOCIATION AT WORK

Despite some of the players' gripes about Upshaw and what many see as his too-cozy relationship with Tagliabue, the players' union has added some important benefits for players over the past few years.

During the 2005 off-season, the NFL and NFLPA agreed on a process that distributes money for the amount of playing time each player gets. Though the pool started at a modest $500,000 per team in the first year, lower-paid players received a majority of the money, measured by the number of downs in which a player participates versus the number of downs he is eligible to play.

Another major modification was in the area of pension payments. Beginning in April 2005, the pensions for more than 2,000 retired pro football players were raised as much as 100 percent, a deal described as "without precedent in American industry." About 625 retirees who played before 1959 saw their pension checks rise from $100 a month for each season they played to $200 a month, with benefits staggered accordingly.

Some of these postcareer benefits were enhanced in the 2006 CBA. "There is significantly expanded postcareer medical coverage for players," Tagliabue said. "They already have five years postcareer [coverage]. There is a health care IRA-type element set aside that the players will get funded in proportion to the length of their career. It's quite a significant improvement in benefits."

Today's NFL players aren't starving. The average NFL salary per player increased to more than $1 million in 2005, and the NFL paid more than $2 billion in salaries that year. Under the 2006 CBA, per-team spending on salaries increased to $102 million the first year and will rise to $109 million in 2007. While that may sound like a lot, the average player's salary still went down about 1.4 percent. And the disparity in payroll spending between the top and bottom NFL teams since the salary cap was implemented in 1993 continued to increase.

The league and the NFLPA have always found a way to work out their labor differences. Indeed, it has been more than 20 years since the NFL had labor problems. It's a record that, like the NFL's revenue-sharing system, is the envy of every other professional sports league. And the other leagues seem to be learning the hard lessons of gross excess.

- In baseball, not even a canceled World Series could force the players' union to accept a salary cap. That's how Alex Rodriguez became the $252 million man. Eventually, the union made modest concessions on revenue sharing and a luxury tax in 2001.
- In basketball, teenagers still in high school were signing some of the biggest contracts in sports history, with rookies becoming multimillionaires before ever stepping on the court. When they realized this farce couldn't go on forever, NBA players accepted a strict and detailed salary structure.
- And in hockey, the average player salary more than tripled between 1995 and 2004, even as the league's franchises reported hundreds of millions in annual losses. It took a whole season without hockey—and few Americans noticing or caring—to get the NHL to rework its finances into a model similar to the NFL's.

The NFL owners, management, and players' union have worked hard over the years to craft and maintain the league's incredibly successful economic model. But I think it fair to say that a large portion of the credit for that model's success goes to its architect, Bert Bell. Through his vision and commitment, Bell was able to bring together a strong-willed group of team owners and forge among them a commitment to building their individual team success on a foundation of shared success throughout the league. Based upon the lucrative salary and revenue-sharing deal that the league and the players union was able to strike in 2006, it's fair to say that players, owners, and league executives still follow the pathway first carved out by Bell.

CHAPTER THREE

ANY GIVEN SUNDAY

HOW BERT BELL BUILT THE NFL'S EVEN PLAYING FIELD

The NFL truly is an equal opportunity organization; some of the league's best teams have come from some of the smaller metropolitan areas. Just look at the teams in the 2005 NFC and AFC championship games. The Carolina Panthers, Denver Broncos, Pittsburgh Steelers, and Seattle Seahawks are from the 37th, 22nd, 21st, and 14th largest metropolitan statistical areas, based on total population. Not represented in the playoffs at all were 11 of the top 12 markets, all of which have NFL franchises. Consider these facts:

- The Indianapolis Colts are in the country's 34th largest market yet have the most sought-after player in all of football, Peyton Manning. He has led the Colts to three consecutive AFC South titles, broken nearly every passing record in the league, and is the highest-paid player in the history of the NFL.
- The Cincinnati Bengals were the NFL's perennial losers for eons. Before finishing 8–8 in 2003 and 2004, the team was 2–14 in 2002, 6–10 in 2001, 4–12 in 2000 and 1999, and 3–13

in 1998. Then they signed quarterback Carson Palmer, hired coach Marvin Lewis, and went on to surprise everyone with an incredible 11–5 record in 2005, earning them the AFC North title and their first playoff appearance since 1981, before losing to the eventual Super Bowl XL winners the Pittsburgh Steelers 31–17 in the first round of the January 2006 playoffs.

Who gets the lion's share of the credit for these phenomenal—and balanced—results? That credit goes to the NFL's shared-revenue model and salary cap. Those systems have created a model that's provided the league with a level playing field in terms of both on-field performance and off-field economics. In today's NFL, any team, no matter how small, can become a star.

But as the league headed into the March opening of the 2006 season, a new revenue-sharing compact among the owners and a new collective bargaining agreement with the players threatened the stability of the NFL. With the old contract still in effect, the salary cap was set at $94.5 million. That would have been about $15 million less than players and teams received had there been no new collective bargaining and revenue-sharing agreement. Before the new deal was reached, many teams had to cut marquee players to stay under the salary cap. The Oakland Raiders released quarterback Kerry Collins to save $9.2 million. The Washington Redskins, more than $20 million over the salary cap, saved $9 million by allowing three-time Pro Bowl linebacker LaVar Arrington to buy out his contract, an almost unheard-of occurrence in the league.

The resolution of the NFL's collective bargaining agreement was critical to the ongoing success of a system that had worked so well and played an integral role in building the NFL's huge following and unprecedented prosperity. To understand just how important the shared revenue and salary cap systems are to the NFL, it's useful to take a closer look at where the league started and how it developed the economic and competitive model that shaped its success.

THE NFL TAKES SHAPE

Many scholars trace the roots of the National Football League to a historic meeting of the American Professional Football Association (APFA) in Canton, Ohio, on August 20, 1920. According to the official NFL history, "An organizational meeting, at which the Akron Pros, Canton Bulldogs, Cleveland Indians, and Dayton Triangles were represented, was held at the Jordan and Hupmobile auto showroom. . . ." A month later, a second meeting was held that included teams from four other states, including the Decatur Staleys and the Racine Cardinals, the only two original NFL teams that survive today. (The Staleys would move to Chicago and change their name to the Bears, while the Cardinals would live on in Chicago, St. Louis, and Arizona.) But not until June 24, 1922, did the APFA change its name to the National Football League. The newly formed league fielded 18 teams, including the Oorang Indians of Marion, Ohio, an all–Native American team featuring 1912 Olympian Jim Thorpe.

The Indians were indicative of the early teams that were formed. The owner, Walter Lingo, was a local businessman in La Rue, Ohio, who raised Airedales and—allegedly—boasted that President Warren G. Harding was an investor in his company. Lingo started the team in 1922 for $100—the price of the least expensive of his pampered hounds, who sold for as much as $500 when trained. When he was awarded an NFL franchise in June 1922, Lingo named his team the Oorang Indians, after his favorite Airedale, King Oorang.

Lingo hired Thorpe, a world-renowned Olympic athlete and graduate of the famous Carlisle Indian Industrial School, as the coach of the Indians. Thorpe and Joe Guyon, a teammate who would end up in the Pro Football Hall of Fame in nearby Canton, started recruiting fellow Native American athletes to join the Oorang Indians. Soon they filled the roster with players such as Ted Lone Wolf, Baptiste Thunder, Xavier Downwind, Red Fang, and Peter Black Bear. Thorpe's Native American name was Bright Path, but Lingo understood the obvious economic and promotional benefits of having him coach and play under his more famous name.

With Lingo's dogs as the central focus, the Indians' games turned into sideshow spectacles, with football relegated to a secondary role. The team would run onto the field at the start of the game yelling war whoops, with buckskins and feathers covering their uniforms. During halftime, instead of resting in the locker room and planning their strategy for the second half, the players would again don their native garb and throw tomahawks, do rope tricks, or help Lingo's dogs chase raccoons up artificial trees. Tackle Long Time Sleep, also known as Nick Lass, sometimes wrestled live bears at halftime. Needless to say, football wasn't the team's number one priority. Chicago Bears tackle Ed Healey recalled the day in 1922 when, after partying at a Chicago bar all night, the Oorang Indians staggered onto the field to play the Bears. "Thorpe hardly played," Healey recalled. "They were tough sons of guns. Just not very good. And they didn't care much." After just two years, the novelty wore off. And in 1923, with an abysmal record of 1–10, the Indians folded.

That would be the story for more than 30 franchises that would come and go over the course of the National Football League's first 10 seasons. These were teams that most people today have never heard of, such as the Buffalo All-Americans, Rock Island Independents, Rochester Jeffersons, Canton Bulldogs, Detroit Heralds, Cleveland Tigers, Chicago Tigers, Hammond Pros, Columbus Panhandles, and Muncie Flyers. The Akron Pros finished the 1920 season with a record of 8–0–3 and were awarded the championship at the league meeting on April 30, 1921. The next year, the league included the Green Bay Packers, Chicago

Cardinals, and the newly named Chicago Bears. These franchises have prospered, while others who joined the league during these early days—the Duluth Kelleys, Providence Steam Rollers, Pottsville Maroons, Racine Tornadoes, and Staten Island Stapletons— remain unknown to even the most stalwart NFL fans today.

By 1933 and the first NFL championship game, the league's roster had been whittled down to just ten teams, including George Halas' Chicago Bears, Earl "Curly" Lambeau's Green Bay Packers, New York bookmaker Tim Mara's New York Giants, Art Rooney's Pittsburgh Steelers, Bert Bell's Philadelphia Eagles, and Charlie Bidwill's Chicago Cardinals. Although they played in Boston as the Braves, George Preston Marshall's Redskins moved to Washington in 1937 and won the 1937 NFC Championship game 28–21 over the Bears. These were the founding teams of what we know today as the NFL.

Bert Bell, Architect of the NFL

Over the next 20 years, the NFL would struggle to establish itself as a business, with only the Chicago Bears making money on a consistent basis. Other teams were on shaky financial ground, and the league as a whole played a weak third fiddle on the national sports landscape, trailing in popularity and prosperity behind both major league baseball and college football, which was considered a purer, less brutish form of the game.

But at the 1935 winter meetings, the groundwork was laid for the league's financial and competitive stability. The architect of the NFL's level playing field and father of the most successful sports league on the planet was a most unlikely hero—a raccoon coat-wearing, Ivy League educated playboy extraordinaire of the Roaring Twenties by the name of Bert Bell.

His father, John Cromwell Bell, was a prominent lawyer who served as Pennsylvania attorney general from 1911 to 1915 and later became the owner of Philadelphia's Ritz-Carleton Hotel.

During the 1880s, John Bell played football at the University of Pennsylvania, and his son DeBenneville—known as Bert—developed a love of football at an early age. "All I ever wanted to be was a football man," he once said.

After a modest career as a middling quarterback at Penn, Bert Bell's career as an early NFL owner and coach was anything but a Pro Bowl performance. In 1933, he and some partners bought the Frankford Yellowjackets, moved them to Philadelphia, and renamed them the Eagles. Two years and $80,000 later, the team went bust. Bell borrowed $2,500 from his fiancée, former Ziegfeld girl Frances Upton and, as the only bidder, bought the team back at auction for $4,500. The team's failure had landed it solely under Bell's control—an event that would turn out to be one of the greatest things that ever happened to the NFL.

From its earliest days, the league shared revenues among member teams. The standard arrangement was a 60–40 split between the home team and visitors, with both teams paying for stadium rental. (Amazingly, that split remains the same today, minus the stadium expenses.) But it was Bert Bell, speaking at the 1935 owners meeting, who sowed the seeds for the spirit of cooperation, both on the field and at the ticket office, by proposing that the league needed to share talent as well as revenues. Later, when describing the meeting, he would say, "I made up my mind that this league would never survive, unless we had some system whereby each team had an even chance to bid for talent against each other."

Bert Bell was absolutely right. In a league that saw more than 30 teams fold in the first 10 seasons, it should be no surprise that a survival-of-the-fittest mentality prevailed. From 1927 to 1932, three teams—the Bears, Giants, and Packers—posted the league's best record in 5 of the 6 years. The first two NFL Championship games in 1933 and 1934 both featured the Bears and Giants. Frustrated with this—and certainly his huge financial losses—Bell made a radical proposal. He put forth the idea that there had to be a way to spread the talent around, make the games more competitive, and ensure that each and every franchise filled the stadium each week, luring fans with one important constant: a good game in which any team could win.

"Gentlemen, I've always had the theory that pro football is like a chain," he said at the 1935 owners' meeting. "The league is no stronger than its weakest link, and I've been the weak link for so long that I should know. Every year, the rich get richer and the poor get poorer." He continued, "At the end of each football season, I suggest that we pool the names of all eligible college seniors. Then we make our selections in inverse order of standings—that is, the lowest-ranked team picks first. We do this round after round until we have exhausted the supply of college players."

No one called it a "draft," but that's exactly what it became. More important than Bell's draft proposal was the idea that the league needed each team to be relatively healthy—financially and competitively—for every team to survive. In short, Bell had laid the ideological foundations for the revenue-sharing system that has made the NFL the economic juggernaut that it is today. Even Halas and Mara, who owned teams in the league's two biggest markets, agreed.

"People come to see a competition," Giants owner Tim Mara said. "We could give them a competition only if the teams had some sort of equality, if the teams went up and down with the fortunes of life."

While the philosophy of financial and competitive parity may bother some staunch American capitalists, it has made the NFL an overwhelming and undeniable success. And it all began when Bert Bell convinced the owners that they must do what was best for the league, not merely what was best for themselves. It was a business strategy, Bell argued, that would, in the long run, prove better than any short-term gains that any one team could realize on its own. His idea, in fact, has turned out to be the single greatest contributor to the NFL's prosperity over the past 84 years.

Bert Bell had only just begun to make his mark on the league. He was named the third commissioner of the NFL on January 12, 1946, earning $20,000 a year. And while his draft proposal would level the competitive playing field for decades to come, it was one of his first acts as commissioner that led the league toward becoming a truly *National* Football League.

THE RISING AND FALLING FORTUNES OF BERT BELL AND HIS EAGLES

Too bad Bert Bell's revolutionary thinking in the boardroom didn't transfer equally well onto the playing field. Following the 1935 owners' meetings, Bell would bounce around the NFL for the next 11 years. These years—as a coach and owner—were mostly disastrous. And, ironically, he seemed to benefit least from the innovative draft system he had proposed.

From 1936 to 1940, Bell's Eagles would finish 1–11, 2–8–1, 5–6, 1–9–1, and 1–10 to place fifth, fifth, fourth, fourth, and fifth in the NFL's 5-team Eastern Division. Over his coaching career, Bell would compile a record of 10–46–2, for a winning percentage of just 0.190, the worst in the history of the NFL for coaches with five or more seasons. As an owner, he also lost tens of thousands of dollars.

All that changed in 1940, when now-legendary NFL owner Art Rooney sold the Pittsburgh franchise and bought an interest in Bell's Eagles. Then, through a convoluted transaction that baffles even some of the most knowledgeable NFL historians (and is mostly ignored for the sake of historical continuity), the Philadelphia franchise ended up in Pittsburgh and the Steelers ended up as the Eagles.

BUILDING THE LEAGUE'S SUCCESS

While the NFL had stabilized by the time Bert Bell took over as commissioner, a few strong teams continued to dominate the league. From 1934 to 1947, the Packers, Bears, Giants, and Redskins took 19 of 20 spots in the NFL Championship games. As Joe Carr, the league's first commissioner, said in 1939, "No owner has made money from pro football, but a lot have gone broke thinking they could."

Indeed, in 1946, the Chicago Bears were the only NFL team to make money. The Cleveland Browns also made money that year, but they were a member of a rival league—the All-American Football Conference (AAFC). The Browns were the AAFC's first champions; the upstart league had risen in just a few years after its formation to challenge the NFL and was well on its way with legendary Ohio State coach Paul Brown at the helm in Cleveland. The NFL tried to ignore the new league but couldn't. Dan Topping, owner of the NFL's Brooklyn Dodgers as well as baseball's New York Yankees, announced that he was defecting to the AAFC, because Elmer Layden, the NFL commissioner who Bell had replaced, had failed to resolve scheduling conflicts between the Dodgers and Mara's Giants.

The NFL faced other challenges as well. By the late 1940s, the AAFC already had two West Coast franchises, the Los Angeles Dons and San Francisco 49ers, while the NFL had yet to expand west of the Mississippi or south of the Potomac. At the January 1946 NFL owners' meetings, Cleveland Rams owner Dan Reeves became the latest of many to propose a West Coast NFL franchise. He was summarily turned down, falling two votes short of the eight needed to make the move. "And you call this a *national* league," he said with justifiable disgust, as he stormed out on the other owners.

Bell, again seeing the importance of working together to make the league stronger, called a hasty meeting with Bears owner George Halas, Cardinals owner Charlie Bidwill, and Washington Redskins owner George Preston Marshall. The compromise was this—the Rams agreed to give teams $5,000 above the guaranteed road payout of $10,000 for the trouble and expense of making the trip to the West Coast. Reeves was lured back into the fold, and the Rams moved to Los Angeles as an NFL franchise.

But being a national league didn't solve all of the NFL's financial problems. The recently relocated Rams lost $161,000 in 1946 and $184,000 in 1947. The rest of the league wasn't doing much better. In 1948, the Eagles defeated the Chicago Cardinals 7–0 to win their first NFL Championship (and to avenge a 28–21 loss to the Cardinals in the 1947 championship game). But during that very year, the Eagles had nearly $625,000 in revenues and almost $710,000 in expenses—in other words, the team lost about $85,000. The Chicago Bears, whose revenues passed the $1 million mark for the first time in 1948, remained the only NFL franchise regularly earning a profit.

BOOSTING ATTENDANCE
THROUGH COMPETITION

While both the NFL and the AAFC continued to lose money through the late-1940s, attendance remained strong in the NFL, while it dropped off sharply for the AAFC. Bell had been absolutely right when he said that fans would not come to see games where the outcome was assured before the opening kickoff. Since the NFL had instituted the draft, average attendance had more than doubled, moving from 15,111 in 1936 to 31,493 in 1946, according to the *2005 NFL Record and Fact Book*. Over the same period, total season attendance had risen from 845,552 to 1.4 million.

Attendance for the AAFC teams was headed in the opposite direction. The league was dominated by Paul Brown's Cleveland

Browns, who went 12–1–1 in the 1947 season, posted a perfect 14–0 record in 1948, and then went 9–1–2 in 1949. Over its 4-year history in the AAFC, the Browns set pro football attendance records in the first two years, averaging 48,556 and 56,108, respectively. But with the Browns beating up on every team they played, attendance took a nosedive. In 1948, attendance fell nearly 19 percent, then tumbled another 30 percent in 1949 to a dismal 31,600.

"A lack of competition had dampened interest in the AAFC in every city," wrote Mike MacCambridge, author of *America's Game*, perhaps the definitive social and cultural history of the NFL. "Cleveland had been the dominant team in the AAFC from day one, and their superiority was becoming so accepted, it began to hurt the gate throughout the league."

The battle for pro football supremacy between the NFL and the AAFC was best illustrated in Chicago, where the AAFC's Rockets went head-to-head with the NFL's Bears and Cardinals. The Bears were formidable simply because they were the Bears. But the Cardinals would prove Bell's theory that competition kept fans in the seats.

In 1943, the Cardinals went 0–10. In 1945, the team improved to 1–9. That same year, Philadelphia running back Steve Van Buren scored more points than the entire Cardinals team, 110–98. A year later, the Cardinals went 6–5 under new coach Jimmy Conzelman, the first time the team finished above .500 since 1935. In 1947, the Cardinals went 9–3 and won the NFL Championship, 28–21 over the Philadelphia Eagles, their first title in 22 years. In 1948, the Cardinals went 11–1 in their last year under Conzelman but lost the NFL Championship game 7–0 to the Eagles.

The NFL's competitive atmosphere kept fans coming to games. By contrast, it only took four years of Cleveland Browns' dominance to bring the AAFC to its knees. The two leagues agreed to merge in December 1949, with the NFL absorbing just three of the AAFC teams: the Cleveland Browns, San Francisco 49ers, and Dallas Texans. In the case of the Texans, Bert Bell convinced Carroll Rosenbloom, a multimillionaire who had made his fortune selling denim to the military during World War II, to take over the Dallas team and make them the Baltimore Colts. Furthermore, he only required the reluctant Rosenbloom to put up $25,000 of the $200,000 price tag that the league was asking for the franchise, with the rest to be paid—interest free—over the next eight years. The Colts also agreed to pay Washington Redskins owner George Preston Marshall a $50,000 territorial rights fee for infringing on the Redskins' market, a financial arrangement that would become commonplace in the coming decades as the league expanded and teams changed cities.

MANAGING THE DETAILS: THE NFL'S CLEAN IMAGE AND FAIR SCHEDULING

In addition to shaping the league's economic model, Bert Bell made other contributions to the stability of the NFL during his years at the helm. In his first year as commissioner, Bell weathered a gambling scandal in which a minor New York mobster, Sidney Paris, tried to fix the 1946 championship game between the Bears and Giants. Paris infiltrated a Giants boosters club that gathered regularly at a local Elks Lodge. Through the club he met Giants quarterback Frank Filchock and running back Merle Hapes. He wined and dined them, offered them lucrative off-season jobs, and then proposed that the Giants lose the game by at least ten points.

Bell got wind of the fix and worked closely with the New York City police and the FBI to avoid a scandal. Furthermore, he instituted what would become a strict NFL policy against gambling. "Bert was death on gambling," Bears owner George Halas said. "He'd watch the odds like a bookie. He'd go into gambling joints right in Philly to check out rumors." Bell also hired retired FBI agents and police officers to keep tabs on gamblers and players.

The NFL's strict policing of gambling continues to this day. In 1963, NFL Commissioner Pete Rozelle fined and suspended two of the biggest stars of the game, Green Bay's Paul Hornung and Detroit's Alex Karras, for betting on their own teams. (It's only fair to note, however, that unlike former Cincinnati Reds player Pete Rose, both football players are in the Pro Football Hall of Fame.) Five years later, Rozelle told New York Jets quarterback Joe Namath, the darling of the league, either to sell his financial interest in the Bachelors III bar or leave professional football. "Bars and the like attract persons who could cast suspicion on professional football," Rozelle said. "I will not allow the suspicion of evil to exist."

Bell's legacy of maintaining a clean image for the NFL continues. During the 2005 season, the NFL told broadcasters *not* to air ads for *Two for the Money,* a Universal Studios film that told the story of a sports handicapper (played by Matthew McConaughey) who made it big picking NFL games. "We felt that the ad constituted affiliating with or endorsing gambling," said NFL spokesman Brian McCarthy, "and our policy dates back to the 1960s. It prohibits any kind of ads concerning gambling." The Fox network obliged, pulling the ads before the second week of the 2005 season. "We were asked by a valuable, long-term partner to make this accommodation, and we agreed," said Lou D'Ermilio, senior vice president of media relations for Fox Sports, which broadcasts the NFL's NFC games on Sundays. Nevertheless, the ad did appear on ABC's October 3, 2005, Monday Night Football broadcast of the Green Bay Packers–Carolina Panthers game.

Bert Bell's other great contribution to the game would come in the area of scheduling. Schedules had long been a source of much infighting among NFL owners. The big-market teams wanted to play each other and leave the small-market teams to fend for themselves. This led to marathon stalemates at the off-season owners' meetings. "The owners who had the staying power were the ones who came away with the decent schedules," said Art Rooney. "The guys who snuck out to get some sleep or go nightclubbing wound up getting murdered the next season, because when they weren't there to defend themselves, we'd give them all the dates we didn't want." Bell, ever the egalitarian, worked to change all that—from his kitchen in the Philadelphia suburb of Narberth. He developed an unsophisticated scheduling system with dominoes and a board that he would tinker with for weeks. "Mother, guess what?" Bert Bell would yell on Sunday afternoons. "It's week four and they're all still in the race."

The league's record attendance and rising revenues helped Bell stifle dissent among owners when he tinkered with the schedule. Some hinted that Bell favored his friends from the founding NFL teams, but he was too strong a commissioner to be moved. And his new system worked.

THE END OF AN ERA: BERT BELL'S LEGACY WITH THE NFL

In spite of the progress made by Bert Bell, the NFL was still on shaky financial ground through the mid-1950s. In an executive summary of a 1957 report, "The Story of Professional Football," Bell noted that in 1956, the 12 league clubs had combined gross receipts of about $10.5 million, with each club netting an average of about $50,000, for a league total of approximately $600,000 in net revenues. Bell also reported, "The most successful club, the Detroit Lions, last season enjoyed six sellouts at home with over 50,000 spectators per game. Their gross receipts from ticket sales at home, their receipts on the road and preseason games, from radio and TV rights, etc., were approximately $2 million, but net profit amounted to only $119,483.22." Bell went on to note: "The federal government in 1956 collected more than $900,000 in admission taxes on professional football games—approximately 33 percent more than the combined net income of the 12 clubs comprising the National Football League!"

Clearly, the NFL needed to figure out a way to generate more revenue. Television was just starting to catch on, and if Bert Bell was ever wrong about anything in his tenure as NFL commissioner, it was his early position on televised football. Only toward the end of his career—and his life—did Bell begin to acknowledge the potential for televising NFL games. In 1956, Bell negotiated the first-ever national NFL TV contract, which banned the broadcast of home games within home markets. In 1957, there was an outcry to broadcast the sold-out NFL Championship game between the Detroit Lions and the Cleveland Browns. Despite pleas from the governor and two senators from Michigan, Bell would not budge. "I don't believe there is any honesty in selling a person a ticket and then, after you've taken his dollars, deciding to put the game on television, where he could've seen it for nothing," Bell said. "As long as I have anything to do with this league, home games won't be televised, period."

Fortunately, just a year later, Bell relented and allowed the 1958 NFL Championship game between the New York Giants and the Baltimore Colts to be broadcast nationally from Yankee Stadium. That televised game, which many still consider to be the greatest professional football game of all time, forever changed the way fans—and Bert Bell—looked at the NFL. For the nation, the drama of the game gave the NFL legitimacy at a time when baseball was still very much the national pastime. For Bell, the wild popularity of the broadcast demonstrated the powerful potential television held for the still-fledgling league.

In 1959, Bert Bell died a fitting death—watching two teams he had once owned play on a field where he had once quarterbacked. A year earlier, Bell's Philadelphia Eagles had moved from Connie Mack Stadium to the University of Pennsylvania's Franklin Field, and attendance had almost doubled. On October

11, 1959, Bell had come to watch the Eagles play the Steelers on his old home field. Never one to sit in the press box, Bell preferred to sit in the stands with the fans and take in the color and excitement of the game. With two minutes left in the game, sitting smack dab in the middle of the world he had created and loved, he collapsed, dead of a heart attack.

"It was like Caruso dying in the third act of *Pagliacci*," wrote sports columnist Red Smith.

Bert Bell's legacy was carved in the granite of football history. He had put the NFL on the all-important path to competitive and economic parity, by creating a system that guaranteed fans would pile into stadiums for decades to come to see teams with a fair chance of winning. "On any given Sunday, any team in our league can beat any other team," Bert Bell, told the Associated Press in 1959. "There isn't any such animal as a weak sister in our league anymore. You knock my brains out this Sunday, and I knock your brains out the next time we meet."

In short, he had set in motion the most important mechanisms that would ensure the league's financial and competitive prosperity for decades to come. Following Bell's death, the mantle at the NFL's league offices passed to Alvin "Pete" Rozelle. This media-savvy former public relations executive and general manager for the Los Angeles Rams would use television to take the NFL to heights never before imagined—even by Bert Bell.

CHAPTER FOUR

A PERFECT TEAM—
TELEVISION AND
THE NFL

The advent of television was the beginning of the transformation of the NFL from an obscure, little-regarded sports league into the economic powerhouse that it is today. From 1948 through 1955, the number of television sets in the United States grew from 172,000 to 25 million, and football awakened to the power of the new medium. In 1956, the NFL got its first national contract with CBS, a major turning point for the league. Two years later, the nation would become enthralled with the NFL through the nationally televised 1958 title game between the New York Giants and the Baltimore Colts at Yankee Stadium. Indeed, nearly every sports historian and writer pegs that game as the catalyst for the NFL's ascendancy to the role of national pastime; by the late 1960s, professional football had replaced baseball as the most frequently watched sport in America.

In terms of financial and competitive success, most sports economists agree that the league's national TV contract differentiates the NFL from Major League Baseball. In 1998, the NFL signed a $17.6 billion national television contract with four networks. The contract gave the NFL $2.2 billion annually and more than $80 million a year to each team. By comparison, Major League Baseball's national broadcast contracts totaled about $570 million a season, giving each team about $19 million. And with the start of the 2006 season, the NFL began a six-year network and satellite television contract that totals about $24 billion.

Ironically, it was at the 1952 *baseball* commissioner's meeting in Scottsdale, Arizona, that legendary owner Bill Veeck first proposed the idea for a nationalized television contract. "It is my contention that the [St. Louis] Browns provide half the cast in every game they play," said Veeck. "Therefore, we're entitled to our cut of the TV fees the home club receives for televising our games. Morally, I know I am right, and I plan to fight this thing to the end." It didn't take long for the end to come. The baseball owners were patently against it. Then–Brooklyn Dodgers owner Walter O'Malley called Veeck "a damned Communist." Little did these baseball owners know that television would be the mechanism by which football would forever eclipse baseball, both in terms of financial success and in capturing the hearts of America's sports fans.

THE NFL'S FIRST EXPERIMENTS WITH TELEVISION

In the early 1950s, professional football was already further along in terms of revenue sharing than any other professional sport. Visiting baseball teams, for example, received only about 30 percent of the home gate, as opposed to the NFL's 60–40 split, with both teams paying for stadium rental. But television was a completely different story; the NFL owners hadn't even discussed sharing television revenues, because there had been little to share.

The Chicago Bears had experimented with televising games in 1948. The gross profits from those events came to less than $5,000. When the Bears—thinking they were on to something—put together a regional network that covered 11 cities, their efforts were rewarded with a loss of about $1,500. The Bears weren't alone. In the late 1940s, the Baltimore Colts got a whopping $50 per game in exchange for the rights to broadcast their games in the local market. By 1949, total NFL television rights were worth only about $75,000, and an early television experiment the next year almost doomed the NFL–television marriage.

The Los Angeles Rams were one of the NFL's most potent offenses in the late 1940s and early 1950s. In 1949, the Rams went 8–2–2, were third in the league in scoring and made their first NFL Championship appearance, losing to the Philadelphia Eagles 14–0. The Rams did even better in the 1950 season. They racked up a 9–3 record, setting 22 NFL offensive records. While the rest of the league averaged 176 yards per game passing, the Rams averaged 294 yards. The Rams also averaged 38.8 points per game during the 1950 season, a record that would stand more than 50 years, until it was broken during the 2004 season by Peyton Manning and the Indianapolis Colts. (The Rams lost the 1950 NFL championship game to the Browns in Cleveland on a Lou Groza field goal, 30–28.)

Despite the Rams stellar performance during the 1950 season, attendance fell almost 50 percent to 26,804 from 49,854 in 1949. The Rams—and the league—blamed it on television. That's because in 1950 the Rams signed a contract with Admiral Television to broadcast all of the team's games—a departure from standard NFL practice, which only broadcast away games back into the home market. The Rams agreed to broadcast their local games, too, but hedged their bets by demanding that Admiral compensate the team for any drop in stadium attendance. Admiral ended up paying the Rams $307,000 in damages.

As a result of the debacle, NFL owners were convinced that broadcasting home games was a losing proposition. The NFL's approach to broadcasting contracts and profits continued to be disjointed and unbalanced throughout the 1950s; the Rams got $100,000 for TV rights in 1953, for example, while the Green Bay

Packers received only $5,000. For the next several years, each team negotiated its own local and regional contracts to broadcast only its six away games.

Bert Bell had solidified this practice by passing a rule that not only prevented home games from being televised but also prevented any other game from being telecast into a market in which a home game was being played. The rule was challenged in 1953, and federal Judge Allan K. Grim (remember that name) agreed with Bell and the league that broadcasting games into a market that was hosting a home game had a clearly detrimental effect on attendance. That decision would come back to haunt the NFL, albeit briefly, when the league wholeheartedly embraced television a decade later.

AMERICA'S FIRST "REALITY TV"

The NFL might have continued its haphazard approach to television programming if it hadn't been for Ed Scherick, a media buyer at New York's Dancer Fitzgerald Sample advertising agency. Scherick looked at the footprint of that tiny 11-station network that the Bears and (now) Cardinals had cobbled together in the Midwest and realized that it almost perfectly matched the distribution footprint of Falstaff Beer, one of Dancer's biggest clients. According to Ron Powers, author of *Super Tube: The Rise of Television Sports* (Coward-McCann, 1984), Scherick approached Bob Kintner, president of ABC television, about buying airtime for advertising. Kintner didn't know that one of his major stations—WBKB, later WLS out of Chicago—was broadcasting football games. Dancer bought half the airtime for a song. "It was the greatest media buy in the history of television," Scherick said.

While the NFL had only seen about $50,000 in television profits in 1951, by mid-decade the DuMont television network was paying the league $450,000 to broadcast just the NFL Championship games alone. And then, in 1958, the televised coverage of the

NFL Championship game between the New York Giants and the Baltimore Colts cemented the bond between television and football forever. More than 15,000 fans made the trip from Baltimore to New York that day to watch the Colts beat the Giants, 23–17, in a game that was watched by more than 45 million people, including President Dwight Eisenhower.

In effect, notes Powers, NFL football became America's first reality TV show. Long before the premieres of *Survivor*, *The Apprentice*, and *The Osbornes*, the live drama of the 1958 NFL Championship game hooked viewers who were hungry for entertainment other than the tightly scripted variety shows of the day. "Those long-ago viewers, their TV expectations already growing numb under the prepackaged neutralities of Perry Como and George Goebel and *Your Hit Parade*," writes Powers, "sat there and watched as a new kind of live video drama—an epic pageant of violence and grace, with real fortunes hanging in the balance—burned itself into their imaginations."

Powers goes on to describe the Colts' winning overtime drive against the Giants: "[Colts quarterback Johnny] Unitas disdained this prepackaged, fail-safe route to victory," Powers writes. "Instead of a cautious field goal, the young quarterback electrified the viewing millions by risking a defiant, flat pass that found Jim Mutscheller on the one-yard line." The next play, Allan Ameche's now-famous one-yard run into the end zone for the winning touchdown, is forever burned into America's collective television memory. When the Colts returned to Baltimore, they were mobbed by fans who nearly overturned their bus, a scene practically unheard of for professional football teams in an era dominated by Major League Baseball and college football. America had found—and fallen in love with—a new type of televised entertainment.

The moment was not lost on Bert Bell. "I never thought I'd see a day like today," Bell said in the press box after the historic game. Bell's death the following year, however, would prevent him from playing a meaningful role in crafting the terms of the NFL's lucrative relationship with television. Fortunately, waiting in the wings was a young man who, perhaps better than anyone, understood the power of television and how it could forever transform the game.

A NEW DAY—AND A NEW LEADER—FOR THE NFL

The story of Alvin Ray "Pete" Rozelle is well known to many who follow the NFL. He grew up in the Los Angeles suburbs, excelled at football, and after a stint in the Navy, attended tiny Compton Junior College, home to the Los Angeles Rams' training camp. He started out as a gofer for Tex Schramm, the Rams' public relations man. By 1957, having shown an uncanny knack for the game and the business, Rozelle had risen to become the Rams' general manager. Two years later, Rozelle, then only 33 and the youngest general manager in the league, was picked as Bert Bell's replacement after 23 votes and 7 days of deliberation. "The reason I was selected was probably that I was the only one who hadn't alienated most of the people in that meeting," Rozelle later said. "They said I'd grow into the job, and that, in effect, is what I did."

Little did the cliquish, eccentric group of NFL owners know how well their new commissioner would "grow into the job." Rozelle, perhaps better than anyone, read the omens in the 1958 NFL Championship game; and he understood that television, more than being merely an adjunct to ticket sales, represented the key to future financial riches for the NFL and its owners. Up to that time, the NFL had been satisfied with its $200,000-a-year contract with NBC to broadcast the championship game. But when the contract came up for renewal in 1959, the rights fees increased more than threefold to $615,000.

It was the beginning of a series of astronomical increases in NFL television rights fees, a trend that continues to this day. Further,

Rozelle would change the face of NFL broadcasting entirely. He would convince a cantankerous, independent group of owners to embrace Bert Bell's 1935 all-for-one mantra and apply it to television. More to the point, he would convince owners with teams in markets like New York, Chicago, and Los Angeles that their best interest lay in sharing television riches with the Green Bays and other smaller-market franchises.

Rozelle had his work cut out for him. In 1960, the business world of NFL television was a mess, and not too many people were happy about it. The Cleveland Browns arguably established the first national television contract through a broadcasting deal with Carling Beer on the independent Sports Network. NBC also had begun national telecasts of Baltimore Colts and Pittsburgh Steelers games, leaving CBS to broadcast games for the other nine NFL teams on regional networks across the country. As a result, some cities were getting three NFL telecasts every Sunday. This rankled CBS, which had paid the NFL for the rights to broadcast games for nine of the league's teams, while the Sports Network and NBC had paid only one and two teams, respectively, to reach the same audience. CBS, angered by the rights-fee disparity with NBC and the Sports Network, was on the verge of giving up on NFL football altogether.

While the NFL's television world was beginning to fall apart, and baseball couldn't—and never would—get its act together, another league's television plans were coming together quite nicely. Lamar Hunt was the latest in a long line of would-be owners who had been rejected by the NFL, a cartel that controlled the supply of its product better than the OPEC sheiks. But Hunt, son of Texas oil billionaire H.L. Hunt, wasn't very good at taking no for an answer.

So he cobbled together a group of wealthy investors—Barron Hilton in Los Angeles, Billy Sullivan in Boston, and Bud Adams in Houston—and formed the American Football League.

MAJOR LEAGUE BASEBALL'S ATTEMPTS TO LEVEL ITS OWN FIELD

Over in the world of Major League Baseball, the idea of a national television contract was being resurrected in 1960. A few baseball owners were making many of the same arguments originally put forward by Bert Bell in 1935, when he convinced the NFL owners to adopt a level playing field across the league to recruit top college talent.

"It has been reported that the American League club in New York City in 1959 realized a gross income of $1,400,000 from radio and television," legendary baseball owner Branch Rickey said in a 1960 speech. "The Washington club in the same league took in approximately $125,000, yet the Washington club plays 11 games at Yankee Stadium. How can Washington ever expect to compete in a competitive market for player contracts where money is king? Any rule or regulation that removes . . . the power of money to make the difference in playing strength is a good rule." To reduce this disparity of riches, Rickey proposed that the home team keep 33 percent of television revenue and 66 percent go into a kitty to be divided equally among the teams. St. Louis Browns owner Bill Veeck pitched his own television revenue-sharing plan to baseball owners in 1952, when he proposed a 50–50 split. Neither plan went very far.

Lamar Hunt, familiar with the demise of the AAFC, wanted to start a league that would challenge and compete with the NFL. Furthermore, he understood that to do that, he needed television. So from the very beginning Hunt built his league around a national television contract—the first of its kind in many ways—that would make the AFL teams solvent from day one. The AFL rules were tailor-made for television. There would be no "fair catch" on punts; there would be the option of running or passing for a two-point conversion after touchdowns; and the players' names would be printed on the backs of their jerseys, making them easily identifiable to even the most casual and novice fans.

The AFL first went to ABC, which had gained great success—and a hefty bank account—by airing college football each Saturday. The league asked ABC for a contract that would guarantee each team $600,000 per year. The network laughed. Instead, ABC ended up offering the AFL a five-year, $8.5 million contract that guaranteed each AFL team $170,000 per year, with incremental increases built into the contract. As a result, in 1960, all eight of the AFL teams were guaranteed to earn more in television revenue than five NFL teams put together. While that was, indeed, a large sum, the most important phrase of the contract was *each team*. In agreeing to distribute ABC's revenues equally among the clubs, the AFL hit upon a revolutionary TV rights formula. The revenue distribution also would reward the networks, putting professional football on a path to becoming the most profitable endeavor in the history of television sports.

Despite its solid financial footing from before the first kickoff, the AFL never became as popular at the NFL. Its ratings on ABC were consistently trounced by CBS' NFL coverage. But the AFL was an important wake-up call for Rozelle and the stodgy NFL owners.

ROZELLE'S PLAN: THE PERFECT SOCIALIST SYSTEM

By 1960, NFL television contracts were in disarray. CBS held 9 of the 12 NFL teams' television contracts, ranging from $175,000 for the New York Giants to $35,000 for the Green Bay Packers. The Baltimore Colts, which had mesmerized the nation in the 1958 title game, had a contract for $600,000 from NBC—almost 10 times what many smaller-market teams were paid. The Steelers had their own network, and the Cleveland Browns' Carling Beer network was broadcasting their games from the east coast to Texas.

With the AFL breathing down the NFL's neck, Rozelle, after just a year in office, opened the 1961 owners' meeting at the Warwick Hotel in New York with a frank discussion about television.

"Much of the past year has been spent in developing a television plan for the future," he said. "The NFL has been credited with harnessing television and using it to greater advantage than any other sports activity. This position, however, will be lost without planning for the future." As one commentator put it, Rozelle had begun laying the groundwork for what would become "the perfect socialist system."

It took two days of intense lobbying, especially with the Mara family, who owned the Giants. With the biggest market, the Giants had the most to lose from a collective TV contract. With some help from Vince Lombardi and the owners of smaller-market clubs (notably the Rooneys, owners of the Pittsburgh Steelers), Wellington Mara and his brother Jack were eventually persuaded that a national television contract was in the best interest of the league. "We should all share, I guess," Wellington Mara said. When he died in October 2005, many of his eulogies noted his role in forming the NFL's first national television contract as his greatest contribution to the league.

But Rozelle needed more than the consent of the NFL team owners. The first national television contract was struck down by U.S. district court judge Allan K. Grim. Remember him? He was the same judge who had allowed the league to black out home and competing games in home markets. In looking at the proposed national television contract, Grim cited antitrust concerns, noting that in granting the league permission in 1953 to black out local games, he hadn't given the league a collective right to do anything it desired in regard to television. As such, he couldn't allow the league to negotiate a national television contract.

Fortunately, for someone of Rozelle's masterful negotiating skills and endless contacts, this legal decision proved to be nothing more than a speed bump on the way to the bank. With the help of Colts owner Carroll Rosenbloom, who had many contacts in nearby Washington, D.C., Rozelle went to work and easily got the football-loving Kennedys and other politicians to move more favorable legislation through Congress. "Carroll Rosenbloom was very, very close to the Kennedys," said Giants general manager Ernie Accorsi, who began his NFL career in 1975 working for Pete Rozelle in the league offices. "He was a big donor in the primaries—a friend of Joe Kennedy."

On September 30, 1961, President Kennedy signed the Sports Broadcasting bill, giving the NFL an exemption from antitrust statutes. On January 10, 1962, a little more than three months after Kennedy signed the bill, CBS and the NFL signed the first national TV contract, for $4.65 million for two years. "The whole thing was equalizing the competition on the field," Rozelle said. "The sharing of income gave everyone the tools, the money, to compete equally."

The decision to share revenue was arguably the most important in ensuring the future economic success of the NFL. And while many were initially skeptical of the plan, the league, primarily thanks to revenue sharing, would become a model to which all others would eventually aspire, a league that guaranteed relative economic and competitive parity. The national television contract placed the highest priority on equality of opportunity for every NFL team over the revenue gains that could have been made solely by any one franchise. In short, it created a revenue structure that guaranteed that a team from Green Bay, Wisconsin, could compete with the New York Giants.

UPPING THE BID

In spite of the greatness of his other accomplishments, Rozelle really excelled in negotiations with the networks. He had an uncanny knack for getting the networks to bid against one another and to continually drive up the price for the NFL's national

NEW YORK GIANT'S MANAGER ERNIE ACCORSI ON WELLINGTON MARA AND THE NFL'S FIRST NATIONAL TELEVISION CONTRACT

Wellington Mara well understood the necessity for sharing television revenues within the NFL. "Whenever I talked to Mr. Mara about it, it was clear that he did not consider it a sacrifice," said Giants general manager Ernie Accorsi in a February 2006 interview. "He knew it was the right thing to do. He knew it meant the salvation of the league." Indeed, Accorsi said, Mara knew that without a national television contract, "There would be no Green Bay."

Accorsi also noted that many football historians give Chicago Bears owner George Halas credit for the survival of the Green Bay Packers, which is true, but it was also the Mara's agreement to share television revenues that ensured that the Packers and every other small-market team would thrive in the 21st century.

Accorsi acknowledges that Halas convinced the Green Bay community that building a stadium for the team was the right thing to do. "But if they [the Packers] didn't get to share in television money," Accorsi said, "they wouldn't have survived."

Wellington Mara's only regret, according to Accorsi, was that his father, team founder Tim Mara, did not live to see the growth in popularity of professional football. "The last game his dad saw was the 1958 Championship game," Accorsi said. "He didn't get to see the TV deal that would guarantee prosperity for the league for decades to come and the all-important role his sons played in making sure that happened. But because he saw that 1958 Championship game against the Colts, he saw the future of the NFL."

---

television package. Indeed, he was such a master tactician that he was able to increase the NFL's national television contract by 25 percent in a year without competitive bidding. The net result was a trend that continues to this day—network NFL contracts for sums beyond anyone's imagination.

In just the first 2 years of the NFL's collective television contract history, Rozelle was able to more than double the league's contract rights. In the first national television contract, CBS paid $4.6 million a year to broadcast NFL games. In 1964, that figure jumped to an astonishing $28.2 million for two years. In part, the contract jump resulted from the bidding between the networks for the rights to telecast two games each Sunday. But the lion's share of the credit for the double-digit increases in rights fees clearly goes to Pete Rozelle.

When the contract came up for renewal for the 1966–67 season, before the AFL-NFL merger, NBC had already acquired the AFL rights for five years for $36 million. ABC wasn't even in the picture. Dissatisfied with its early experiment with the AFL, ABC went back to the comfort of broadcasting college football, leaving CBS unopposed in its bid for the NFL contract. Certainly the network wouldn't have to pay more for NFL rights, you'd think. Think again.

Rozelle, ever the shrewd negotiator, threw the network a curve. He said that, if CBS didn't agree to the league's price, the NFL would start its own network, and he went on to explain to the network how he would do it by leasing dedicated telephone lines from AT&T. Unwilling to give up the NFL and its growing audience—especially the all-important 18–49 male category that Madison Avenue lived for and the NFL drew better than any other programming—CBS agreed to a new contract and a 25 percent increase, paying $37.6 million for two years of regular season games.

And so it would go for decades. In 1974, the NFL earned $63 million for its national broadcast rights. Five years later, the figure jumped to $164 million. In 1982, it was $427 million; in 1987, it jumped to $468 million; and in 1990, it rose to $925 million. As the following chart shows, today—and through 2011—the NFL gets about $3.75 billion a year for broadcast rights.

New NFL Network and Satellite TV Contracts That Begin with 2006 Season

ESPN (announced April 18, 2005) Monday night broadcasts
- Eight years (2006–2013)
- $1.1 billion per year
- No Super Bowls

NBC (announced April 18, 2005) Sunday night broadcasts
- Six years (2006–2011)
- $600 million per year
- Super Bowls in 2009 and 2012

Fox (announced November 8, 2004) Sunday afternoon NFC games
- Six years (2006–2011)
- $712.5 million per year
- Super Bowls in 2008 and one other year during deal

CBS (announced November 8, 2004) Sunday afternoon AFC games
- Six years (2006–2011)
- $622.5 million per year
- Super Bowls in 2007 and one other year during deal

DirecTV (announced November 8, 2004) Sunday Ticket satellite
- Five years (2006–2010)
- $700 million per year
- No Super Bowls

Source: Author compilation

All the NFL television contracts were up for renewal in 2005. The NFL sold its Sunday afternoon packages to CBS and Fox for about $8 billion, with $4.3 billion coming from Fox for the NFC games and about $3.7 billion coming from CBS for the AFC games. The annual rights fees that the NFL will receive from Fox and CBS increased by 25 percent to 30 percent in the new deals. The NFL also agreed to a five-year, $3.5 billion contract extension with DirecTV for the Sunday Ticket package, which broadcasts every game, through the 2010 season. Broken down annually, the

DirecTV contract went from about $400 million a year to about $700 million.

And of course, these ever-escalating contracts not only continue to astonish television, advertising, and league executives alike but put the NFL in the stratosphere when compared with other professional sports franchises.

THE BROADCASTING STAKES TODAY

As the following Kagan World Media chart shows, over the past 30 years, the NFL has consistently obliterated the other stick and ball sports leagues in terms of television revenues. In 2000, the NFL television contract, which earned the league $2.27 billion a year, was worth nearly 19 times the NHL television contract, 6½ times the Major League Baseball contract, and 3½ times the NBA contract. The NFL performed equally well in terms of ratings. For the 2000–01 season, the NFL's average regular season rating of 10.8 was more than 3 times the audience the NBA drew, about 4 times the average baseball audience, and 18 times the audience drawn by the National Hockey League.

What's more impressive is that the NFL continued to increase the value of its national television contract at the same time that televised sports in general were seeing a significant decline in advertising revenue. During the 2000–01 season, network television grossed about $2.7 billion from ads sold during almost 7,000 minutes of major league sports programming. But with total network sports broadcast rights of $3.4 billion—the lion's share of which went to the NFL—the networks lost about $695 million.

ABC, CBS, and Fox paid about $2 billion in 2000 for NFL rights. But the networks earned just $1.7 billion in ad dollars. By contrast, NBC and Fox spent about $550 million on Major League Baseball broadcast rights in 2000 and took in $317 million in ad revenue, resulting in a $233 million loss. Only the NBA made money for the networks, costing NBC about $440 million but

National Broadcast TV Rights Fees: Average per Year ($ mil.)

Year	NHL	NBA	NFL	MLB
1974	–	9	63	43
1975	–	9	63	43
1976	–	11	63	52
1977	–	11	63	52
1978	–	19	164	52
1979	–	19	164	52
1980	–	19	164	97
1981	–	19	164	97
1982	4	28	427	97
1983	4	28	427	97
1984	4	28	427	183
1985	8	28	427	183
1986	8	56	427	183
1987	8	56	468	183
1988	17	17	468	183
1989	17	17	468	183
1990	17	17	219	366
1991	6	219	219	366
1992	14	219	219	366
1993	14	219	219	366
1994	44	278	278	193
1995	44	278	278	193
1996	44	278	278	300
1997	44	278	278	345
1998	44	660	660	345
1999	120	660	660	345
2000	120	660	660	345
2001	120	660	660	–
2002	120	–	–	–
2003	120	–	–	–
2004	–	–	–	–
2005	–	–	–	–

bringing in $710 million in ad revenue, for a tidy profit of about $270 million. Baseball's six-year contract with Fox (through 2006) covered the regular season, All-Star game, and postseason, for a total worth of about $2.5 billion. Major League Baseball, following in the NFL's footsteps, also announced plans to launch its own cable network in 2006.

"We've acquired wide-ranging rights to fuel all of the multimedia businesses of ESPN that today number over a dozen and will continue to grow," ESPN and ABC Sports president George Bodenheimer said. That's all well and good, but it's still about five times less than what the network paid to acquire the rights to Monday Night Football, the game that took the NFL into the television stratosphere and changed the game's popularity, style, and reach forever.

And so, thanks to the efforts of Pete Rozelle, the NFL commands the largest television contracts in sports. This is especially true for the Super Bowl, a television spectacle that has taken on a life all its own and dwarfs every other broadcast in terms of ratings and advertising fees. And the Super Bowl television bonanza wouldn't exist today if it weren't for Monday Night Football, which debuted in 1970. Monday Night Football represents more than football's birth as one of the world's most sought-after advertising vehicles; by introducing football to a prime-time audience, Monday Night Football launched an expansion of the NFL's fan base that continues to this day.

CHAPTER FIVE

THE NFL GOES
PRIME TIME

MONDAY NIGHT FOOTBALL AND
MAINSTREAM AUDIENCES

I doubt that Pete Rozelle had "The Bone Lady" in mind when he created *Monday Night Football*. The Bone Lady is actually Debra Darnall of Columbus, Ohio, who jumped on the Cleveland Browns bandwagon when the team returned to the NFL in 1999. Before every Browns home game, she and about 10,000 other fanatical Browns fans can be found in the "Muni Lot," the municipal parking lot that sits across Highway 2 from Cleveland Browns Stadium. I met her before the Browns' 2005 regular season opener against their in-state rivals, the Cincinnati Bengals. There she was, festooned in her orange skirt plastered with Cleveland Browns slogans, her faux beehive hairdo covered in doggie treats that look like hair rollers and barrettes, and a large dog biscuit in her hand. "I followed the little voice in my head," she said of her decision to paint her car orange, put a big bone on the roof, and take on the persona of The Bone Lady. "That's what happens when you have too much beer and too much glue."

While Darnall's a bit of an extreme example, many women are avid followers of NFL football. According to the NFL, about 375,000 women attend NFL games each week, and 45 million watch the games on TV. In fact, women today account for almost 50 percent of the NFL audience. And this growing love affair all began when *Monday Night Football* introduced the NFL to prime time—and the female audience.

As a result of that success—and the NFL's prescient nod to female fans in recent years—women are the fastest-growing segment among the league's fan base. In a September 2004 Harris Poll, 30 percent of women said NFL football was their favorite sport—that's almost more than the other major sports combined. Major league baseball came in at 14 percent, college football at 10 percent, NASCAR at 8 percent, and the NBA at 7 percent. The NFL even comes out ahead of more traditional female sports like gymnastics and figure skating. And the Super Bowl? Forget about it—the Super Bowl draws more women viewers than the Academy Awards. According to a recent survey, about 37 million women watch the Super Bowl, while only about 27 million watch the Academy Awards.

Women NFL fans aren't just spectators, either. More than a million girls participate in the NFL's Pepsi Punt, Pass, and Kick competition each year, and more than 10,000 women attend one of the NFL 101 Workshops for Women that teams present in each market. "It's standing room only," said Sandra Van Meek, marketing director for the Atlanta Falcons. Since Home Depot cofounder Arthur Blank took over the team five years ago, the Falcons have grown their fan base significantly, and many of those new fans are women.

"We sell out every NFL 101 Workshop we have," Van Meek said. "Women are just dying to get in and learn more about the game." Of the women who participate in the fast-growing fantasy sports world, more than 75 percent play fantasy football, while about 38 percent play fantasy baseball and 35 percent play fantasy basketball. The NFL has started to recognize these trends and tap into the growing female market.

"There are more women becoming avid fans of the NFL than any other sport," said Susan Rothman, the NFL's vice president in charge of merchandising. "What they love is that it's the one time of the week that the family all gets together." And the more women know about football, the more comfortable and avid they become as fans. Says Rothman, "The number of casual fans to rabid fans is growing faster than ever in the NFL, and many of them are women."

This expansion into a new fan base—and a massive new source of revenue—kicked off when *Monday Night Football* moved the NFL to prime-time entertainment and brought it to the attention of mainstream audiences. *Monday Night Football* boosted the NFL's standing as a sports franchise and introduced professional football to a female audience; in doing so, it forever changed the economics of the league.

THE NFL HITS PRIME-TIME TELEVISION

The NFL's ascendancy to prime-time network television began when Pete Rozelle announced the AFL-NFL merger in 1966. The rotten deal that CBS got from the merger illustrates what a ruthless negotiator Rozelle was when it came to national television contracts. Rozelle bludgeoned CBS into agreeing to a 25 percent increase in NFL rights fees for the 1966–67 season (the uncontested year). He also got the network to agree to pay $2 million for rights to each of the NFL Championship games in 1966 and 1967. But before the network could broadcast either of those games, Rozelle secretly negotiated the merger between the NFL and the AFL, thus relegating CBS' $2 million purchase of the NFL Championship game to nothing more than a divisional title, namely the National Football Conference (NFC) Championship game. When CBS executive Bill MacPhail asked Rozelle why he hadn't told the network of the pending merger of the two leagues, Rozelle calmly said, "Because it was our business and nobody else's." In fact, Rozelle already had plans for a new championship game to be called the Super Bowl.

NBC wasn't too happy with the NFL, either. After the merger, NBC continued to broadcast the AFL games, while CBS began broadcasting the NFL. Starting in 1970, NBC became the network of the American Football Conference, while CBS retained the rights to broadcast the NFC games. NBC complained that its broadcasting rights mostly gave it the NFL's second-tier cities. With the exception of New York and the Jets, NBC was right; many of the AFC (formerly AFL) teams were in places like Buffalo, Denver, and Houston. So in 1970, Rozelle convinced Baltimore, Cleveland, and Pittsburgh—NFL teams that had become part of the NFC after the merger—to move to the AFC to address NBC's concerns and balance out the television demographics and ratings.

So in 1970, just 10 years into his 30-year tenure as NFL commissioner, Rozelle had convinced the league to negotiate national broadcasting rights, increased those rights at least twofold every time the contract came up for renegotiation, and managed to broker an AFL merger with his league. But that wasn't enough for Rozelle. His dream was to have the NFL play in prime time. Rozelle undoubtedly saw a prime-time NFL broadcast as a means to add another zero to the end of the national television contract. Furthermore, he knew that a prime-time game would further enhance the NFL's credibility with the segment of the American television audience that hadn't yet embraced it.

Still, in 1970, prime-time football was a pipe dream. While viewers today take 150 cable and satellite channels for granted, during the early 1970s, ABC, CBS, and NBC ruled the airwaves. Prime-time broadcasting was dominated by shows like *Gunsmoke*, *Carol Burnett*, and *All in the Family*, and even the unbelievable broadcasting fees Rozelle had managed to win from the networks paled in comparison to what the networks were getting for prime-time programming. More important, in 1970, sports still had second-class citizenship in the network hierarchy. Yes, sports directors had a seat in the boardrooms at ABC, CBS, and NBC; and sports, particularly college football, was a cash cow for the networks. But for the most part, the sports division was still looked down upon by network executives who considered it a necessary evil that had to be tolerated.

Yet, even in this highly prejudicial environment, Rozelle had convinced NBC in 1968 to experiment with some prime-time NFL broadcasts on Monday nights. Rozelle knew going into the negotiations that NBC would likely agree to a Monday night package, because the lineup at CBS was so strong (and ABC was still a third-tier network). Unfortunately, the game ran until after midnight, preempting the start of the *Tonight Show*, which sent Johnny Carson into a fit. That abruptly ended any interest NBC had in broadcasting prime-time NFL games. The experience further convinced network executives that broadcasting NFL games in prime time was a losing proposition, because the duration of the games was unpredictable, making it a bad fit for the network television programming schedule.

Over at CBS, they were still stinging from the shenanigans Rozelle had pulled with the merger of the NFL and the AFL, in which the network lost its championship games with the stroke of a pen. Further, CBS had the strongest Monday night lineup on television. No way was the network going to change programming to accommodate the NFL. Even for Rozelle, the master negotiator, CBS was a dead end.

That left fledgling ABC, which in 1970 was struggling as a distant third to CBS and NBC in ratings and prestige. The network initially turned Rozelle down. ABC Sports president Roone Arledge didn't want to say no, but he was under pressure from network executives who thought ABC was foolish even to consider a prime-time NFL broadcast. Never one to take no for an answer, Rozelle returned a few days later and told ABC that he had a deal with the Hughes Sports Network to carry the NFL's prime-time Monday night broadcast. The network was owned by, yes, Howard Hughes. The eccentric billionaire was in the midst of forging another new business venture, this one to launch a fourth television network to compete with ABC, CBS, and NBC. As much of a long shot as that was, the networks took the challenge from Hughes seriously and tried to thwart him at every turn.

ABC had reason to reconsider Rozelle's proposal. The majority of Hughes' affiliates that had shown interest in broadcasting a prime-time NFL game were independent stations in flyover country that CBS was trouncing in Monday night ratings. These stations were strongly affiliated with ABC but would clearly defect for the promise of the NFL's ratings. Rozelle and Arledge eventually convinced ABC to take a gamble on *Monday Night Football*—and Rozelle himself couldn't have scripted the first season any better.

The first regular season telecast of *Monday Night Football* featured Joe Namath, the telegenic quarterback of the New York Jets. The upstart former AFC team had slain one of the NFL's giants, the Baltimore Colts, 16–7 in Super Bowl III at Miami's Orange Bowl. While some people scoffed at the idea of a prime-time NFL game—especially network executives who still looked down their noses at sports programming—the game was an undeniable success. In its first season, ABC's *Monday Night Football* drew an average share of 31 percent, meaning that nearly one-third of all Americans watching television were tuned to the game. More important, that was well above the 24 share that ABC had said it needed to make the show work. *Monday Night Football* had laid down a strong prime-time footprint, and audiences around the country were tuning in.

THE MAKING OF A PRIME-TIME STAR

The unmitigated success of *Monday Night Football* continues today. It is consistently one of the highest-rated prime-time shows on television. Indeed, the other two networks often use Monday nights from September to January to air experimental pilots, knowing full well that they have no chance of eclipsing the ratings of "that football game."

I went to a half-dozen Monday night games during the 2005 season, and the games clearly felt like something special. These games *are* special, in part simply because they're night games. The appeal of night games for many harkens back to Friday night high school football games, which form the root of organized football for most people. Night games also clearly distinguish the NFL from college football, which is almost always played on cool crisp Saturday afternoons in autumn. The Monday night games look different, too—on television and at the stadium. The uniform colors are a bit brighter and the helmets sparkle a little more under the intense floodlights. The grass seems greener, the white lines on the field seem more distinct, and the zebra stripes of the referee uniforms in sharper contrast. Finally, the crowd at the stadium senses that the game is being broadcast during prime time, and that gives the entire event a special feel. These fans know that they're taking part in what is probably the biggest television event of the week, and their excitement is palpable.

The television spectacle of *Monday Night Football* is an increasingly important part of the stadium experience. For instance, when I attended the 2005 Monday night game between the Kansas City Chiefs and the Denver Broncos, a publicity person for the host Broncos actually came out and warmed up the crowd. One side of the stadium was given blue-and-orange placards. On cue, they turned them over, and one whole side of the stadium was transformed into the Broncos logo. A camera in the blimp hovering overhead zoomed in on this and transmitted the picture around the world. While the beneficiaries of this visual display were primarily in the TV audience, the people in the stands clearly felt that they were a part of the broadcast.

These are just some of the reasons that *Monday Night Football* has become a prime-time cash cow. Perhaps more importantly, the unfolding drama and excitement of a live football game are perfectly suited to prime-time television. As Ron Powers, the author of *Super Tube*, noted about the early days of *Monday Night Football*, "It did not require the stultifying presence of jaded, formula-deadened Hollywood scriptwriters and producers, because the players on the field became their own characters and improvised their own narrative destinies."

PLAYING TO THE CAMERA: LONG SHOTS, HIGHLIGHTS, AND INSTANT REPLAYS

Of course, by 1970, the unscripted drama of the NFL had been playing out on NBC and CBS daytime broadcasts for nearly a decade. But those broadcasts were fixed and formulaic. The NBC and CBS cameras recorded the game's movement on the field but told you little about the players and what the games meant for them and their teams. "This austere technique, or lack of technique," Powers said, "goes far toward explaining why professional football was perceived as a dehumanized, corporate-militaristic allegory on the older networks, and why, through ABC's prism, it became a parable of the personal and the grand."

While *Monday Night Football* was Rozelle's idea, the credit for its successful execution clearly has to go to Arledge and his skilled director, Chet Forte. *Monday Night Football* was exactly the vehicle Arledge had been looking for to bring together all the elements—technical and dramatic—that he knew a network sports telecast could be.

Arledge had actually laid out the basics a decade earlier in a 1960 memo to ABC executives:

We will utilize every production technique that has been learned in producing variety shows, in covering political conventions, in shooting travel and adventure series to heighten the viewer's feeling of actually sitting in the stands and participating personally in the excitement and color of walking through a college campus to the stadium to watch the big game. To improve upon the audience, we must gain and hold the interest of women and others who are not fanatical followers of the sport we happen to be televising. Women come to football games, not so much to marvel at the adeptness of the quarterback in calling an end sweep or a lineman pulling out to lead a play, but to sit in a crowd, see what everyone else is wearing, watch the cheerleaders, and experience the countless things that make up the feeling of the game.

Super Tube author Powers notes that Arledge understood his viewers and their interests very well:

If the three networks have been accused of prurient dwelling on the faces and long legs of beautiful cheerleaders, Arledge's corollary dwelling on the male athletes' sexual appeal has received almost no comment— but it helped attract women to *Monday Night Football*, and women provided its margin of ratings success.

Throughout the 1960s, Arledge used ABC's college football broadcasts to hone his sports broadcasting skills. For instance, it was Arledge who thought to mount a camera on the roof of Veterans Hospital in Pittsburgh and peer down into Pitt Stadium, long before blimps were a common sight above stadiums. And while CBS was the first to use instant replay during the 1963 Army-Navy game, it was Arledge who mastered it later in the decade. Indeed, as Bob Boyles and Paul Guido note in *Fifty Years of College Football,* the technology was so new that CBS football announcer Lindsay Nelson kept yelling, "This is a videotape. They did not score again," when CBS showed a replay of Army quarterback Rollie Stichweh running for a touchdown.

Indeed, the ABC Sports crew embraced technology like no one else, and that instinct was continually fostered by Arledge, who never stopped listening to his engineers and technicians. They constantly brought him new technology—miniature cameras and microphones, tape machines, slow-motion effects—that Arledge adapted masterfully to the game and the broadcast. Arledge made the most of existing technologies, too; instead of using just a few cameras to cover the game, Forte's crew used 12. Thanks to Arledge's mastery of television technology and football's continuing meteoric rise into the American sports psyche, *Monday Night Football* became, as Powers said, "state-of-the-art television covering state-of-the-art sport."

THE RATINGS GAME

Within just a few years of its first broadcast, ABC's *Monday Night Football* was an overwhelming success. In fact, it was a little too successful for some rival network executives. In January 1972, Robert D. Wood, president of CBS, penned a pointed letter to Rozelle, noting that he believed that the NFL was playing scheduling favorites with *Monday Night Football.* Looking at the past two seasons, Wood wrote, "In each of these seasons, we expected that for the 13 [Monday night] games, each of the 26 teams would appear on one occasion. Instead, we found that in 1970, five teams did not appear at all on prime-time television while five other teams played twice on Monday nights."

Rozelle was unfazed. He continued with a formula that he knew was a proven winner. And 10 years later, he was still commanding double-digit increases in the NFL television contract. Indeed, in 1982, Rozelle negotiated a new set of contracts that sent shudders through even the high-dollar world of television advertising. From ABC, he got a 5-year, $680 million contract in exchange for putting the network into the Super Bowl rotation for the first time. From NBC, Rozelle extracted—some would say extorted—$700 million, an enormous sum when you consider that, even with adjustments in the league, the AFC package was considered to be less lucrative because the teams were in smaller markets (Kansas City, Denver, Houston, and so on). From CBS, Rozelle negotiated $720 million, a 150 percent increase over the previous contract with the network. That made the total 1982 NFL television package worth more than $2 billion.

The NFL had come a long way from that initial 1962 national television contract of $4.6 million a year. And Rozelle's legacy continues today. In 2006, ABC, CBS, ESPN, and NBC will pay the league $3.7 billion a year. And these rights fees continue to go up, even though the networks have lost money—on paper anyway— on NFL broadcasts for decades. That's because the price to broadcast NFL games grew so high that there was no way the networks could ever recover the fees. But network executives understood—then and now—that the NFL brings something much more valuable than advertising revenue. It brings ratings. *Monday Night Football* is consistently one of the highest-rated prime-time broadcasts on television.

Indeed, every network executive knew before they even signed the 2006 NFL television contract that they'd never get back in advertising during the games what they paid to broadcast the games. But the ad revenue that the networks generate during the broadcasts themselves is just part of the accounting equation. That's because the NFL consistently delivers—better and more broadly than any other programming—the most valuable demographic in television: males 18–49.

The networks also are willing to pay to broadcast NFL games because by maintaining a larger audience, they also maintain their "major network" status. The networks may not make their money back during NFL broadcasts alone, but the ratings from those broadcasts so inflate the network's average ratings and audience, that they boost ad rates for programming across the board. That, in short, is how the networks recoup the exorbitant fees they pay for NFL broadcasting rights. And, as we'll see in later chapters, the networks also pay for NFL rights to get the playoff and Super Bowl broadcast rights.

A CLOSER LOOK AT THE NFL RATINGS

The NFL typically delivers a regular season television rating of about 10. By comparison, basketball delivers about a 3, Major League Baseball a 2.5, and hockey less than 1. For the playoffs, the NFL rating jumps to the midteens, while baseball goes to about 7, basketball to about 5, and the NHL about 3. When it comes to the Championship games, the NFL blows the other sports leagues out of the water in ratings. The 10 most-watched TV programs of all time in terms of total viewers are all Super Bowls. About 91 million Americans watched the Pittsburgh Steelers defeat the Seattle Seahawks on ABC in Super Bowl XL. The last time the Super Bowl's average audience exceeded 90 million was in 1996 when the Steelers lost to the Dallas Cowboys.

In the United States, the most watched game was the 1998 Super Bowl between the Denver Broncos and the Green Bay Packers, which received a 44.5 rating and 67 share—representing about 90 million homes. By comparison, the final episode of M*A*S*H in February 1983 drew a higher rating of 60.2 but a total audience of only about 50 million households. In terms of household percentage, the most watched game was Super Bowl XVI in 1982, which was watched in 49.1 percent of households (73 share), or more than 40 million households.

THE MOVE TO ESPN

Today, *Monday Night Football* is an event. People plan their week around it; the game and the outcome dominate office conversation every Tuesday from September through January. About the only televised sport that beats it in popularity is the Super Bowl, which continues to be one of the biggest days in television.

The 2005 season was the last for ABC's *Monday Night Football*, but hold on, lest you think the network finally decided the broadcast fees were too high. Walt Disney, the parent company of ABC and ESPN, merely decided that it made more economic sense to move *Monday Night Football* to ABC's cable cousin, ESPN. With the NFL's 2006 move to ESPN, Disney pays the NFL almost $1 billion a year for the rights to make the broadcasting move, knowing full well that it will mean a significant ratings decline for ABC. To understand the economics behind this move, a little history is in order.

From 1998 to 2005, when it acquired the rights to *Monday Night Football*, ESPN's deal for broadcasting Sunday night games had an average annual cost of about $600 million, or a total of $4.8 billion. That's double what ABC was paying for *Monday Night Football* and made ESPN the biggest spender for NFL television rights. As part of the network shuffle that began with the new NFL national broadcast contracts in 2006, NBC took over the Sunday night NFL broadcast that had been on ESPN. In the last seven weeks of the 2006 NFL season, the NFL also planned to experiment with flexible broadcasting, something it had never done before; as a result, NBC, in cooperation with the league, is allowed to move games from the Sunday afternoon broadcasts on CBS or Fox to NBC's Sunday night slot. This, in effect, gives NBC the power to broadcast the greatest matchups each week as the season unfolds. For that flexibility, NBC pays about $600 million a year and gets the extremely lucrative Super Bowl broadcasting rights for 2008 and 2011.

So why is Disney, the parent company of both ABC and ESPN, willing to pay the higher broadcast fees for ESPN but not for ABC? In short, Disney believed that ABC's ratings were not growing enough to justify the fee increase for the NFL's Monday night package. And that's in line with what experts predicted would happen back in the early days of cable. A 1982 study from National Economic Research Associates, Inc., for example, noted, "The impact of pay TV on the value of league network contracts, and on the number of network sports broadcasts, will be signifi- cant but small." The group also accurately predicted that the total number of broadcasts (free and pay) would increase. As pre- dicted, the NFL eventually saw cable television as a better vehicle for broadcasts, because cable subscription rates produced more revenue, as compared to free network television. Thus, the ABC/ ESPN swap in 2006.

The economics work for Disney at ESPN, because that net- work has more revenue sources than ABC. And while ABC's rat- ings will almost assuredly decline with the loss of the *Monday Night Football* broadcast, the gains at ESPN will offset those losses and keep parent company Disney's ratings and audience size where they need to be, allowing the company to recoup the costs associated with *Monday Night Football* through ad rates across its networks.

RIDING THE REVENUE STREAM

The 2006 broadcast rights shuffle also revealed what Rozelle inherently understood long before the network executives: Once hooked on the unparalleled demographics and ratings that come with the NFL, networks would find it very hard to give up such a powerful revenue stream. Looking at the 2006 contracts, it's clear that ABC took the risk of losing ratings while NBC, which hadn't broadcast an NFL game since 1997, was forced to risk spending large amounts of money to regain network ratings.

All the while, the NFL just keeps getting richer. The new television contracts with CBS, DirecTV, ESPN, Fox, and NBC more than doubled the NFL's annual television revenues to about $3.75 billion in 2006. That's more than the total national TV money spent annually on the NBA, Major League Baseball, NASCAR, the PGA Tour, the NCAA basketball tournament, and the summer Olympics—combined. The only risk for the NFL is that its broadcasts are no longer offered exclusively on free television. With the *Monday Night Football* broadcast migrating to ESPN, viewers will have to have cable to see it. But with cable in about 60 percent of U.S. households, the NFL's gamble is small.

Of course, despite this phenomenal record of ever-increasing television contracts and ratings that no other programming can consistently deliver, some think the NFL train is perilously close to going off the tracks. A July 2004 panel at the Wharton School at the University of Pennsylvania predicted that the money networks were willing to shell out for sports programming was about to drop off.

"The growth rate is certainly going to slow," said Robert DiGisi, an adjunct marketing professor at Wharton. He said that some of the fundamentals that led to an economic boom for network sports in the 1990s have changed for good, noting that Fox spent billions to secure rights to professional football in the early 1990s as it was establishing itself as the fourth broadcast network. "You could argue that sports built the Fox network," DiGisi said.

He and other Wharton economists argued that splitting the media pie by driving content to cable, satellite, and other forms of new media such as wireless and the Internet would put pressure on the league's television revenue model. "They are eating into their revenue sources," said J.P. Dolman, vice president and director of ESPN ABC Sports customer marketing and sales. "We believe a certain amount of sports dollars are out there, so the more networks there are, the more you have to split up the pie."

A Wharton panel that looked at sports broadcasting rights before the 2006 NFL contracts were finalized predicted that the league's double-digit gains in broadcast revenue would begin to slow. But, in fact, that didn't happen. The NFL contract that expired in 2005 was worth about $2.2 billion, double the previous contract of $1.1 billion. The panel further predicted that the NFL contract beginning in 2006 would only increase by 5 to 10 percent. The new round of NFL television contracts that began with the 2006 season, however, were worth $3.75 billion a year—a 70 percent increase from the previous contract. "The bottom line is that . . . they are making it difficult for us to make our money back," ABC's Dolman said.

Maybe so, but overall ad spending continues to increase, with much of it going to NFL broadcasts, particularly the playoffs and Super Bowl. During 2005, an estimated $200 million more was in the ad marketplace, with average prices up over 10 percent. Dolman's network, ABC, sold over 80 percent of its available Super Bowl ads before the big game at an average price of $2.2 million per 30-second spot. Those rates represented a new high—15 percent more than the $1.95 million Fox had received the year before. In the end, the cost for a 30-second spot during the 2006 Super Bowl topped out at $2.5 million, a 4 percent increase from what Fox had charged to advertise during the 2005 Super Bowl in Jacksonville. Furthermore, Ford, Microsoft, and Gateway—just to name a few big-name sponsors—became NFL sponsor/partners for the Sunday night, regular season broadcast package.

But there is some validity to what Dolman said. The financial advising firm of Morgan Stanley Dean Witter predicted that ABC, CBS, and Fox would lose a total of $2.9 billion on their combined NFL contracts. Further, Fox publicly admitted to writing down $387 million of NFL losses as part of a $909 million sports reconciliation. And no one is sure what impact satellite television will eventually have on NFL broadcasting rights fees. DirecTV has about 10.7 million subscribers, and digital cable systems have passed 17 million subscribers on the way to a projected 40 million over the next several years. The emergence of cable and pay-per-view could have a profound effect on future NFL television rights fees—all, I'm sure, in the NFL's favor.

BROADCASTING GAMES ON THE NFL NETWORK

Starting with the 2006 season, the NFL complicated the television revenue picture by doing something the league (and its chairman, Pete Rozelle) promised it would never do—broadcasting its own games. The NFL Network, which broadcasts on cable and satellite television and on Sirius satellite radio, began broadcasting on November 4, 2003; by the end of the 2005 season, the network could be seen in about 40 million homes. In its first two years, the NFL Network's lineup was primarily pregame and postgame talk shows, interviews, and current season highlights. The network also has a show devoted to fantasy football, as well as historic replays of games taken from the vast archives of NFL Films. But in January of 2006, commissioner Paul Tagliabue announced that the NFL Network would begin broadcasting the league's games, premiering with a game on Thanksgiving night.

In addition to airing on the NFL Network, the games also will be shown on local stations in the teams' home markets. "After discussing this new package of games with many potential partners, we decided it would be best presented on our own, high-quality NFL Network, which has developed so rapidly that the time had come to add live, regular season games to the programming," Tagliabue said. "In the end, we wanted these games on our network, which is devoted 24/7 to the sport of football, and not on a multisport network."

"This turns the NFL Network into a serious force to be reckoned with," said Robert Thompson, professor of television and popular culture at Syracuse University. "If you're really going to make the brand of the NFL Network mean something, you're going to have to have some NFL games on it."

The NFL television package is worth about $4 billion a year. Analysts estimate that the NFL gave up a few hundred million dollars in potential television revenue by agreeing to broadcast the eight games on the NFL Network. The longer-term concern is that the NFL will eventually put all its games on its network and charge cable and satellite networks to carry the NFL Network and the games.

Another unintended consequence of the eight-game, Thursday night package could be the impact on fantasy football players. As you'll learn in the next chapter, this segment of NFL fans—once a small pocket of "stat geeks" amid the NFL's larger fan base—has grown exponentially over the past few years. Fantasy players typically finalize their rosters on Friday afternoons; the Thursday night NFL Network game package will force them to do it earlier. At the time of this writing, we have yet to see whether there will be any fantasy player backlash during the 2006 season.

Of course, the NFL has not only maintained growth in its national television contract—earning the league, teams, and players more money than ever before—but, as the next chapter also reveals, the league has further benefited from an early and fairly successful strategy of harnessing the power of new media. The NFL has been particularly savvy in its use of satellite television, the Internet, and video games. And through team Web sites, NFL Network broadcasts, and other new media efforts, the NFL has increasingly catered to the fantasy football crowd, demonstrating that the league understands just how important these fanatical fans are for building NFL brand loyalty.

CHAPTER SIX

SPORTS BARS, SATELLITES, AND FANTASY FOOTBALL

NEW MEDIA, NEW MARKETS

For a sense of how new media has transformed the NFL, just look at fantasy football. Current estimates put the number of people playing fantasy football each year at anywhere from 20 to 30 million. Over 3 million fantasy football magazines are sold before each season. Every major sports network has added fantasy football components to their broadcasts: Web sites, newspapers, and television shows. And while over 80 percent of these fantasy footballers have played for five years or less, most are only one or two years into the experience.

As in any fantasy sports game, fantasy football players act as the president, owner, manager, and coach of their own franchise. Putting together a team of actual players and competing against other teams within the fantasy league requires enormous amounts of statistical analysis and tracking. Not that long ago, all that was done with paper and pencil. Players had to have their rosters in to the commissioner—a designated league organizer, statistician, and arbitrator—by Friday afternoon at the latest, usually by fax. The commissioner then coordinated all the team rosters and changes—by hand—before the Sunday games. Often, the commissioner would have to wait until the Monday morning newspaper to get all the statistics needed to tabulate scores. And then, of course, there was the Monday night game.

The really good fantasy football league commissioners would have it all figured out by Tuesday afternoon and have put the results in the mail immediately, so players would get them by Thursday—just in time to make their roster moves for the next week. In the meantime, the players would have to scan the newspapers to look for roster moves and injury updates in the real NFL.

"It was pretty low-tech," said Jon McDaid, a writer from Philadelphia who started playing fantasy football in 1997. "It was Amish fantasy football."

No more. NFL fantasy football is real-time and, by most estimates, here to stay. Moreover, the NFL hopped on the fantasy football bandwagon early and has ridden it deftly during its meteoric rise over the past five years. Although fantasy football doesn't make the NFL a ton of cash, it's one of the best brand builders to come along in decades. While it sometimes tests fantasy footballers loyalty to their hometown team, it has made everyone care a whole lot more about the NFL and pay strict attention to what's going on in football. By any marketer's measure, that's never a bad thing.

But fantasy football is just the latest example of how the NFL has been an early and adept adopter of new media. The NFL was one of the first to master the network television model and has continued to adapt as new technologies have emerged: cable and satellite television, the Internet, and satellite radio. As a result, today's NFL fans, whether or not they live in their favorite team's home city, are better connected than perhaps any other major league sports fan to their "home team" of choice.

In fact, teams like the Washington Redskins and Atlanta Falcons are using their Web sites not only to stay connected with fans year-round but also to give them real-time video of press conferences, in-depth player interviews, and insights into the team that even the mainstream media sometimes doesn't get. From sports bars carrying satellite broadcasts of every game to wireless game broadcasts and league updates, the NFL has taken advantage of the digital revolution to forge deeper and more continuous bonds with its ever-expanding fan base.

SATELLITE TELEVISION BROADCASTS DELIVER THE NFL TO ITS FANS

As you learned in previous chapters, television was the springboard that vaulted the NFL past major league baseball to make it the most popular sport in America. Television was the new media of the 1950s, but the later developments of cable and satellite television drastically changed the way the NFL marketed itself. Those new media helped the NFL and its teams to build their brand not only locally but also across the country and the world.

To see the astounding impact of these broadcasts on the NFL and its fans, all you need to do is walk into a place like TNT's Sports Bar and Grill in Morton, Illinois, on any Sunday during the NFL season. There, as in similar sports bars around the country, you'll find more than a dozen televisions tuned to every game in the league. When I went to TNT's one October afternoon in 2005, TVs were showing the Green Bay Packers versus the Minnesota Vikings, the Detroit Lions versus the Cleveland Browns, and the Indianapolis Colts versus the Houston Texans—all at the request of fans who pack the bar every week and are easily identifiable by their team hats, T-shirts, and jerseys. This mosaic of fans, glued to televisions broadcasting games between their favorite NFL teams, might seem unremarkable to you. But to executives from the NFL, the networks, and their sponsors,

TNT's—or any corner tavern, chain restaurant, or sports bar car-rying the games—represents a marketer's dream come true.

To put it in marketing terms, new media like cable and satellite television, the Internet, fantasy football leagues, and wireless broadcasts allow the NFL and its 32 franchises to build incredible brand loyalty. This, in turn, fuels the NFL's $3.5 billion annual merchandise business. More importantly, behind all these new media are billions of dollars in NFL rights fees, as well as tens of billions of dollars in local, national, and international advertising.

Of course, following your favorite NFL team wasn't always this easy. Just ask Randy Williams, Sr., a retired marketing execu-tive from Caterpillar Corporation who I met at TNT's. Will-iams—a native of Richmond, Virginia—spent large chunks of his nearly 40-year career overseas, trying to tune in to Armed Forces Radio broadcasts of his beloved Washington Redskins.

"Back then, everyone who worked overseas owned a Zenith TransOceanic Radio," Williams recalled over orders of chicken wings, pizza, and Coors Light, as he watched the Redskins beat up on the San Francisco 49ers 52–17. "With a little ingenuity, you could get Armed Forces Radio, which always seemed to carry the Redskins games. I guess because the station was based in Wash-ington."

Armed Forces Radio's signal is transmitted around the globe for the benefit of U.S. troops overseas. But getting the broadcasts wasn't always easy. "I used the radiators in our apartment in Paris as an antenna," Williams said. "When we were living in Greece, I used the fire escape." How times have changed. Today, instead of fiddling with a finicky antenna to get a spotty radio broadcast, all Williams has to do to watch his beloved Redskins is make the ten-minute drive from his home in Morton to TNT's.

On this particular Sunday, the Redskins–49ers game was on the big screen in the back room at TNT's. On the bar's other big-screen TV, the Packers–Vikings game was being closely followed by Todd Curtis, Brian Manuel, and a number of other Green Bay

Packers fans—all dressed in green and gold T-shirts, jerseys, and ball caps. Decked out in his #4 Brett Favre jersey, Curtis cheered loudly as the Packers easily handled their struggling NFC North rivals, the Minnesota Vikings, before the Vikings kicked a 56-yard field goal in the fourth quarter to win the game. Curtis has been a Packers fan since he was seven years old, but before cable TV, it was hard to follow his favorite team. Back in the old days, they weren't on TV a lot," Curtis said. "It was all Bears."

Brian Manuel agreed. "My whole family were Bears fans," Manuel said. "I wanted to be different, especially after they won the '85 Super Bowl and that's all you heard: Bears, Bears, Bears." The only solace for Manuel—as for many Packers fans living in the heart of Bears country in those days—was a buddy with a satellite dish. "It was one of those gigantic dishes that you used to have to put out on your lawn because they were so big," Manuel recalled. "We could pick up the Packers' signal from Wisconsin."

In its infancy, satellite TV didn't carry commercials during the game, which also gave viewers access to unscripted and uncensored commentator coverage. "You'd hear the announcers during the commercials, checking out some hot chick in the stands or talking about how much the team sucked," Manuel said, "stuff you'd never hear them say on air. It was great." As far as Brian Manuel is concerned, satellite and cable TV have everything to do with why football has grown so much in popularity. "It's what put the NFL on the map," he said.

Putting games on cable and satellite continues to be a good strategy for the NFL. In 2006, 27 percent of U.S. households subscribed to satellite service—up from 19 percent in 2004 and 12 percent in 2000. And thanks to advances in technology, subscribers no longer have to put a huge and unsightly satellite dish in their yard to pick up the signal. Today's smaller satellite dishes are easier to install, even in places like New York City, where many naysayers said satellite TV would never work. As a result, any fan, almost anywhere in the country, can follow the action of their favorite team through live broadcasts.

Satellite broadcasting is helping the NFL to reach a bigger audience not only in the United States but around the world as well. Consider, for example, Robin and Demi Collins of Manchester, England, who were in Cleveland for the 2005 home opener against the Cincinnati Bengals. While it may seem odd to find Cleveland Browns fans hailing from the hometown of the world's most recognizable sports team—Manchester United of England's Premier (soccer) League—the Collinses are as rabid as any Browns fans from Ohio.

"I love dogs," said Robin Collins, who works for a Manchester sportsbook, the equivalent of an American off-track betting parlor. When he learned about the Dawg Pound, a rowdy section of fans behind the east end zone in Cleveland Browns Stadium, he knew, "That was it for me." His wife was hooked, too. "I'm a typical female fan," said Demi. "I was swayed by the good-looking quarterbacks in tight pants."

Thanks to the NFL's growing number of international broadcast alliances, primarily through satellite television, the Collinses are part of an ever-expanding international fan base. In 2005, the NFL announced partnerships that would take the league into 234 countries and provide more than 190,000 hours of programming. During the 2005 season, NFL content was broadcast across 24 time zones and in 31 languages.

That same year, the NFL increased distribution of the NFL Network, the league's 24/7 channel, to nearly 5 million households in Mexico, Canada, and the Caribbean. The league signed a deal with the North American Sports Network (NASN), the European broadcast network, to provide NFL Network programming in 21 countries in Europe. The NASN also acquired the exclusive pay-TV rights to televise NFL games through 2008. The network carries all playoff games, the Super Bowl, Pro Bowl, and the NFL Europe League. SKY Sports, the UK satellite network that brings the Collinses their beloved Browns, now broadcasts two NFL games live every Sunday and every NFL playoff game, including the Super Bowl.

Meanwhile, back in the United States, it's a rare occasion these days when Brian Manuel and his Packers-loving friends from Peoria make the six-hour trip to Green Bay for a game at Lambeau Field. Thanks to DirecTV's $3.5 billion, five-year contract to broadcast NFL games, they don't have to. In fact, no matter where an NFL fan lives, a satellite broadcast is likely delivering NFL games and content to a bar or restaurant nearby. And these satellite broadcasts are only one way that the NFL is leveraging new media to reach its fans—and expand its revenues.

THE NFL ONLINE

While it's easy to find a bar showing your favorite NFL game every week, the Internet has made it even easier to find other fans with whom to watch the game. Just go to *www.packers.com/fans/ fan_clubs*, for example, and you'll find a listing of bars in most major cities—and some not-so-major cities—where you can watch games with other rabid Packers fans. And the Packers aren't alone online.

Every NFL team has its own, unique, branded Web site with game-day updates, stats, player appearances, off-season events, and fan clubs. Each team also has its own strategy for leveraging the Internet. Some, like the Washington Redskins and Atlanta Falcons, adapt the latest technology to broadcast real-time streaming video, game highlights, and press conferences. Other teams, like the Buffalo Bills, Pittsburgh Steelers, and Cleveland Browns, use the Internet to reach out to their fan base across the country.

The Internet is one of the few areas where the NFL doesn't micromanage nearly everything at the local level. In a rare departure from its usual Mother Hen role, the NFL very much believes that each team is in the best position to manage its Web site and knows best how to reach out to its fan base. Like other aspects of the NFL's finances, there are shared and nonshared Internet revenues. The league maintains *NFL.com* and has sponsorship deals that work like national television sponsors: These revenues are shared equally with all 32 NFL teams.

The NFL Internet strategy seems to be working. In September 2005, *NFL.com* and team Internet sites had record traffic with 16 million unique visitors, up from the previous monthly record of 14.5 million in September 2004 and 5.4 million users in September 2000. The NFL is ranked second among sports-related Web sites, behind only *ESPN.com*, with its 18.7 million users. According to Media Metrix, *MLB.com* gets only about 10 million visitors, NASCAR 4 million, the NBA 3 million, and the NHL a little more than 2 million.

Part of what's driving the increased Internet traffic to NFL Web sites is the services that are offered. For instance, most teams offer streaming video of press conferences and player interviews during the regular season. In the off-season, the teams e-mail fans roster updates, trades, and waivers, and they even host draft parties online and at local sports bars. The teams are allowed to sell their own ads, and—as with the revenue from premium tickets and parking—they're not required to share this ad revenue with the rest of the league.

Clearly the biggest chunk of NFL Internet revenue comes from the national contracts, five-year deals with America Online, SportsLine, and Viacom. Ad sales and e-commerce also bring in revenues for the league, all of which are shared with the 32 franchises. And, while the league hasn't gone to pay content on *NFL.com*, some teams have, especially when it comes to fan clubs and newsletters; with paid membership, these sites offer fans faster and more in-depth content than is available on the team's basic Web site. For example, the Pittsburgh Steelers have Black ($30), Gold ($75), and VIP ($160) level memberships for Internet content. The Steelers' VIP memberships were sold out in 2005. In the near future, I think fans can expect to find teams offering pay services for real-time video and fantasy football.

Even today, some teams offer online content that hasn't been made available to the beat writers and reporters who follow the team for local radio, TV, and newspapers. In fact, the Washington Redskins angered local media in January 2006, when the team announced that it had re-signed popular defensive coordinator Gregg Williams to a lucrative, three-year contract but that he was not interested in doing interviews. Imagine the surprise in Washington, D.C. newsrooms when a live interview with Williams was streamed on the team's Web site. "The world is changing," said Redskins owner Daniel Snyder, in response to media complaints about the team breaking the interview online.

The strategy not only cuts out traditional sports reporters, who may be critical of the team, but also makes fans feel as though they're in an exclusive club that even the media sometimes can't join. "That leap—that direct communication between teams and their fans—is going to increase," said Marc Ganis, a sports business consultant in Chicago.

While that may rankle some reporters, it's seen as a win-win by the Redskins and other teams. "They wanted to build the Web site, bring fans closer to the team," said Larry Michael, who worked at Westwood One Radio for 20 years but in 2005 was named executive producer of media for the Redskins. "It's been incredible how many people have accepted what we do."

For instance, during the NFL Combine in Indianapolis, where coaches and scouts gather to evaluate potential players, Redskins coach Joe Gibbs agreed to let Michael and his staff follow him around for an hour. "That's unheard of," Michael said, "but we built that relationship because we work with him every day. And it's access that ESPN or any number of other media outlets don't have."

For the Redskins, it's all about building brand loyalty among its fan base. During the 2005 season, the Redskins averaged 30,000 to 40,000 hits a day on its video content. The single-day high was 113,000. That's still small by Google or AOL standards, but it's growing, and it's still new territory for many NFL teams and their fans. "We do highlight packages, take fans on a trip through the training room, the locker room," Michael said. "We try to show them every aspect of the team. . . . We're a news department in one respect," he said, "but we're an entertainment department, too."

And while some of the content annoyed reporters in Washington, Michael said that much of the focus of the Redskins' Internet strategy is to keep in touch with fans who are spread across the country and around the world. "One of the purposes that we serve is to keep displaced fans in touch with their hometown teams," he said. "'Hey, thanks for keeping us posted' is typical of the responses we get. That's because the depth of coverage we give fans was never available before."

SATELLITE RADIO AND WIRELESS BROADCASTS

Another new medium for delivering the NFL to fans near and far is satellite radio. The advantage of satellite radio—like satellite TV—is that no matter where you live, you can hear your favorite game. Satellite radio has the added benefit of offering far-flung listeners broadcasts hosted by home-team announcers.

Both XM Satellite Radio and Sirius Satellite Radio, the big players in this relatively young medium, are potentially billion-dollar businesses. XM Satellite Radio, for example, has over 3 million subscribers. In 2005, XM agreed to pay Major League Baseball $650 million to broadcast every game beginning with the 2005 season. That means that New York Yankees fans in California can hear every game, just as though they lived in the Bronx.

Many sports economists and media analysts think satellite radio's increasing popularity could put the local sports radio industry at risk. While the Yankees, Mets, and Braves have fairly large and secure local radio deals, some teams in smaller markets have had to renegotiate their local broadcast agreements or take their rights in-house. Major League Baseball's XM deal may also hurt local ad revenue. Under the terms of the agreement, XM will broadcast the local feeds, including advertising. But it will also create its own pre- and postgame programming around which it will sell ad spots.

Sirius Satellite Radio, with a little more than one million subscribers, has an exclusive broadcast contract with the NFL. However, due to the NFL's independence from radio broadcasting, the deal is not as extravagant as XM's contract with Major League Baseball. The Westwood One radio network also inked a multi-year agreement to extend its partnership with the NFL in 2005. The agreement included play-by-play rights for regular and post-season games, the playoffs, the Super Bowl, and Pro Bowl. Terms weren't disclosed, but Westwood One said the added benefits of the deal offset the higher cost. "The NFL is a significant piece of our programming," said Shane Coppola, president and CEO of Westwood One, which has carried the NFL since 1987.

The NFL also is leveraging digital content to expand its offerings to television viewers. As part of its new 2006 national television package, the NFL signed a new agreement with DirecTV that includes a number of cutting-edge programming enhancements. For example, NFL Sunday Ticket customers who subscribed to the premium package had access to new interactive services in 2005, including viewer-selected camera angles and replays. Premium subscribers also got the new Red Zone channel, which switched to games when a team was in the red zone—inside the 20-yard line—and poised to score. Subscribers could also index, search for, and view specific NFL teams, players, or types of plays from games broadcast that Sunday.

DirecTV customers with a digital video recorder (DVR) also received expanded and unique NFL-related content and highlights that they could download to their DVR hard drives. DirecTV also negotiated the right to provide remote access to NFL Sunday Ticket games and content to subscribers via broadband or wireless devices, as well as rights to broadcast every game in a high-definition format. But what fans really enjoyed in 2005 was NFL Sunday Ticket's mosaic channel, which showed multiple games on one screen. DirecTV also began showing an exclusive fantasy football show with NFL footage each season.

Finally, the NFL is also going wireless. In 2005, Sprint and the NFL announced a deal that made Sprint the official wireless telecommunications provider for the NFL. In addition to branding and advertising at the games, the agreement will allow Sprint to deliver exclusive and original NFL content to mobile phones, including game highlights and live updates with scores and statistics as well as live video and video on demand. "It represents a clear departure from the standard sports sponsorship and delivers exclusively into the hands of Sprint customers and fans an entirely new and interactive experience," said Tom Murphy, vice president of sponsorships at Sprint.

A WHOLE NEW GAME: THE EXPLOSION OF FANTASY FOOTBALL

Fantasy football is a serious—and growing—phenomenon among NFL fans. Despite the name, fantasy football is a game firmly grounded in reality. Fantasy football players act as the commissioner, owner, manager, and coach of their own football team. Teams are made up of actual NFL players. Just as in the real NFL, fantasy football leagues hold a draft—usually near the start of the season—and draft real players. The players' value is based upon their NFL contract and performance. Fantasy teams have a salary cap, just like the real NFL, and must assemble a team within budget.

Game action all takes place online, through membership-controlled Web sites. Fantasy teams score points based upon their players' performance in the real games. Running backs score by running, receivers score by catching passes, and quarterbacks score by throwing touchdowns. Similarly, defensive players score by making tackles, sacking the quarterback, and intercepting passes.

Fantasy football leagues typically are made up of 10 teams, with each fantasy football player kicking in about $100 to cover Web site hosting expenses and to fuel the pot that's divided among the top three teams at the end of the season. This may sound complicated to a novice—and it was in the days of pen and paper—but today, with nearly every fantasy league playing on a Web site, the calculations are done automatically, and league players are free to enjoy the action of the game.

By most estimates, NFL fantasy football has, in a relatively short time span, eclipsed rotisserie baseball, which dominated the fantasy sports world for decades with players using paper and pen instead of Web sites and electronic spreadsheets. According to Ladd Biro, a syndicated fantasy football columnist who runs a sports management consulting firm at *www.championmgt.net*, there were somewhere between 15 million and 20 million fantasy football players, by best count, during the 2005 season. And those numbers include men and women from diverse social, cultural, and geographic groups—even celebrities, such as Meatloaf, who in a 2005 story told the *New York Times* that he was in 18 fantasy leagues.

"It's my escape," he said. "I get so many phone calls. There are so many decisions I have to make. It gets me thinking about something else other than what's going on in my life." Like so many fantasy football players, Meatloaf uses DirecTV's NFL

Sunday Ticket as well as Sirius Satellite Radio to follow his team's progress in the "real world."

And while the NFL doesn't make a ton of money from fantasy football, it has been perhaps one of the best brand-building tools for the league over the past five years. As NFL fantasy football has exploded, fantasy players have become obsessed with the real players, coaches, trades, and stats. In short, these people are gaga about NFL football. Even though the revenue stream is diffused, any marketing or advertising executive will tell you that having a horde of rabid fans buzzing about your product is never a bad thing.

The Fantasy League–Friendly NFL

"There has been tremendous growth in fantasy football," said Biro, the fantasy football columnist. "Most players are not satisfied with merely being in one league. They want to be in two or three. People are getting obsessed with it." So great is national interest, some newspapers are starting to run regular columns on fantasy football. That's where I found Biro, in the sports pages of the *Cleveland Plain Dealer* during opening week of the 2005 season. It's one of eight newspapers in which he appears. In Dallas, where he lives now, his column runs three times a week alongside other fantasy football content.

Biro acknowledged that the Internet is one of the primary reasons that fantasy football has taken off so quickly over the past five years or so. "It has made fantasy football easy for the common man," said Biro. "You don't have to track all your scores on paper anymore. Back in the old days, we had to calculate our scores and compare them with what our opponent figured. The Internet changed all that."

The NFL format also makes it fantasy league–friendly. "Every team plays every week and only once a week. That makes it easier to follow," Biro said. He also noted that the NFL adapted quickly to the growing popularity of fantasy football and now embraces it as yet another means of expanding the NFL brand and fan base. The league, for example, had to come to grips with the potential for betting associated with the fantasy games. Noting the NFL's long history of stamping out any suspicion of gambling, Biro added, "I think they've gotten over that. Look on *NFL.com*. There's a lot of fantasy content. DirecTV is pushing fantasy football, too." The fact that people win NFL fantasy pools "may be a remote concern," Biro said, "but it's such big business and it isn't going to go away. I think it was something that they knew they had to be a part of."

Fantasy Football Comes of Age Online

To gauge the increasing popularity of fantasy football, just listen to a sampling of fantasy footballers who spend increasing amounts of their leisure time following this rapidly growing offshoot of the NFL.

Jon McDaid, 36, a writer from suburban Philadelphia, is a perfect example of the typical fantasy football player. He was lured into it in 1997, partly out of curiosity, partly out of necessity. "A buddy of mine and his older brother had been running the league for a few years," McDaid said. "They had nine players and they needed a tenth."

Of course, 1997 was the dark age—or the analog age—of fantasy football. It was still primarily the domain of stat geeks who reveled in hours of manual number crunching. "When we started, you contacted the commissioner by fax or had to call his office by end of business Friday," said McDaid, who has won his season-long league championship twice. Before the digital age, *commissioner* was the name typically given to the fantasy football league member who crunched the numbers and kept track of the standings. It was a thankless job: disputes over scoring often erupted. "You would sometimes ask questions, especially if your guy scored on a weird play," McDaid said.

Today, McDaid and his buddies, like a lot of fantasy leagues, use CBS Sportsline, one of the original fantasy sports Web sites. But other sites abound: Yahoo!, AOL, and most Internet service providers have online fantasy leagues, some free and some costing up to $125 for a season. The scores are tabulated online. In many leagues, players can make changes up until Sunday morning. Some sites will send you alerts when a certain player is traded or hurt.

All of this has made fantasy football mainstream. It's not just for geeks anymore.

"Ten years ago, I would have avoided it like the plague," McDaid said. "Our commissioner, who did the job for years, was really into it, and the amount of work he put into it was great." But now, "It takes a little bit less time and a little bit less knowledge."

And ease of use has made NFL fantasy football appealing to so many people. "It has changed the way everyone watches football," McDaid said. "If you go into a bar now and ask who's winning, they'll tell you the score and then start rattling off fantasy stats. They've become the lingua franca of NFL fans." And if you meet a guy who has the same player on his fantasy team, "You're instant friends."

Fantasy football has also made fans care about faraway games that in years past they wouldn't have even tracked. "Jacksonville–Houston? I never would have watched that game before," McDaid said. "But if one of my fantasy players is on one of those teams, I care what happens."

Of course, as with any other activity that goes online, the digitization of fantasy football has the potential for eliminating some of the camaraderie of the old predigital days of the sport. For many married guys, the annual fantasy football draft, which coincides with the real NFL draft in April, was a regularly scheduled day out of the house. It was a day for getting together with their buddies, drinking beer, and being 15-year-old sports geeks again. But today, a lot of fantasy drafts are simply conducted on-line. "It's still about doing the draft and having a party," said Mc-Daid, whose league gets together in person for their annual draft. "But everything else we do online."

The loss of camaraderie has been especially noted by the players in the Al's Bar Fantasy Football League. The suburban Minneapolis league has been around since the early 1990s, before fantasy football went online. In addition to gathering for the annual draft, the players would get together every week at Al's Bar to go over the results. "In the old days, you *had* to go to Al's Bar," said Ben Koster, 38, who has been in the league since 1994 but has never made the playoffs. "We'd get together, the commissioner would pass out the results, and we'd all watch the Monday night game together. We don't do that anymore."

While eliminating the delay in information exchange, the digitization of fantasy football has challenged some fans' allegiance to the hometown team. Koster used to get annoyed when his cousin, Paul Happe, would come into Al's Bar and cheer for an opposing player to score against the Vikings simply because it was good for his fantasy team. "I'd scream, 'What are you doing?'" said Koster, "and he'd reply, 'I can win money.'"

Although Koster laments the potential for fantasy football to become mostly about gambling and winning money, as a diehard Vikings fan, he admits that sometimes he finds himself rooting against his favorite team. At the same time, he acknowledges that fantasy football has increased the general level of interest in the NFL for most fantasy players. "Before, I just cared about the Vikings," Koster said. "Now I follow all the teams."

While the Internet might have destroyed some of the camaraderie once enjoyed by the fantasy football league at Al's Bar, it has kept together a group of buddies from Cincinnati. Sean Brown, 38, a software application developer, has hung out with the same group of guys since he was 12. Most of them started playing fantasy football in the 1980s, when they were in college at Ohio State. But because Brown went to school at the University of Miami at Ohio, he couldn't play in their league. "In the 1980s, you had to be in the same city," said Brown. "When I'd visit on weekends, I'd trash-talk fantasy football with them, but that was about all I could do."

That all changed when they got out of school. Brown, thanks to his work background, was one of the early pioneers who figured out—long before there was Yahoo! and AOL—how to digitize his fantasy football league. First, he developed a software application, and then he found a vendor to sell him the data. Historically, real-time NFL stats were managed, for all practical purposes, by a monopoly; only a few professional firms, like Stats, Inc., made them available. Because there were so few subscribers, the cost was about $45,000 a year, which made access to the stats prohibitive for most fantasy leagues.

Eventually, however, Brown found a vendor that would give him the stats after *Monday Night Football* and charge his league only $75 a week. He and his buddies would load the stats into their program and then analyze them manually. Because the stats were delivered electronically, Brown and the members of his group, who had scattered to the four corners of the earth, could all play fantasy football together. They no longer had the barriers that they did when they were in college. "I'm the only one who came back to Cincinnati," said Brown, whose friends moved to Texas, Alabama, and elsewhere. "With everything online, it doesn't matter where we are."

Today, there are still just a handful of vendors for real-time NFL stats, but because the number of fantasy football players has increased exponentially, into the tens of millions, Web sites can spread the costs and even make a little money hosting leagues for about $100 a season for ten teams. "Yahoo! and others can afford to pay Stats, Inc. and the handful of other real-time stats providers, because their online fantasy football leagues have hundreds of thousands of users," said Brown.

The ease of online play has vaulted football to the top of the fantasy sports world, once clearly dominated by baseball. "Baseball versus the NFL? It's not even close any more," said Brown. The availability of online leagues has also encouraged women to join the ranks of fantasy sports—a pastime once completely dominated by men. "Now that it's easier and more social, huge numbers of women are into fantasy sports," said Brown. "People in our office do fantasy NASCAR." And it's not just a fad. "I see fantasy sports doing nothing but growing," said Brown. "I don't think this is a recent craze. Now you can't watch an NFL game without a ticker with fantasy stats scrolling across the bottom."

Brown is also one of those fantasy players who got DirecTV, partly for its NFL Sunday Ticket. "I didn't get the multiscreen function, but I got Red Zone." The multiscreen function allows viewers to watch 8 games at once; the Red Zone feature jumps to games when a team is on the 20-yard line or closer and may be about to score. Brown said that fantasy football was a big part of the reason he invested in DirecTV. "We all got into this originally because we're football fans," said Brown, "but now I find myself watching games, and if one of my fantasy players is against Pittsburgh, my favorite team, I'm against the Steelers."

Columnist Ladd Biro, through his interactions with fantasy footballers every week, believes that interest in the games is one of the factors changing the face of professional football today. Just as Sean Brown noted, Biro sees that the NFL's inroads into new media have redefined the concept of "home teams." "I think fantasy football has, in many ways, supplanted loyalties to your own team," Biro said. He was quick to note, however, that, "In the long run, it helps the NFL more than hurts."

Team loyalties aside, like Brown, McDaid, and Koster, fantasy football fans around the world are watching the NFL more intently than ever. For the NFL, therefore, the growing fantasy fan base translates into very real advertising and merchandising dollars.

BUILDING NFL BRAND AWARENESS, ONE FAN AT A TIME

Just as the switch to online play has made fantasy football easier and more accessible, the NFL's broad investment in new media has made the experience of following league games much easier and more enjoyable for fans around the world. But I think it's fair to say, the NFL hasn't made that investment simply to enhance the lives of football fans in Morton, Illinois, or Manchester, England. The NFL owns one of the world's most recognized and valuable brands, and every inroad into the market's awareness represents newer and larger revenues for the league.

In the next chapter, I explore yet another way that the NFL is building brand awareness (and filling league coffers): through its vast and growing merchandising program. Every NFL team jersey, cap, bumper sticker, coffee mug, beer sleeve, paperweight, and poster represents both merchanding dollars and free advertising for the wealthiest sports league on the planet. And, as you'll learn, although the NFL wasn't always adept at marketing its products, all that has changed. Today's NFL runs a savvy and sophisticated merchandising program that helps to define the league's image around the world, even as it generates billions of dollars in revenue.

CHAPTER SEVEN

NFL MERCHANDISING

THE EMPIRE'S NEW CLOTHES

In January 1983, just days before Super Bowl XVII in Pasadena, California, the National Football League went to court seeking a restraining order to keep vendors from selling unlicensed NFL merchandise. Leaving no stone unturned, the league sought relief in Washington and Miami, home cities of the two Super Bowl teams, as well as Los Angeles.

Judge Charles R. Richey of the U.S. District Court in Washington said that, if he issued the restraining order sought by the NFL, it would "invite catastrophe" through "a nightmare of jurisdictional flaws, deprivations of due process, and windfall litigation that could ensue for years to come." Furthermore, he said it would cause a "physical spectacle" in the streets, with potential violence erupting between bootleg vendors and NFL security.

While the NFL cast its net far and wide in January 1983, everyone knew who the league was most concerned about: the Hogs. That was the affectionate nickname Joe Bugel, the Redskins' offensive coordinator, had given to the offensive line of the Washington Redskins, made up of Joe Jacoby, Russ Grimm, Jeff Bostic, Mark May, and George Starke. The Hogs became legendary, both on and off the field. As one pundit said, they "transformed offensive linemen from unheralded blockers to NFL celebrities."

They also angered the team of lawyers and marketing managers who oversaw merchandising at the NFL. That's because the linemen were smart enough to cash in on their celebrity by forming Super Hogs, Inc. Their business created, marketed, and sold hundreds of thousands of dollars of Hog merchandise, including T-shirts, posters, and the ultimate Hog accessory, a plastic pig snout—none of which had been officially licensed by the NFL. The Hogs ended up winning the 1983 Super Bowl game against the Dolphins 27–17; they also won the lawsuit, thanks to Judge Richey's ruling. Following the victory, the company sold more than $500,000 worth of merchandise. And there was absolutely nothing the NFL could do about it.

Times have certainly changed. As the NFL has become the most financially sophisticated and market-savvy league on the planet, it has legally tied up all the loose ends that allowed a group of chunky linemen to sell several hundred thousand dollars of unlicensed merchandise. Today, the NFL oversees—more closely than ever—the sale of everything from T-shirts and caps to blankets and bobbleheads. Because it has more control than ever, the NFL has revitalized its merchandising line and made its jerseys, sweatshirts, and bumper stickers some of the most sought-after goods in sports merchandising.

THE NFL TAKES CONTROL OF ITS BRAND

Although NFL team merchandise has been for sale since 1957, when the Los Angeles Rams opened the league's first team store, NFL merchandising was arguably the last of the league's traditional businesses to mature into the smart, sophisticated marketing model that defines the NFL today. For years, merchandising was an unorganized business, with individual teams taking care of most of their own products and advertising, thus giving the NFL very little control over the quality, quantity, and types of products being made and sold.

Like much of the NFL's business operations, the tide started to turn when Pete Rozelle became commissioner. While Rozelle is largely remembered for his keen understanding of television, he understood sales and marketing, too. When he was still with the Rams, Rozelle recognized the revenue potential of official NFL merchandise. To make sure the Rams did it right, he brought in Larry Kent, a salesperson for Roy Rogers, Inc., which was selling $30 million a year in Roy Rogers toys and souvenirs. In 1962, just three years into his tenure as NFL commissioner, Rozelle established NFL Properties—the NFL business unit that now handles the league's apparel and merchandising activities. But not until the 1983 dispute with the Hogs did the NFL realize it needed to watch its merchandising business much more closely. That incident was just a symptom of larger problems looming on the horizon for the NFL and merchandise sales.

A BRAND IS BORN

Back in the 1960s, the NFL wasn't known for its fashion sense, and the term *team apparel* applied only to the players' uniforms. Most coaches stalked the sidelines in rather formal dress, usually suits and ties. Tom Landry, perhaps the least flamboyant of the 1970s-era coaches, understood the marketing power of his signature fedora and sold his own line of hats. Minnesota Vikings coach Bud Grant, who often wore khaki pants, a golf shirt, white socks, and black cleats, was one of the league's more casual dressers; Grant was clearly in the minority.

The real sea change for NFL sideline fashion was started in the 1980s by a trio of prominent coaches, New York Giants coach Bill Parcells, New York Jets coach Joe Walton, and Chicago Bears coach Mike Ditka. Every week, these popular coaches could be found on the sidelines wearing big sweaters and pullover jackets that bore their teams' colors. Fan demand for the sweaters and jackets materialized almost overnight, and a lightbulb went on over the NFL offices in Manhattan. "The NFL and various teams began to see the kind of calls and interest they were getting, and the thought was, 'Hey, we could grow a business out of this,'" said Dennis Kayser, senior director of on-field operations for NFL Properties, in a November 19, 2003, interview with the *Washington Times*.

From those humble beginnings in the 1980s grew the NFL merchandising business, which today racks up about $3.5 billion in annual sales. The profits that the NFL sees from the sales of NFL-branded merchandise amount to about 8 to 12 percent of the wholesale price, mainly from licensing revenues. Sales of officially licensed merchandise from the NFL, NBA, Major League Baseball, NHL, and major colleges grew dramatically in the 1990s, peaking in 1996 at $13.8 billion. Although sales of NFL merchandise dropped steadily from 1996 through 2001, sales have since rebounded. Today, the demand for retro-themed jerseys and other memorabilia helps drive the sale of NFL merchandise, as does the fast-growing category of women's apparel and accessories. The success of the NFL brand, however, has been achieved only through concerted effort on the part of the league and its business managers.

MAKING THE BRAND "OFFICIAL"

In 1999, the NFL's business was roiled by a trademark dispute between the league and the players' union, the NFL Players Association (NFLPA). The source of this turmoil was an advertisement for Coors beer that used the phrase *Official Beer of the NFL Players*. The ad was part of a marketing agreement between Coors and the NFLPA. The NFL argued that the "official beer" designation was fraudulent, because active players cannot endorse alcoholic beverages. The league also said that, because the

NFLPA did not represent all NFL players (quarterbacks have their own union), the statement was untrue. A New York judge found the ad an unauthorized use of *NFL* by both the NFLPA and Coors and ordered Coors to stop airing the ad.

The temporary injunction was the latest salvo in an ongoing war between the NFL and Players, Inc.—the marketing arm of the NFLPA. The long-running feud basically concerned whether the players union and its sponsors had the right to use the league's name in advertising campaigns. At the time, the NFL had sponsorship agreements with Coors' primary competitors, Anheuser-Busch and Miller Brewing, which reportedly threatened to withhold payments if the Coors ad wasn't stopped. The Coors deal with the NFLPA was for $1.6 million; at the same time, Miller was paying the NFL $9.5 million, and Anheuser-Busch was paying $2.2 million for advertising rights as one of the official products of the league. The judge ruled that Coors could say it was the "Official Beer of Players Inc.," but not "of the NFL." "It is abundantly clear that Coors would not have entered the contract without receiving the rights from Players, Inc. to use the term *NFL Players,* the judge said. "A licensing agreement that only gave the right to say Players, Inc. would simply not have been valuable."

In 1999, the league and the players union also got into a dispute over designating Bally's as the "Official Training Center for NFL Players." All this was smoothed over two years later, when NFL Properties, Inc. and Players, Inc. reached an agreement to share sponsorship revenue with players. The deal also allowed league sponsors to use NFL players in their marketing and advertising campaigns, but it prohibited Players, Inc. from pursuing its own deals with direct competitors of NFL sponsors. In its best year, 1996, Players, Inc. generated an estimated $30.5 million in licensing agreements.

LOGO WARS: STREAMLINING THE NFL'S
MERCHANDISE PROGRAM

When the sales of NFL merchandise began a five-year slide in 1996, the sports apparel market was flooded with merchandise tied to the 1996 Olympics in Atlanta. At the same time, upscale apparel companies like Tommy Hilfiger, Polo, Nautica, and FUBU had started getting into logo-branded apparel. "The market was saturated," said Susan Rothman, the NFL vice president who oversees licensing.

Further complicating matters, the NFL's business model was in disarray. The league had more than 350 licensing agreements, making it very hard to control the quantity and quality of products, which are basically broken down into two categories—hard goods and soft goods. Hard goods are coffee mugs, seat cushions, video games, footballs, trading cards, and bobbleheads. Soft goods are T-shirts, outerwear, sweatshirts, caps, sweaters, and players' jerseys emblazoned with the team and NFL logos.

One of the people that the NFL tapped to turn around its licensing business was Chuck Zona, a veteran of the apparel business who now consults for a number of clients, including the J. Peterman Company. When Zona and his team took inventory of NFL Properties in the late 1990s, they realized that the league was overlicensed and caught in a vicious, downwardly spiraling business model. "NFL Properties–licensed business had meteoric growth through the 1980s and 1990s," Zona said. "The NFL's licensed merchandise supply couldn't meet the fan base's demand for product, largely because of a dysfunctional business model. NFL-licensed merchandise was selling in every retail channel, from mass merchants [Wal-Mart and Kmart] to specialty stores [Champs and Dick's] with no distinct product differentiation."

Overlicensing created an inventory glut in the marketplace, and oversupply put tremendous pressure on profit margins. With margins squeezed, retailers reduced the retail floor space devoted to NFL apparel, and the business began to shrink. That, along with the emergence of competing fashion brands, threatened to turn NFL merchandise from a specialty item into a commodity. "That's the worst thing that can happen to a world-class licensee like the NFL, which depends on the caché and quality of its product to drive sales and profits," Zona said. "Once your product becomes just another commodity, you're forced to make low-quality merchandise with less fashion and functional detailing."

Zona realized that his most important challenge was to restore the profit margins for NFL merchandise—something that couldn't be done overnight. "You have to create the dynamic of supply and demand," Zona said. To create that dynamic, he and his team did an analysis of all of the NFL's licensees in each business, then invited vendors to bid on the right to become an NFL licensee. "You have to ask if the bidders are willing to commit the human and financial resources of their company to effectively operate as an NFL licensee," Zona said. "That's no small task. They basically have to set up a separate business within their company to exclusively service the NFL."

The net result of Zona's restructuring of NFL Properties was a much more streamlined, controlled, and sophisticated business model for merchandising NFL products. The NFL cut licensing agreements from 350 to about 125. To further lock down merchandising, the league created a master agreement to manage its trademarks and merchandising deals and got the team owners (with the exception of Dallas Cowboys owner Jerry Jones) to cede control of licensing.

With the overwhelming success of the restructuring of the league's merchandising, NFL Business Ventures, the business unit that handles everything from sponsorships to merchandising, has been able to negotiate other lucrative deals with on-field vendors. One such deal, for example, gives Motorola the right to handle all of the NFL's game-day communications.

THE NFL DEVELOPS ITS "LOOK"

Prior to Zona's restructuring of the NFL's apparel merchandising, NFL Properties gave out the team rights to licensees, and then each one of those teams worked with that licensee on uniforms, practice wear, and sideline apparel. Before the reorganization of the merchandising business, a half-dozen different companies, including Nike, Champion, Adidas, Puma, Logo, and Starter, were each working with any number of the 32 NFL franchises. Zona and his team decided to award the on-field apparel licenses for all 32 teams to a single licensee. The company that won the license for official apparel was Reebok, which paid $250 million in 2002 for a ten-year contract. "There are very few companies that have the internal structure to handle all 32 teams," Zona said. "It came down to a few competent companies, with Reebok ultimately getting the rights."

That change streamlined the entire NFL apparel merchandising operation and created more uniformity among the teams, especially for the sideline apparel worn by coaches and staff. "The first year was a little bumpy," Zona admits. "Reebok had to service all 32 teams with an entire organization focused on the NFL. That requires a tremendous amount of commitment." But looking at it with the benefit of hindsight, Zona believes the transition was worthwhile. "I think it has helped the NFL in terms of service," Zona said. "If there's a uniform issue with a team, it now takes two phone calls to fix it: one to the NFL and one to Reebok." And it improved things on the commercial side as well. "The league is now working with one on-field licensee," he said. "You can control all aspects of the business against an agreed-upon standard."

If you don't believe Zona, just take a look at the sidelines the next time you watch a game. While there's some latitude for personal taste—younger coaches tend to like bolder styling, while older coaches are more conservative—the clothes that coaches wear are now relatively uniform (no pun intended). "The NFL sidelines are crystal clear in terms of branding," said Zona, whose family have been lifelong New York Giants supporters. "You see all the coaches wearing agreed-upon hats, shirts, and jackets. Even injured players wear specific garments, often in team colors."

And that helps tremendously in the retail market. "If all the Giants coaches are wearing the same shirt, you can take that to retail," Zona said. "It translates to retail in terms of control, timing, and consistency. Now you can place product in the store for the fan to purchase."

Being able to design and market team wear led to the popular Reebok commercials that show fanatical fans sneaking into locker rooms and hiding in laundry bins, all to get official NFL apparel. The ad campaign's signature tagline drives home the point that fans don't have to go to extremes anymore to get officially licensed apparel just like the coaches and players wear. Now all they have to do is go to the team shop, a local sporting goods store, Wal-Mart, or the online NFL shop at *www.nfl.com*.

The NFL also showed more strategic thinking by making the Reebok deal a ten-year agreement, compared with past licensing agreements that typically ran for just five years. That not only locks things up for the NFL but also makes Reebok a lot more comfortable. "If you're going to build an NFL-licensed business, it's nice to know you have a ten-year window," Zona said. "Reebok can develop short-, mid-, and long-term marketing strategies with the NFL."

Indeed, the Reebok contract led to an apparel strategy never before seen in the NFL—or any other league. Reebok now works 18 months ahead to develop sideline apparel. The process begins with initial sketches and ends with game-day use, similar to the way clothing is designed for a Paris or Milan debut. After the NFL and Reebok come up with designs and color schemes for the season, Reebok designers and marketing executives visit each

NFL team, soliciting opinions from the coaches, managers, owners, players, and wives. All apparel design is finished in time to give Reebok 12 months to take orders from retailers and to stock team stores.

The designs and materials Reebok uses in its apparel are different for each team, culture, and climate. After the initial design and consulting period, Reebok develops about 30 items of clothing for each team, which are split into 3 groups based on weather. (So Houston's team, for example, is as comfortable playing at home in September as in a January playoff in Pittsburgh.) Reebok develops polo shirts for warmer days, light jackets and sweaters for fall-like weather, and thick parkas for late in the season. Even the NFL's bulky winter wear is more stylish today, and as well-branded. In other words, don't expect players and coaches to be draped in the blanketlike capes that teams like the Packers and Colts wore on the sidelines in the 1950s.

THE BOOMING MARKET IN NFL WOMEN'S APPAREL

A major thrust of the NFL's new merchandising strategy was to try to grow the women's business, and Reebok, which already had name recognition within that market, was a good partner for that strategy. Today, the women's market is the fastest-growing consumer apparel segment for the NFL.

Before he left the NFL, Zona and his team began developing jerseys and other apparel specifically for women, who now account for more than 40 percent of the NFL audience at home and at the stadium. Jerseys are the league's number-one selling apparel item, but in the past, women had to buy a men's small- or medium-size jersey and make do. "We developed an entire game-day jersey program for women," Zona said. "The garment is sized specifically to properly fit a woman." The program that Zona started was picked up and expanded by his successor, Susan

Rothman, who joined the NFL in 1995 when the league was look-ing very hard at its demographics.

"We started a concerted effort in the mid-1990s," she said. "We wanted to understand what [women] liked and didn't like in our game. We had many focus groups. We talked to them about a line of apparel." At first, most women said they didn't need a separate line of apparel. "Then the moderator started showing them women's products, and they got it," Rothman said. "Sitting behind the one-way glass at these focus groups, I could see the light bulbs going on over the heads of these women at the conference table. They really liked this idea a lot."

Although Reebok was one of the stronger sports apparel brands among women, Rothman said the company didn't ini-tially see the potential of the women's market. "While they were excited and committed to the NFL business, they didn't see it translating to the female fans," Rothman said. They're now be-lievers, as are retailers. "The retailers who bought it the most quickly were the team stores," Rothman said. "We were doing a very nice business in polos, T-shirts with feminine graphics, clothing that was made to fit women."

Then for the 2004 season, the NFL developed a line of pastel pink caps designed specifically for women. "People thought we were crazy," said Rothman. "They said we'd never sell them." But Rothman saw firsthand how popular the caps were when she wore one to an early season Philadelphia Eagles game. "I couldn't walk five steps without having someone stop me and ask where I got my cap," she said.

The Eagles quickly sold out of their first, experimental run of pink caps. By the end of the season, the Eagles had sold 42,000 of the caps, more than double the sales of the caps that Eagles play-ers wear on the sideline. The NFL further enhanced the caps' popularity by announcing that it would donate a portion of the sales to breast cancer research. As a result, the caps have become so popular that they're available at almost every NFL stadium, along with a slew of other women-specific apparel and products.

Today, fans can purchase official NFL camisoles, jewelry, handbags, scarves, off-the-shoulder jerseys, and skirts with lace-up fronts that resemble players' pants. All this variety has helped sales of women's products triple over the past few years. "Once you get noticed, the business grows exponentially," Rothman said. "It seems to have happened overnight, but it didn't. We've been building this business slowly for a long time."

"I love pink," said Lisa Brzostowski, 29, who was wearing a pink #99 Julius Peppers jersey on the club level of Bank of America Stadium for a 2005 *Monday Night Football* game between the Carolina Panthers and Green Bay Packers. "It helps girls get into the game. And I like the fact that the women's jerseys aren't as bulky," added Brzostowski, who was also wearing one of Rothman's pink caps. "They fit me better."

Early in the 2005 season, Rothman said 24 percent of Wal-Mart's NFL apparel business was for women. "That's a staggering number and bodes well for the growth of the business," she said. "And we're growing the women's business without cannibalizing the men's business. Growth in women's does not seem to have come at the expense of the men's business."

"This is for real," said Mike May of the Sporting Goods Manufacturers Association. "It probably should have started years ago, but the industry was late in understanding the potential."

The explosion in women's apparel hasn't gone unnoticed by Reebok's Eddie White. "In 2005, the Indianapolis Colts had a magical season," he said. "But the hottest-selling team merchandise isn't Peyton Manning's jersey or the jacket [coach] Tony Dungy wears on the sideline. It's a new women's ski jacket with faux fur on the hood. We sold out."

The reorganization of the licensing business, the improved quality of the products, and the rapid growth of the women's market has made NFL Properties a hot commodity again. Although NFL jerseys are flying off the shelves, "The business is tightening a little bit," Rothman said in a September 2005 interview. "Our product was so hot with the hip-hop crowd and urban kids that it was bound to drop a little. But we're going to be okay as long as hot young players keep coming into this league."

NFL-LICENSED VIDEO GAMES AND OTHER MERCHANDISE

Zona and his team also streamlined the hard goods business, significantly cutting the NFL's more than 100 licensees. But that side of the merchandising business is harder to trim. "It's a different business," he said. "It's more item focused. Almost every unique item is made by a different licensee." And sales are better than ever—for traditional products, such as trading cards, footballs, and thick throw blankets as well as for some truly innovative stuff.

One example of such innovative products comes from Coopervision, a high-tech contact lens specialty company. Coopervision recently started shipping officially licensed NFL Crazy Lenses, a contact lens that features NFL team logos. The lenses were the brainchild of Dr. Mitchell Cassel, a New York City contact lens specialist who provides unusual eye effects for television and movies. Coopervision initially introduced nonprescription lenses for seven NFL teams—the Baltimore Ravens, Buffalo Bills, Minnesota Vikings, Oakland Raiders, Philadelphia Eagles, St. Louis Rams, and Tennessee Titans. The company has since introduced prescription contact lenses for all 32 NFL teams.

The lenses retail for $120 to $150 and come in a lens case with a football helmet on it. The logos encircle the pupil, which prevents the decoration from interfering with the wearer's vision. Initial production runs were limited to 1,000 pairs per team, but Coopervision was getting calls before the first pair ever hit the optometrist's office. "Fans enjoy incorporating their favorite teams into their daily lives," said Susan Rothman. "NFL Crazy Lenses offer an exciting and new avenue of team spirit."

While team-themed contact lenses are indeed a niche product, the real driver of the NFL's hard goods business is electronic games. Madden, an NFL-licensed video game that features *Monday Night Football* commentator and former Oakland Raiders coach John Madden, racked up $1.5 billion in retail sales in its first 16 years. EA Sports paid the NFL and the NFL Players Association more than $400 million to license the game. Not surprisingly, Madden 2006 debuted at number one.

Another video game manufacturer, Midway Games, Inc. of Chicago, shot itself in the foot in 2005 with its updated release of NFL Blitz. The game, which debuted in arcades in the mid-1990s and eventually migrated to game consoles, was a good seller. But the 2005 version of Blitz went too far for the NFL by including violent action that fell outside the buttoned-down corporate image the league likes to portray. For instance, players could snap the bones in an opponent's leg during a tackle. Midway admitted that it modeled that scene after a 1985 hit on Washington Redskins quarterback Joe Theisman by New York Giants bad-boy linebacker Lawrence Taylor. The replay of the tackle literally snapping Theisman's leg in two is considered one of the most gruesome images in the history of the sport, and many people found the Blitz scene even more repulsive.

"It was absolutely disgusting," said former congressman and NFL quarterback Jack Kemp, who first saw a commercial for Blitz while watching a 2005 NFL game with his grandson. "I think the league showed real integrity by not accepting that kind of stuff. It was just awful. We all just sat there after the commercial was over and didn't know what to say."

Players in Blitz also can moon fans, shoot steroids, and pick up cheerleaders. As owners, players can deal with crooked politicians for favorable stadium deals. "What we're doing is portraying what actually happens in professional football," Dave Zucker, CEO of Midway, said in defense of the game. But it was too much for the NFL, which refused to endorse the game. Midway was forced to shorten the game name to simply Blitz, omitting the NFL reference. Midway did create a toned-down version of Blitz that would have satisfied the NFL, but it disappointed gamers, according to the company.

While there hasn't been much buzz around the new Blitz game, stores can hardly keep Madden on the shelves. When its 2005 version debuted, the game shot to number one, selling 2.5 million units, up from 2.1 million units the previous year. By August 2005, EA Sports, together with NCAA Football 06, had captured 43.1 percent of the video game market.

CLEANING UP THE MARKETPLACE

All of this translates to big business—and big revenues—for the NFL. And the league knows it. In a 2005 NFL Total Access interview with reporter Rich Eisen, NFL commissioner Paul Tagliabue discussed the importance of NFL merchandise and the NFL Trust, which distributes league marketing and merchandising dollars equally among the 32 teams.

"I think it's [NFL merchandise marketing] more important as a promotional set of arrangements, as a way for teams in their markets to build partnerships with local businesses and companies and employees of companies with sponsorships and things like that," Tagliabue said. "At the league level, it's very important with our Gatorade relationship, our Pepsi relationship, and some of our youth programs that some of those sponsors will invest in."

In addition to servicing clients and properly managing apparel quality and quantity, the NFL also has tried to clamp down on illegal sales of unlicensed merchandise, both in the United States and abroad. "That's another benefit of trimming the number of apparel licensees—it cleaned up the marketplace," said

Zona. "By controlling two handfuls of licensees instead of a hundred, the licensee becomes more interested in policing. You end up with your licensed partners helping you."

Zona, a New Jersey native who is all too familiar with lower Manhattan's Canal Street and its market of knock-off Gucci and Coach handbags, said that limiting the number of licensees also helps the league track down the bootleggers. "If you really clean up the marketplace, you can narrow down and identify the sources that are making the illegal merchandise," he said.

And the NFL has expanded its hologram program by placing a silver sticker bearing an official NFL hologram on all NFL merchandise. Granted, the hologram can be copied, but it adds cost to the illegal merchandise, taking away some of the margin for would-be merchandise pirates. The NFL's legal department has started to crack down as well, especially around the Super Bowl. According to Zona, "There are four cities the NFL has to worry about regarding Super Bowl illegal merchandise: the two home cities that have teams in the Super Bowl, the host city, and Las Vegas." (In Las Vegas, Super Bowl day has become the single biggest betting day.)

In January 2003, the NFL went to court in San Diego and got permission from a judge to seize any unlicensed merchandise it found in stores or on street corners. In the week leading up to the Super Bowl that year, the NFL seized 2,000 counterfeit hats and 600 counterfeit T-shirts in the Los Angeles garment district. Previously, the NFL had seized about 10,000 counterfeit items during the playoffs. The NFL expected to sell about $100 million in Super Bowl merchandise during the San Diego Super Bowl.

Jerry Cohen, who owns Payless Sports Memorabilia in Wilmington, Delaware, rented the San Diego Wigs & Beauty Supply space in the Gaslamp Quarter for Super Bowl week. In an interview, he told the *San Diego Union-Tribune* that counterfeiters rarely sell their illegal goods to licensed retailers. "They know we won't take their stuff, because if the NFL finds out about it, it will be seized, and they might just shut down our whole shop," said Cohen.

During the 2005 Pro Bowl in Honolulu, police and NFL officials seized more than $4,000 worth of illegal goods. At the 2005 Super Bowl in Jacksonville, police seized 3,000 fake NFL items worth an estimated $69,000. In addition to policing game-day parking lots, the NFL now has to watch the Internet for illegal sales of unlicensed merchandise. But thanks to the NFL's tighter control of its merchandising business, unauthorized sales have declined.

REAPING THE REWARDS OF
SAVVY MERCHANDISING

Team owners seem to be happy with what the NFL has done to revamp merchandising. In March 2004, the owners renewed the NFL Trust for 15 years. After taxes and operating expenses, the NFL's $3.5 billion merchandise business provides each of the 32 teams about $4 million a year. The only signs of a rift came from the Dallas Cowboys' Jerry Jones, the Washington Redskins' Daniel Snyder, and the Miami Dolphins' Wayne Huizenga, who asked the league to look into modifying the NFL Trust's revenue-sharing arrangement. Jones is the only NFL owner who sells his own merchandise. Snyder and Huizenga are part of the new class of entrepreneurial NFL owners who think that teams should work hard at generating local sales and get to keep much of the revenue. Commissioner Paul Tagliabue added the group's concerns to the agenda of the nine-member committee that was looking into all aspects of the NFL's revenue sharing, but it's fair to say that, with the NFL on the precipice of a labor dispute in March 2006, the NFL Trust was the least of its economic worries.

The same kind of business savvy that helped reinvent the NFL's merchandise licensing program has also contributed to the ever-growing media monster that is the Super Bowl. In fact, you need look no further than Super Bowl XL in Detroit for evidence of the popularity of NFL merchandise. The weekend before the Super Bowl, vandals broke glass windows on storefronts in downtown Detroit. What were they after? Super Bowl XL merchandise and memorabilia. While theft is certainly not the kind of endorsement the NFL is looking for, it's yet more evidence that, of all its merchandising efforts, the Super Bowl may be the league's greatest success story.

CHAPTER EIGHT

THE SUPER BOWL

WHO REALLY WINS?

"We just went wild," said Tampa mayor Pam Iorio.

"The biggest thing that's ever happened to me was watching my son being born," said Paul Catoe, executive director of the Tampa Bay Convention and Visitors Center. "This wasn't as exciting, but it was close to it."

"It means a whole helluva lot of money for this area," said Joe Redner, owner of several Tampa strip clubs. "We raise the prices, and we have more people. It's just a bonanza."

What could these people possibly be so ecstatic about? They're all reacting to the news in 2005 that Tampa was awarded the Super Bowl for 2009.

You'd think that by now they'd know better. Tampa was the site of three previous Super Bowls—1984, 1991, and 2001—each supposedly more stupendous than the last in terms of local economic impact. In 2001, the Super Bowl brought about 100,000 visitors, each of whom—according to various Tampa-area chambers of commerce, paid consultants, and the NFL—spent on average about $2,500 during their stay. Based on those numbers, the NFL figured the economic impact on the local community to be about $250 million.

"I think those [numbers] are gross exaggerations," said Allen Sanderson, a University of Chicago sports economist. Sanderson, like many of his colleagues, argues that you have to subtract from that $250 million the spending by people who would have come to a warm city by the Gulf of Mexico in the middle of winter regardless of whether or not it was hosting a Super Bowl. You also have to trim revenues generated by hotel spending, because a lot of that money only briefly touches the host city before being transferred to corporate headquarters elsewhere. Next, you must subtract the millions of dollars that won't be spent at area malls, theaters, and other entertainment venues because of Super Bowl–related events. And finally, you have to subtract what it cost the city to host a Super Bowl in infrastructure improvements, extra security, and marketing and advertising; in 2006, those costs were estimated to be between $12 million and $15 million.

"The NFL says $300 million, but I'd say it's closer to $50 million," Sanderson said. Other economists who have studied the impact of the Super Bowl on local economies say it's more like $25 million or $30 million. In fact, according to some economic analyses, the Super Bowl can actually end up costing a city money—especially when a January or February Super Bowl is in a city in California, Florida, or Texas, which would attract visitors from Wisconsin, Pennsylvania, New England, and other cooler climates, regardless of who's playing.

But what you may find even more ironic is the fact that Super Bowls aren't always a financial boon for the teams that play in them. "I would expect to lose a little bit of money on the game," Atlanta Falcons president and general manager Rich McKay said just before the start of the 2004 playoffs. McKay, one of the most respected general managers in all of football, isn't alone in his assessment of the cost of participating in a postseason NFL game; he has history on his side. The Green Bay Packers estimate that they lost about $1.5 million during their two Super Bowl appearances in 1997 and 1998. The St. Louis Rams also reported losing money during their Super Bowl winning season in 2000. The same goes for the San Francisco 49ers. Here's why Super Bowl champions lose money.

As I've shown in previous chapters, the NFL shares most revenues equally. The 2006 labor and revenue agreement confirmed that. But during the playoffs that arrangement changes. The NFL keeps all ticket revenue. Teams get to keep stadium-related sales from concessions and parking, but the league only pays teams about $500,000 for early playoff appearances and about $1 million for the NFC and AFC championship games. Super Bowl teams average about $3 million each, but the game is played at a neutral site so they lose parking, concessions, and suite revenue.

Teams also lose money because they have to pay playoff bonuses to players, coaches, and other staff and move equipment, players, and staff. And they have other traveling and host expenses, such as entertaining VIPs like past Hall of Famers and important local-market sponsors and advertisers. "Expenses usually exceed whatever you get from the league," said John Jones, chief operating officer of the Green Bay Packers and a former NFL corporate officer.

Players don't do much better during the playoffs and the Super Bowl. While a top-rated player like Peyton Manning may make upwards of $1 million a game during the regular season, postseason salaries are paid by the NFL and are paltry by comparison (but don't count against a team's salary cap). Every player is paid the same salary during the playoffs, whether they're the quarterback or the backup holder on extra points. Although an MVP performance during the Super Bowl can do much for a player's career, maybe even landing him in the Pro Football Hall of Fame, the only immediate upside is for the guys who work hard every week on the offensive line and special teams.

So who does profit from the Super Bowl? Most sports economists agree that, while the Super Bowl may not be so good for the host city, team, or individual players, it's absolutely great for the NFL, television networks, and sponsors and advertisers. With 144 million guaranteed viewers, advertisers are paying unprecedented rates to score a spot on the most widely viewed sporting event in the world. Today, Super Bowl advertising supplies the NFL with a lucrative source of income, even as it provides some of the televised event's most memorable moments. As professor Charles Tomkovick of the University of Wisconsin has noted, "It started out as the Super Bowl, morphed into the Bud Bowl, and now could accurately be called the ad bowl."

Official NFL sponsorships cost tens of millions of dollars. Super Bowl advertisers not only had to pay $2.5 million for a 30-second spot during the Super Bowl, but the ads had to be funny, clever, and memorable. Creating a truly great ad can cost 5 times what the sponsor pays for airtime. Despite those ever-increasing costs, many companies obviously think it's worth it. But once you cut through the hoopla surrounding the Super Bowl spectacle to take a hard look at the cold economics of the event, who emerge as the winners and losers? Let's see if we can separate the promises from the payoffs in this multimillion-dollar media bonanza.

SPORTS ECONOMISTS TAKE A
HARD LOOK AT THE NUMBERS

Phil Porter is the guy Super Bowl host committees and NFL executives love to hate. The University of South Florida economist has been one of the most outspoken critics in analyzing the claimed economic impact of Super Bowls and other megasporting events on local economies. His findings won't please taxpayers who fund these extravaganzas or the leagues that try to sell them as economic dynamos for the local economy.

In one of his many studies, Porter examined the economic impact of six Super Bowls and concluded that the numbers touted by mayors, city councils, chambers of commerce, tourism boards, and the NFL are as hyped as the Super Bowl halftime show.

"Three Super Bowl impact studies [1991 Tampa, 1995 Miami, 1996 Phoenix] as well as conventional wisdom predict huge windfalls for the communities that host Super Bowls," Porter wrote in his analysis. "But in these and every other instance studied [1976 and 1979 Miami and 1984 Tampa], no windfall materializes."

For instance, in looking at Miami's 1995 Super Bowl, Porter found that Miami-area hotel rates and occupancy levels were only 4.4 percent higher in 1995 than they were in January 1994 and January 1996. When he looked at the impact of Super Bowl XXXIII, played January 31, 1999, before 74,803 fans in Pro Player Stadium in Miami, Porter found, "A simple comparison of taxable sales data for south Florida for January/February 1998 . . . reveals that Super Bowl XXXIII could not have contributed, by any reasonable standard, more than $37 million to the south Florida economy. This represents approximately 5 percent of the impact the NFL attributed to the game."

In looking at Super Bowl XXXIX, played February 6, 2005, in Alltell Stadium in Jacksonville, Florida, in front of 78,125 fans, Porter found that the Super Bowl resulted in a $41.3 million increase in taxable sales. While that sounds like a significant amount, what you have to look at, Porter argues, is how much tax was collected. At a 7 percent rate, that $41 million of increased sales only translated into about $3 million more tax revenues for the municipality. When you factor in that hosting a Super Bowl costs local government roughly $15 million in infrastructure improvements; security; and overtime for police, fire, and EMS personnel, you realize that hosting Super Bowl XXXIX cost Jacksonville and Duval County about $12 million.

Houston didn't make out much better when it hosted Super Bowl XXXVIII in 2004, according to University of Texas economists Craig Depken and Dennis Wilson, authors of "What Is the Economic Impact of Hosting a Super Bowl," which appeared in the January 2003 issue of Texas Labor Market Review. These authors took a close look at the predictions of the Super Bowl's economic impact upon host cities provided by the NFL, local government groups, and representatives of area hotel and restaurant associations. Their study found that, for various Super Bowls held between 1992 and 2006, these sources predicted that the events would generate a net real economic impact of "between $220 and $350 million." The authors concluded that those numbers were not accurate.

Depken and Wilson noted that, in fact, most economists consider the promised economic impact to be inflated. Indeed, as Porter mentioned in his analysis of the economic impact of the Super Bowl on Jacksonville, the valid measure is the net change in economic activity associated with the event, usually measured in direct and indirect economic impact.

"Direct impacts include new spending by local residents and out-of-towners that would not have been spent otherwise (e.g., on hotels, restaurants, rental cars, taxi services, shopping, and visits to local attractions)," Depken and Wilson said. "An accurate measure of direct spending must include only new spending, not merely money spent at the event that would have been spent anyway (e.g., attending the Super Bowl instead of attending the theater)."

This is precisely the point that Porter and other sports economists like Robert Baade, Mark Rosentraub, and Art Rolnick make. In Rolnick's case, the Minneapolis federal reserve economist makes the same points, whether he's arguing the merits of hosting a Super Bowl, building a new stadium, or luring the newest GM or Toyota plant to town. "I don't care if it's a stadium or a factory," Rolnick said. "If the state has to subsidize it, there's usually a pretty good reason why private enterprise—the free market—hasn't put it there already."

Calculating the Promise of "Indirect Benefits"

Where the economic waters really get murky is when the debate turns to "indirect benefits," economic activity that is harder to see because it is the result—often called the "ripple effect"—of direct spending. To calculate indirect benefits, economists assume that at least some of the money spent locally on the event will trickle down into other parts of the community.

The calculations of these indirect benefits typically account for the difference between the league's and cities' estimates of the economic benefits of a major sporting event and those of most economists. There are three sources for those differences.

First, there is what economists call practitioner bias, which simply means that those preparing the estimates might be prone to presenting somewhat inflated figures, because those figures best support their own interests. "Practitioner bias arises because promoters and hotel/restaurateurs generally desire large estimated impacts to justify any public subsidization of the event," Depken and Wilson said. "The economic impact studies by local advocates are rarely subject to scholarly review, and inflated estimates can go unquestioned and perhaps unconfirmed after the event."

Another source of difference in the estimates stems from measurement errors. As Porter has noted, for example, many event advocates calculate the impact of hotel occupancy and higher room rates as if the hotels would have been vacant without the event. Of course, nothing could be further from the truth, especially in places like Miami and San Diego, which have healthy tourist trades in January and February when there isn't a Super Bowl.

And, finally, there is the problem of *leakage*, a term economists use when referring to money that is spent locally but doesn't necessary end up in the local economy. Again, the best example is hotels. "It is unlikely that the majority of revenue increases at a company-owned Marriott or Holiday Inn will remain and be respent in the local economy," Depken and Wilson argue. "Much of the revenue increases may be transferred to a parent company in another city, state, or country."

"They swipe the credit card in Detroit, but that's about all Detroit will see of that money," says Professor Porter. Furthermore, he argues that higher hotel rates and occupancy have more of an impact on hotel investors in Riyadh than on taxpayers in Detroit.

All of these factors make up the indirect economic impact, the most hotly contested factor when calculating the impact of a major sporting event like the Super Bowl or the Olympics.

Debating the Economists' Findings

Kathleen Davis, executive director of the Sports Management Research Institute in Weston, Florida, is one economist who thinks that the Super Bowl is all that. She admits that hosting a Super Bowl could cost a city upwards of $5 million but believes the NFL's claims that a typical Super Bowl generates somewhere around $300 million in economic activity for the host city. "The average income of people that come [to south Florida] this time of year is $53,000," Davis said. "The average income of a Super Bowl attendee ranges anywhere from $90,000 to $120,000. What does that tell you? It tells you that, hypothetically, they might purchase more."

Depken and Wilson admit that the exact impact of megasporting events like the Super Bowl is hard to measure. They also acknowledge that hosting a big game is often an opportunity for a city to show off its attributes to visitors who might not otherwise visit the city. Furthermore, a positive experience at an event like the Super Bowl might cause a corporation or group to return for a convention; it even could be a factor in deciding to locate a corporate headquarters or regional office in the host city.

That's the argument the city of Jacksonville makes, both in regards to the expansion NFL franchise it was awarded in 1993 and the Super Bowl it hosted in 2005.

"The day the NFL named Jacksonville the 30th franchise is the day that this city changed entirely," said Jerry Mallot, executive vice president of the Jacksonville Regional Chamber of Commerce. "We have cachet; we have a sense that we are different, up to date, leading edge," he said. "That was not the attitude of this city prior to the Jaguars."

Hosting Super Bowl XXXIX in 2005 was icing on the cake. Before the game, Mallot was working on 52 prospective businesses that were thinking of locating their headquarters or regional offices in Jacksonville. A few months after the Super Bowl, he was working on 69 business deals. "That's a one-third increase in three months," he said. "It's not all because of the Super Bowl, but the exposure of our market played a role in how rapidly we gained a bunch of new prospects."

But at what cost?

Phil Porter noted that hosting a Super Bowl opens a city up as much to ridicule as to accolades. He said that some of the media coverage around the 2005 Super Bowl in Jacksonville pointed out how boring the city was. Media coverage of the 2001 Super Bowl in Tampa focused on the business boom the big game created for local strip clubs.

The Super Bowl economics debate even entered the political fray in Texas, when comptroller Carole Keeton Strayhorn announced that the state would kick back $8.7 million to the city of Houston, the Super Bowl host committee, and Harris County to help defray expenses from Super Bowl XXXVIII, which the city hosted on February 1, 2004, before 71,525 fans at Reliant Stadium. The reason for Strayhorn's announcement of the proposed rebate was Texas Senate Bill 275, which requires the comptroller to forecast revenue gains from increased collections from sales, motor vehicle, hotel occupancy, and alcohol taxes in the market area of a major sporting event. The law was used for the first time with Super Bowl XXXVIII. Based on a formula in the law, a portion of the expected tax revenue increase will be placed in a new "Other Events Trust Fund" to help defray expenses related to the Super Bowl.

The rebate from the state represented the anticipated extra sales tax revenue that the Super Bowl was expected to generate. "Approximately 104,000 happy visitors will take back warm memories of Texas—after they leave quite a few dollars here," Strayhorn said. "Texas will be a winner, no matter who wins the big game."

Strayhorn estimated that visitors would spend an average of $373 per day for 4.3 days, leaving $165.5 million in the Houston area. In addition, the Houston Super Bowl host committee would spend $10.1 million dollars on preparing Reliant Stadium and other facilities, media and team hotels, transportation, security and law enforcement, deploying 10,000 volunteers, and hosting nearly 4,000 members of the worldwide media.

"You probably will not find an academic economist who isn't critical of these numbers," said Coates, the University of Maryland sports economist. "You will only find a comptroller or paid consultant coming up with those numbers." Indeed, some sports economists told the *Houston Chronicle* that Super Bowl XXXVIII would have a $20 million to $50 million economic impact on the Houston economy, while others said it would have little or no effect on taxable sales.

To arrive at the $8.7 million rebate figure, Strayhorn's office used a multiplier of 2.3 to calculate indirect spending and total spending, a figure often used by economic development officials, whether it relates to a new stadium or public investment in any other private-sector project. Tamara Plaut, a senior economist in

Strayhorn's office, called that multiplier "pretty conservative," noting it was derived from economic models commonly used by Texas state officials and offices.

"Oh, my God, I think that's outrageous," said Coates. "That's absolutely ludicrous. That's way too high." Coates argued that a more accurate figure is one derived by Stanford sports economist Roger Noll, who puts the multiplier at about 1.2. Our old friend Porter also said the multiplier was way too high and that the NFL, the host committees, and the comptroller's office were using economic models designed to overstate the economic impact of the Super Bowl.

"I can guarantee you that there won't be any $8.7 million increase in state taxes due to the Super Bowl," Porter said.

"Reasonable minds will differ," said James LeBas, chief revenue estimator for the comptroller's office. "I welcome diversity of opinion."

Questioning the League's Numbers

Perhaps the most definitive study of the impact of Super Bowls was completed in 2003 by economists Robert Baade of Lake Forest College in Illinois and Victor Matheson of Williams College in Williamstown, Massachusetts. (Called "Super Bowl or Super (Hyper)Bole? Assessing the Economic Impact of America's Premier Sports Event," the full report can be viewed at *www.williams.edu/Economics/wp/mathesonSuperbowl.pdf*.) Baade and Matheson note that civic boosters and NFL officials regularly estimate the economic impact of the Super Bowl at between $300 million and $400 million. In addition to hyping the Super Bowl, the study makes a case that these sources have an ulterior motive for promoting these inflated estimates.

"The National Football League has used the promise of an economic windfall to convince skeptical cities that investment in new stadiums for their teams in exchange for the right to host the event makes economic sense," they write. The authors go on to note, "The evidence indicates that, at best, the Super Bowl contributes approximately one-quarter of what the NFL promises."

In regard to a 1999 NFL study that estimated the impact of Super Bowl XXXIII on the south Florida economy at $393 million, the authors ask, "Can a study either commissioned or performed by the NFL be unbiased if the NFL has used the promise of a future Super Bowl as an enticement for cities to build new facilities? . . . Modern sports stadiums generally receive some form of public funding, and the NFL at least indirectly has rationalized public financial support on the grounds that the economic impact from a single Super Bowl approximates the cost of building a new stadium. Coincidence?"

The authors go on to present information that appears to answer their question with a solid no. As I noted earlier, more than 20 NFL stadiums have been either built or refurbished since 1995. Indeed, from 1995 through 2003, about $6.4 billion dollars, or an average of $304 million per stadium, was spent to build or substantially refurbish 21 NFL stadiums. The public contribution was about $4.4 billion, an average of $209 million, or roughly 69 percent of the construction costs.

"This substantial transformation of NFL infrastructure has been accomplished in part through league incentives to include hosting a Super Bowl in some cases and using league-shared club seat revenues to help finance stadium construction," the authors write. The shared incentives the authors refer to stem from the NFL's G-3 program, which takes revenues from the national TV contract and some stadium seating, puts it into bonds, and then uses the proceeds to help teams fund stadium construction. I talk more about the stadium-building boom in Chapter 9.

In addition to the economic analysis by Porter and other sports economists, Baade and Matheson cite their own 1999 study that looked at the economic impact of 25 Super Bowls from 1973 to 1997. They found that hosting a Super Bowl resulted in "an average economic impact of roughly $30 million or roughly one-tenth the figures touted by the NFL." In conclusion, the authors found that, "cities would be wise to view with caution Super Bowl economic impact estimates provided by the NFL. It would appear that padding is an essential element of the game both on and off the field."

What about the Jobs?

The estimates for NFL stadiums' impact on employment are on even shakier ground. As we saw with the Atlanta study, the estimate of new jobs created as a result of hosting the Super Bowl was 2,736. Again, Baade and Matheson have done some of the best work in analyzing the validity of these estimates. They have calculated that the average metropolitan area sees about 537 jobs created as a result of hosting a Super Bowl. Furthermore, they found that most of the work was short term and often part-time. Again, their conclusion is that, "while the Super Bowl did contribute jobs to the local economy, job creation attributable to the game fell considerably short of that predicted in studies commissioned by the NFL."

Baade and Matheson also note that, in 1999, the average job in the United States paid $40,000 in annual wages and fringe benefits. After multiplying that by their jobs number, adjusting for earned income, inflation, population growth, and other standard economic factors, the authors concluded that the economic impact of Super Bowl XXXIII on south Florida was, at most, just under $37 million. "In terms of magnitude, this is in keeping with our estimate of an economic impact on average for Super Bowls in the neighborhood of $30 million, about one-tenth the impact the NFL attributes to the game."

Depken and Wilson, the University of Texas economists, are a little more pointed in their analysis of alleged job gains as a result of hosting a Super Bowl. "Most likely those who are already employed, especially in service sectors where overtime is compensated (e.g., police and fire services), ultimately experience the greatest economic benefits from the Super Bowl, while elected officials gain substantial political capital."

Detroit's Experience

The estimated impact of a Super Bowl may be greater, however, in cities that don't have large winter tourist populations. Detroit, which hosted Super Bowl XL in February 2006, is a great example. While the economists remain skeptical, the Detroit Super Bowl hosts were positively buoyant about the event's estimated economic impact on that city, despite past history and economic analysis. "We used some data from the NFL and put them into a model that the convention and visitors bureau has," said Susan Sherer, executive director of the Detroit Super Bowl XL host committee. "It was right around $400 million." And, yes, she's heard the predictions from economists Porter, Samuelson, and others that the impact isn't that great. "There were naysayers who said that in San Diego and Miami, you're just replacing one person with another," Scherer said. "That's not true here. A weekend in February is not a busy time. The hotels will clearly see more revenue with four-night minimums and the highest published rates for a weekend in Detroit."

Of course, the Detroit host committee also touted the infrastructure improvements that were made, all of which would benefit the residents of Detroit long after Super Bowl XL had passed. But that begs the question: Should a city—especially a model of modern urban decay like Detroit—need an impetus like the Super Bowl to improve basic services and infrastructure? Many people think not.

Ted Johnson, a 48-year-old sound technician from suburban Detroit, nearly wrecked his van while driving on one of the city's suburban highways in the weeks leading up to Super Bowl XL.

Three street sweepers and a road crew were picking up trash. "I've lived here my whole life, and that's the first time I've seen street sweepers on the highway," said Johnson.

He isn't alone. Detroit natives watched in amazement as their city, long the poster child for urban decay, undertook a massive effort to clean itself up for the 100,000 out-of-town guests expected for Super Bowl XL. Major highways were repaved. Long-abandoned buildings were demolished or, at a minimum, had their facades painted and fixed up. Authorities even got the homeless off the streets for Super Bowl weekend. All this—at an admitted cost of about $100 million in public and private money.

"It's great that they did all this for the Super Bowl," said Johnson, "but think about how that makes those of us who live here feel. They let Detroit rot for 40 years, but when they got a Super Bowl, they fixed things. The message was: It's okay to do things for the fat cats who are coming into town for a weekend, but if you're one of the poor dumb schmucks who lives here, you're not worth it." Wilson's attitude was shared by a lot of people I spoke to leading up to the Super Bowl—with one exception: the homeless.

On Super Bowl Sunday, the Detroit Rescue Mission served nearly 200 homeless men and women, who came in out of the cold to sit on big easy chairs and couches; partake of a typical Super Bowl buffet of hot dogs, chili, chips, and popcorn; and watch the big game.

"I needed to see the game somewhere," said David Riley, a 29-year-old homeless man who said he hadn't worked in 7 years.

"This is great," said Phil Summers, 42, who was sitting in a big easy chair, balancing a bowl of chili in one hand and a Coke on his knee. "I think they should have the Super Bowl every year."

It's still too early to tell what the long-term impact of Super Bowl XL will be on Detroit, but the bevy of sports economists who track it don't have much hope. "Most economic impact studies implicitly assume the hotel occupancy would have been zero without the event," said University of Texas economists Depken and Wilson.

"The athletes, the chain hotels, and the restaurants receive money from the Super Bowl and take the money out of the area," notes King Banaian, economics chairman at St. Cloud State University in Minnesota. "This reduces the impact on the local economy."

"With leaguewide revenue sharing and other external commitments, most of the game-related money will leave Detroit faster than the corporate jets on Super Bowl night," said University of Chicago economist Sanderson. "The one thing that remains will be the costs."

ADVERTISERS SCORE BIG AT THE SUPER BOWL

So if the teams and the host city aren't the big winners of the Super Bowl's financial bonanza, who is?

One group of winners is the advertisers—at least *some* of the advertisers. Paying more than $2 million for a 30-second spot during the most-watched television event of the year will pay huge dividends, if you're advertising the right product. But if you're in the wrong product category, you might as well throw your money out the window.

Those are the findings of Charles Tomkovick and Rama Yelkur, two University of Wisconsin marketing professors who have studied the success—and failure—of Super Bowl advertising. One of the biggest winners in Super Bowl advertising, they've found, is Hollywood. The professors, who have published their work in the *Journal of Advertising Research* and other publications, found that films and entertainment were among the categories positively linked with Super Bowl ads. By advertising a new film during the Super Bowl, "Hollywood has found that it can spend $2 million to make an extra $50 million," Tomkovick said.

THE AD BOWL TIME LINE: A SUPER BOWL CHRONOLOGY

- *1967.* NFL commissioner Pete Rozelle created the Super Bowl, initially a war between staunch rivals (the NFL and the AFL) to be played during the dead of winter in sunny climes like Florida and California. Super Bowl I was split between the two television networks with NFL broadcast rights, NBC and CBS, who outdid themselves promoting their respective halves of the game.
- *1969.* Joe Namath guaranteed that the upstart New York Jets of the AFL would upset the Baltimore Colts, one of the most storied franchises in the history of professional football, in Super Bowl III. The Jets won, and the Super Bowl replaced the Kentucky Derby as the number-one gambling event of the year, a title it has not relinquished since.
- *1976.* In another nod to the increasingly important entertainment factor of the big game, the NFL re-created the Fourth of July in the middle of January.
- *1984.* The commercials became bigger than the game. *Blade Runner* director Ridley Scott shot a $400,000 ad to introduce Apple's Macintosh PC. More than 8,000 Macs were sold the next day, and the following year, Super Bowl ad rates jumped nearly 40 percent with a half-minute spot going for $525,000.
- *1989.* Billy Joel sang the national anthem at Super Bowl XXIII, launching a Super Bowl trend of megastar pregame and halftime entertainment. In advertising, American Express stole the show when Saturday Night Live regulars Dana Carvey and Jon Lovitz went to the Super Bowl, one carrying Visa and the other American Express. You can figure out the rest.
- *1991.* Diet Pepsi won the increasingly competitive advertising wars. A truly global cast, from African Bushmen to British butlers, sang Ray Charles' Diet Pepsi jingle, "You've got the right one, baby."

(continued)

THE AD BOWL TIME LINE: A SUPER BOWL CHRONOLOGY

- *1992, 1993.* These two Super Bowls were actually dominated by the NBA, as Michael Jordan and Bugs Bunny battled basketball bullies in plugs for *Space Jam.* The next year, Larry Bird and Jordan played an entertaining game of H-O-R-S-E.
- *1995.* The first season of the NFL Europe. Its most important function was to prime a worldwide audience for the Super Bowl. It worked; today the Super Bowl is beamed to more than 200 countries.
- *2001.* Ad highlight: Cedric the Entertainer's plans to seduce a beautiful young woman go awry when his bottles of Bud Light start exploding.
- *2002.* Paul McCartney played in the pregame show. Ad highlight: An amorous housewife tries to lure her husband to the bedroom with a case of Bud Light. Diving for the beer, he slides across their satin sheets and out the window.
- *2004.* Janet Jackson's "wardrobe malfunction" left CBS with egg on its face.
- *2005.* Bye-bye MTV: The NFL took charge of producing the Super Bowl halftime show and played it safe; Paul McCartney earned about $100,000 per minute delivering his $1 million halftime performance.
- *2006.* A 30-second spot during Super Bowl XL cost $2.5 million.

What other product categories get a big bang for their buck? Food and beverages are the no-brainers, the professors said, especially beer.

"Many viewers watch the Super Bowl in groups of four or more creating a party atmosphere, so it makes sense that ads for food and beverage products would do well on the Super Bowl," said Yelkur.

"Certainly for Anheuser-Busch and Pepsi, they dominate across the spectrum of mass media," said Tomkovick. "Their commercials are previewed; there's lots of Web site activity. You have a two-week period to do it."

Companies also do well if they tie in onsite promotions to their television ads.

"The companies that are official NFL sponsors and advertise during the Super Bowl are buying access, which they can merchandise internally," Tomkovick said. "It's like tickets to the Academy Award parties. It works well with a company's customers and distributors. It gives the impression that you're a player on the event scene."

A SURE BET

No question about it, the Super Bowl is a guaranteed advertising spectacle. According to the professors, about 50 percent of the people who watch the Super Bowl do so partly to watch the ads. And the percentage of people who watch exclusively for the ads "is in the double digits," Tomkovick said. "That's mind boggling. That's a very intensive audience."

In fact, consulting firm Penn, Schoen, and Berland found that 58 percent of Americans would rather miss part of the game than the ads. AOL has tapped into the popularity of Super Bowl ads by replaying them online and allowing visitors to vote for their favorites. In 2004, the site drew 3.5 million online voters; that's almost double the number of people AOL drew after the 2004 NCAA basketball tournament (2 million) and more than double the 1.5 million after *Sports Illustrated* released its annual swimsuit issue.

This research is especially valuable for advertisers when Super Bowl ad rates continue to climb. In 2006, the average Super Bowl ad cost $2.5 million for a 30-second spot, a slight increase from $2.4 million in 2005, which was 6.7 percent higher than 2004

Super Bowl rates and 20 percent higher than the $2 million cost in 2002.

Rob DiGisi, a Wharton sports and entertainment marketing lecturer and president of Ironhorse Marketing in Wilmington, Delaware, thinks there's a certain caché to paying huge sums for Super Bowl advertising. "There's always an incentive to advertise on the high side," he said. "It makes you seem more in demand." DiGisi estimates a fudge factor of 5 to 15 percent on the premium ad rates for Super Bowl airtime. And by some measures, so-called "industry leaders" *must* advertise during the Super Bowl.

"If you are perceived as the industry leader and you are not in the Super Bowl, people might ask, 'Why not?'" said Schmittlein. "There is a lot of . . . paranoia that, if you're not going to advertise in your product category, then the field is wide open for your competitors. Maybe you don't have a great idea to use the Super Bowl to your advantage, but you're afraid your competitor will, and you don't want to give them a free pass."

While some TV events come close to the Super Bowl, nothing is as predictable in its ability to reach viewers—or produce revenues. "The Academy Awards come close in terms of ad spending," Yelkur said. "Target or JCPenney will spend about $1.6 million for a 30-second spot during the Oscars. Cosmetics companies are big advertisers as well. . . . You really can't beat the Super Bowl in terms of ad impact and the predictability of the audience."

And consumers aren't always the only target of Super Bowl advertising.

"Making your employees feel they are working for the best company in the industry may be better achieved through the Super Bowl than with a longer company newsletter," he says. According to Len Lodish, certain companies advertise during the game to draw the attention of wholesalers and trade customers. "When combined with other events, it may be useful for getting your distribution channels behind your product," he said.

Advertising Super Stars

Super Bowl commercials have transcended their basic marketing function and are now seen as a reflection of American culture. When Super Bowl advertisements work, they can fuel water cooler conversations for years after they air, changing the fortunes of the companies and advertisers who produce them. Apple and Budweiser are perhaps the two strongest examples of such companies.

"Advertising executives speak in hushed tones about the greatest Super Bowl of them all, 1984," wrote ad guru Jerry Della Femina in a January 2001 piece in the *Wall Street Journal*. He was speaking about Apple's 1984 ad that introduced its Macintosh computer; the ad—featuring a young woman in shorts and headband throwing a sledge hammer at a Big Brother–like face—still stands out for many as the Super Bowl's greatest play. "No, there is not a single one of these executives who can remember which two teams competed. But they all can tell you it was the year of the greatest Super Bowl commercial, a beautifully produced take-off on George Orwell's *1984* that featured one rebel sticking it to dictatorship and authority. Sales of the Apple Macintosh, which was introduced in this commercial, zoomed out of sight. The commercial's producer, Chiat Day, became world famous."

Other companies have used Super Bowl advertisements to reinvent their image and open up new market segments for their products; Budweiser is a prime example of these successes. "The ads with the frogs and 'wassup' works with the target audience," said Wharton marketing professor Len Lodish. "Bud used to have an old, stodgy image. Now it's cool to drink Bud."

Hollywood executives have found that it pays to play during the Super Bowl. *Independence Day* was the first blockbuster film to advertise during the Super Bowl (1996), even though its release date wasn't until July 4. Fox spent $1.1 million to promote the film, which earned more than $500 million worldwide.

That was enough to convince Hollywood that Super Bowl advertising was a good investment. During the 1999 to 2001 Super Bowls, 5 movies were advertised each year. In 2002, the figure increased to 9 and then 10 in 2003. Of 18 films that were advertised during the 2002 and 2003 Super Bowls, 15 were number one at the box office the weekend they opened, 2 finished second, and 1 claimed the number four spot. Even at $2 million per 30-second ad, the cost of the ads was less than 2 percent of the films' U.S. box office gross. In 2005, about a dozen movie ads were shown during the Super Bowl, accounting for about 20 percent of the ad time sold during the game.

Why the increase? The ads pay huge dividends.

"There is a clear difference in the box office return of the Super Bowl–promoted movie," Tomkovick said. "Even controlling for release size, budget, and other factors, data shows a 40 percent better return on your investment, if you're a Hollywood studio and advertised during the Super Bowl."

The professors looked at Super Bowls and films from 1998 to 2001 and found that the average Super Bowl–promoted film earned twice as much in first-weekend, first-week, and total U.S. box office revenue than a non–Super Bowl promoted movie. Even when controlled for release date and budget, they found similar results. In 2003, all 10 movies promoted during the Super Bowl opened at number one in terms of box office revenues.

Of course, Tomkovick admits, the movie has to be good. But if it is, Super Bowl advertising almost guarantees a studio the number-one spot at the box office when the film opens. "Worst case, you'll get a close second," Tomkovick said. "If you're a Hollywood studio, you like your odds when your investment turns into number one at the box office."

One surprising winner in the Super Bowl ad blitz that has emerged of late is financial services companies, such as Accenture and Met Life. "There is evidence that you get a short-term bump in your stock price by advertising during the Super Bowl,"

Tomkovick said. "You get a bump the day you announce you'll run an ad and the day after the Super Bowl. But most Super Bowl ads fall off the cliff after you get beyond a week or two after the game."

Ads for erectile dysfunction products, such as Levitra and Cialis, have done well also. "Some of those advertisers have seen a significant increase in the number of prescriptions that were written shortly after the Super Bowl," he said.

"The Super Bowl isn't just the biggest day of the year for two football teams," Della Femina said in his January 2001 *Wall Street Journal* article. "In my world—advertising—the Super Bowl is judgment day. If politicians have election day and Hollywood has the Oscars, advertising has the Super Bowl."

Super Bowl Ads That Don't Work

But some advertisers see the Super Bowl as a losing proposition. Other research conducted by professors Tomkovick and Yelkur found that oil and credit card companies aren't superstars in Super Bowl advertising. "Credit cards don't do well, because the Super Bowl is just after Christmas and many people are reminded of the high credit card bills they have to pay off," Yelkur said. "And oil companies don't do well, because there's no real connection to the game. You don't see an ad for motor oil during the Super Bowl and say, 'Oh, that's right. I have to get my oil changed.'"

Other businesses or products just simply aren't a good fit for the Super Bowl event and its audience. "We've done movie research with high school and college students, and there's a significant recall," Yelkur said. "If you ran an ad for Holiday Inn, you would not get . . . that overwhelming connection." In the same vein, if a Super Bowl watcher has a favorable impression of a movie, they'll likely go see it, but not everyone who sees a great car ad is going to go out and buy that automobile.

Of course, some ads have crossed the line with viewers. There was the 2005 ad for ABC's *Desperate Housewives*, for example, that featured actress Nicollette Sheridan dropping her towel in the pregame locker room to entice Philadelphia Eagles bad-boy wide receiver Terrell Owens to watch the show. While the ad featured no nudity, the message was clear enough that the NFL and ABC, which was broadcasting the Super Bowl that year, got a good amount of negative feedback from viewers.

Still other Super Bowl ads have been rejected before they were even shown. For instance, the NFL and Fox refused to air an ad for Airborne, a natural cold remedy, that showed 84-year-old actor Mickey Rooney's backside. "Our standards department reviewed the ad, and it was deemed inappropriate for broadcast," said Fox Sports spokesperson Lou d'Ermilio.

Airborne co-owner, Rider McDowell, said the commercial was harmless. "It's tantamount to showing a baby's bottom," he told a newspaper, noting there was "nothing sexual about the ad." Mickey Rooney agreed. "There's nothing sensual about the brief exposure of my backside," said Rooney. "It's not gratuitous. It's a fun spot, and the public deserves to see it."

Maybe they don't have to, Mickey. According to Eisner Communications, a marketing research firm, 29 percent of the U.S. population said they knew about the Airborne ad although it never aired. Without paying for airtime, Eisner estimated that Airborne reached about half the audience it would have had the ad aired.

The NFL and the networks also rejected political advertising in 2004, including ads against incumbent president George W. Bush. The controversial liberal advocacy group, MoveOn.org, wanted to air the first political Super Bowl ad that year, with a spot that would have asked, "Guess who's going to pay off President Bush's $1 trillion deficit?" The ad was rejected by CBS, which also told People for the Ethical Treatment of Animals (PETA) in a letter that it would not run ads on "controversial issues of public importance."

"We have a policy against accepting advocacy advertising," said CBS spokesman Dana McClintock.

That same year, the network rejected another advertisement from PETA, which would have promoted vegetarianism. The PETA ad showed two scantily clad women snuggling up to a meat-eating pizza delivery man. "Meat can cause impotence," read text that accompanied the ad. CBS said the spot raised "significant taste concerns." "They just want to be able to present their jiggly women," said PETA spokesperson Lisa Lange.

And finally, some ads are just too clever for their own good. Wharton marketing professor Lisa Bolton said that advertisers use the Super Bowl to build brand equity, which has two key components: awareness and association. "With the Super Bowl, there's a lot of competition for [viewers' attention], so the ads have to do a good job of cutting through the clutter," said Bolton. But sometimes ads are too successful in drawing attention to their own creativity, rather than the product they are promoting. "They build awareness for the ad, and people forget the brand," she said. "That can be a danger if an ad is too clever in its execution." A prime example of this was the controversial GoDaddy.com ads that aired during the 2005 Super Bowl, a year after the Janet Jackson "wardrobe malfunction." While the ad, which featured a buxom blonde nearly losing her tank top, was the most popular and memorable of the dozens of clever ads that aired during the game, if you stopped someone on the street today and asked them what GoDaddy.com did, they wouldn't know.

"Many companies have wasted a lot of money over the years, especially the dot-coms," said Wharton professor Len Lodish. He pointed out in a Wharton study of Super Bowl advertising that dot-com companies spent millions in Super Bowl advertising, but didn't have the sales—or the profits—to justify the expense. "It made no sense for companies operating on such a small scale to advertise [during the Super Bowl]," he said.

"The 17 dot-coms that advertised in the 2000 Super Bowl drove the price of 30-second spots to over $2 million, thereby effectively freezing out well-established companies that had something real to sell," wrote Della Femina in the *Wall Street Journal.*" And for what? It was impossible to figure out from those commercials what these Web sites did. Some of the worst examples were Epidemic.com with a commercial about a bathroom attendant . . . WebMD pushing poor Muhammed Ali. . . . *LastMinuteTravel.com* with cowboys and twisters. . . . OurBeginning.com featuring a commercial called 'Battle of the Brides.' . . . There were sock puppets singing about cat food, dancing monkeys, and, lest we forget, Lifeminders.com, which boasted in its commercial that it had just wasted $2 million."

"I'm convinced the end of the dot-com economy came, not when the Nasdaq nosedived in March and April but at last year's Super Bowl," Della Femina wrote in 2001. "On that afternoon in January, 88 million Americans saw the spotlight shining on the dot-com economy and found it to be bankrupt intellectually, long before it was bankrupt financially."

THE NFL AND THE BUSINESS OF THE SUPER BOWL

Despite its now-and-then controversies, the Super Bowl remains the most watched program on TV. Indeed, the top-ten rated American TV shows of all time are all Super Bowls. More importantly, the Super Bowl is one of the best-run businesses in the country. And that brings us to another of the Super Bowl's big winners—the NFL.

The Super Bowl is made up of two types of activities: those events coordinated by the NFL (staged events, such as *The NFL Experience*) and those events surrounding the Super Bowl that are put on by the host committee. The host committee earns revenue from corporate sponsorship, fees from accommodating businesses such as hotels and rental services, government grants, and gate fees from staged events. The committee's budget depends on its business plans for the Super Bowl two-week period but is usually between $5 million and $8 million. Super Bowl national revenues are paid in advance as part of the national television contract negotiated by the league every few years. In exchange, the TV networks get the ad fees for the (in)famous commercials. This structure typically allows the networks to get enough money from ad revenue for the Super Bowl to cover the rights fees paid to the NFL.

Those rights fees amount to big business for the NFL. Many companies become official sponsors and make official products of the NFL simply to tap into a Super Bowl audience that's increasingly focused on the ads. This realization struck home with me as I traveled to NFL stadiums during the 2005 season. I knew which advertisers were the official sponsors and making the official products of the NFL, but clearly their impact was being diminished significantly at the stadiums themselves by local marketing agreements, some with direct competitors to official NFL sponsors. This competition was particularly evident on the club levels, where I saw the official NFL beer—Budweiser—for sale alongside direct competitors, like Miller, as well as upscale brands such as Sam Adams and Guinness. Seeing all this, I kept asking myself, "What's the benefit of being an official NFL sponsor?"

I got my answer from Dick Sullivan, the former head of marketing for Home Depot, who followed cofounder Arthur Blank to the Atlanta Falcons and is now president of the team. "It's all about the postseason," he said. "What the official NFL sponsors are paying for is not stadium signage and pouring rights during the regular season but for the highly intense spotlight they garner during the postseason, particularly at the Super Bowl."

Sullivan and other team marketing and advertising executives agreed that what official NFL sponsors really pay for is exposure at the Super Bowl, where signage is controlled by the NFL, not the individual teams. "They're paying for those 144 million eyeballs on television and the 100,000 in the stadium," Sullivan said. Indeed, as Wisconsin economics professors Tomkovick and Yelkur pointed out, they're paying to be *at* the Super Bowl. "The real key is that they merchandise their brand with boots on the ground [at the Super Bowl]," Tomkovick said. "If you're a beer company, it means you have signage in all the bars, hospitality tents—everywhere. It requires a very coordinated effort. You have to get your logo everywhere. And that's what these national sponsors are paying for: first billing at the Super Bowl, both in terms of television advertising and a strong presence in the host city."

Of course, the Super Bowl is just one demonstration of the NFL's remarkable expertise at managing the business of marketing its brand. Every NFL stadium in the country plays host to the league's advertising blitz. In fact, teams make most of their advertising money on local sponsorships at the stadium. And while the 2006 revenue-sharing agreement modified that to a small degree, the teams get to keep most of the money generated from NFL stadiums—including the vast revenues brought in by premium memberships, club seating, and other luxury features. In other words, newer, larger, more luxurious stadiums are big business for the NFL. The deal grows even sweeter for the league, as you learn in the next chapter, because the vast majority of these stadiums are still paid for primarily by taxpayers.

CHAPTER NINE

STADIUM FEVER

WHO PLAYS AND WHO PAYS?

It was a sunny August afternoon in Minneapolis. Perfect for having lunch at Hubert's, the quintessential sports bar, which sits across the street from the Hubert H. Humphrey Metrodome. The place was packed with Minnesota Twins fans going to a day game against their American League Central Division rivals, the Chicago White Sox. Everyone was happy, eating burgers and brats and drinking beer. A few days later, 62,000 Minnesota Vikings fans, who fill the Metrodome to capacity for almost every home game, would file in for a 2005 preseason game against the San Diego Chargers (which the Vikings won, 19–16).

Nothing could be better, right?

Wrong.

I was having lunch with Art Rolnick, the brilliant economist from the Minneapolis Federal Reserve Bank. He's made a name for himself in the Twin Cities by pointing out—much to the chagrin of state and local politicians, sports columnists, editorial writers, and team owners—that the only net economic development the city of Minneapolis has realized as a result of the construction of the Metrodome is the patio at Hubert's, where we were having lunch.

"This is it," Rolnick said with a smile when I met him at the bar.

All of this, of course, is lost on most of the giddy pregame patrons, who don't know that the stadium they're about to walk into is one of the biggest wastes of taxpayer dollars in history—a statement that applies to almost every other professional sports stadium in the country. The reason most of them don't know that stadiums are a huge rip off of taxpayer money is because there are a bevy of local politicians, developers, consultants, and league officials who appear at every press conference to tout the economic benefits of building a new stadium. Taxpayers are told that the new facility will result in millions of dollars in economic development and create thousands of new jobs. In fact, nothing could be further from the truth.

Indeed, if the NFL has one chink in its well-oiled, well-communicated, tightly controlled, market-savvy armor, it is stadium financing. Reduced to its simplest elements, stadiums are the most expensive playgrounds that state and local governments have ever built. And the cost keeps going up.

So do the luxury amenities at new and renovated NFL stadiums. If pepper-crusted tenderloin of beef, Gulf shrimp scampi, and grilled asparagus don't sound like football-stadium fare to you, then you probably aren't a member of the Atlanta Falcons Owner's Club, a $5,000-per-season, members-only bar and restaurant that opened in 2005 at the Georgia Dome. It's where Atlanta's business elite—CEOs, the mayor, and team executives—rub shoulders over glasses of cabernet sauvignon and top-shelf single malt scotch before, during, and after Falcons home games.

For their $5,000, members get parking near the stadium, gourmet food, and three well-appointed cash bars. The club features dark wood paneling, muted lighting, and tastefully framed Falcons photos. Members eat dinner in deep, overstuffed red leather chairs with no fewer than nine large, flat-screen TVs within easy view. There also are cozy tables for two along the floor-to-ceiling smoked-glass windows, each with a 19-inch, flat-screen TV showing the week's NFL highlights and the pregame show.

The club's 250 memberships sold out almost instantly, and now there's a waiting list. For those of you keeping track at home, that $1,250,000 in annual memberships is going directly into the pockets of the Atlanta Falcons, because the NFL doesn't require teams to share revenue from private clubs and suites when they're paying off stadium debt. And while the 2006 revenue-sharing agreement calls for the 15 highest-revenue teams to share their stadium windfalls with the rest of the league, sharing will barely dent this lucrative revenue stream for the team.

That's because membership fees are just the beginning. Premium seating; special events; and premium food, alcohol, and cigars are just a few of the other luxury offerings that NFL teams are using to rake in piles of mostly unshared cash. These favorable economics have fueled stadium fever in this country. Indeed, in 2006, the NFL was nearing the end of a stadium-building boom that saw more than 20 teams build new or renovate old stadiums over the past decade. This movement has changed the stadium experience for the haves and have-nots who attend the games, even as it has significantly realigned the revenue economics of the NFL.

TAXPAYER-FUNDED STADIUMS:
WELFARE FOR BILLIONAIRES

Taxpayers still overwhelmingly pay for new stadiums, covering about 65 percent of new construction costs, including stadium clubs and other luxury amenities. Sports stadiums are among the worst investments a community can make. The returns are lousy, and—for the most part—the stadiums benefit only the NFL owners and the privileged few who can afford their luxury amenities. According to economists, public financing of sports stadiums is nothing more than giving taxpayer money to billionaire owners so that their $10 million players have a $500 million place to play. It's that simple.

And the owners are laughing all the way to the bank. In addition to paying for the stadium, many cities allow teams to keep most of the revenue from ticket sales, parking fees, concessions, advertising, and naming rights, which can be hundreds of millions of dollars. Even the revenues from luxury boxes and club seats, the single biggest source of locally generated revenue for most teams, go into the team's bank account—all thanks to the generosity of the taxpayers.

The evidence of the economic folly of publicly financed sports stadiums is overwhelming. Entire books have been written on the subject. *Field of Schemes* and *Major League Losers* are two of the best. To prove their theorems, economists have calculated the net economic impact of every ticket, hot dog, parking space, luxury suite, and beer vendor job associated with a season of professional sports. The clear consensus is that the benefits of building a stadium don't even come close to outweighing the costs.

Perhaps no one has done a better job of pointing out the folly of publicly financed stadiums than Art Rolnick. Some economists have pointed out the economic shortcomings of stadium financing but still excuse it by arguing that there's a caché to having a pro franchise, to being able to call yourself a "major league" city. Rolnick, on the other hand, is unflinching in his declaration that sports stadiums return little or no value to a community. "If one of my quotes ends up in your book, I want it to be this," he said over cheeseburgers on Hubert's patio. "There is literally no— none, zero, zilch—positive economic impact from the public financing of stadiums. None."

Nonetheless, most Minnesota Vikings and Twins fans were happy to retire Metropolitan Stadium in Bloomington, now the site of the Mall of America. By 1982, when the Metrodome was built, baseball fans had had enough of sitting in cold drizzle in April, and all but the hardiest Vikings fans were eager to avoid subzero temperatures in mid-December. Building a domed stadium in a city where the April temperature hovers closer to the mean low of 36 than the mean high of 59 seemed like a no-brainer to almost everyone—except Art Rolnick.

He's fond of reminding people that the Vikings kicked in just $7 million—a mere 12 percent—of the Metrodome's $55 million cost. Even more egregious is that next to none of the economic development promised by stadium backers has materialized. The neighborhood around the Metrodome is not home to the new jobs, restaurants, businesses, upscale condos, and hip urban scene that taxpayers were told would arise. Instead, crime, poverty, substandard housing, empty lots, and shuttered storefronts have spread around the Metrodome, which sits within earshot of one of Minneapolis' most notorious drug-infested neighborhoods.

In fact, the only good thing to come to the area as a result of the taxpayer's lavish gift to the Vikings and the Twins is Hubert's patio. The bar was here long before the Metrodome, but shortly after the stadium opened, the owners added the patio. Today, they cook brats and burgers on a big, open-air grill for fans waiting to go in and watch the Twins and Vikings. This, in essence, is what the taxpayers got for their $48 million. And Rolnick doesn't let them forget it.

It's important to note that Rolnick isn't some antisports zealot. He grew up in Detroit listening to legendary broadcaster Ernie Harwell call Tigers games on the radio and suffered through the worst seasons with the Lions. No, Rolnick is intellectually consistent on this subject. He is against government funding of private enterprise. He believes that if a private endeavor is such a good idea, then it should have no trouble finding private financing.

"Whenever government uses public money to finance private enterprises, it's nothing more than a futile exercise to justify an old Keynesian idea," said the unabashedly free-market economist. "If you take it to its extreme, it's no different than the old Soviet model." Rolnick's fundamental objection to public stadiums is that government is choosing one private enterprise over another. Worse, it's choosing one that historically delivers a pretty lousy return. "It's taking from Peter to give to Paul, and when government does that, Paul is usually a friend," Rolnick says with a laugh.

SPORTS ECONOMISTS TALLY THE SCORE

The economic impact numbers commonly bantered about at city council meetings, economic development seminars, and Capitol rotunda press conferences are well known among the small fraternity of sports economists. They're experts at determining how much value a pro sports franchise adds or detracts from a major metropolitan area. (If you want to learn more about sports economics, check out *thesportseconomist.com*.)

At the high end, advocates often argue that stadiums have an economic multiplier of about 2.5. That means that for every $1 the community spends building a new stadium, it will experience an added $2.50 in related economic activity. The same multiplier is used for jobs; for every job visible at the stadium, there are allegedly 2.5 less-visible jobs created somewhere in the local community.

The lower end of the estimates for these stadium multipliers, often produced by economists with no vested interest in stadium construction, are closer to 1.25. Others, like Art Rolnick, think it's zero. "You have to take these multipliers with a grain of salt," Rolnick argues. "All stadium advocates want to talk about are the positives. But for every positive multiplier, there is a negative as well, and it's probably greater than the positive."

Adding Up the Costs, Scrutinizing the Benefits

Myriad studies dispel the myth of the economic benefits that politicians and developers claim will flow freely from the construction of a new stadium. One of the best is from the first quarter 2001 edition of the Kansas City Federal Reserve Bank *Economic Review* (available at *www.kc.frb.org/publicat/econrev/PDF/ 1q01rapp.pdf*), completed toward the end of the nationwide stadium-building boom that began in the early 1990s. In "What Are the Benefits of Hosting a Major League Sports Franchise?" economists John Rappaport and Chad Wilkerson make a pretty compelling case that the benefits are few.

By the end of 2004, nearly 70 percent of big league sports franchises were playing in stadiums or arenas that either had been opened or renovated in the previous ten years. From 1995 through 2003, about $6.4 billion dollars were spent to build or refurbish substantially 21 NFL stadiums—an average of $304 million per project. The public contribution was about $4.4 billion, or roughly 69 percent of the construction costs.

While stadium backers inevitably produce impact studies promising generous returns for these investments, few of those returns ever materialized. "Many of the studies look at only the positive effects of hosting a major league franchise," the Kansas City Fed study said. "Taking account of negative effects such as offsetting job losses, however, would produce much lower estimates of the net impact on local economic development. Moreover, the impact studies almost always fail to measure benefits in a form that can be compared with public outlays."

One way to perform such a comparison, the authors argue, is to contrast the growth rates of metro areas with big league teams to those without. For instance, one study looked at the growth of per capita personal income in 48 metro areas from 1958 to 1987 and found "no significant difference between metro areas with major league teams and those without." A similar study of 46 metro areas from 1990 to 1994 found "a negative relationship between economic activity and the presence of a sports team."

A 1997 study by economists Robert A. Baade and Allen R. Sanderson, "The Employment Effect of Teams and Sports Facilities," looked at the subsequent growth of cities that acquired new teams between 1958 and 1993, and they, too, found "no significant increases in employment or output." A number of other economic impact studies, including a 1996 study by Baade and a 1999 study by economists Dennis Coates and Brad Humphreys, have found that per capita income actually falls in most metropolitan areas that add sports franchises.

So what about the economic impact of specific teams? Economists Bruce Hamilton and Peter Kahn looked at the annual returns that Maryland residents saw from the addition of the Baltimore Ravens football team. While the community saw a net economic impact of roughly $1 million, that paled in comparison to the $14 million annual public cost to finance the new stadium.

Indeed, the stadium is owned by the Maryland Stadium Authority, which paid almost $200 million of the $220 million construction costs. Of the Ravens' roughly $20 million contribution, $5 million was generated from the sale of personal seat licenses, a fee that season ticket holders pay for the privilege of having seats. Furthermore, the Ravens pay no rent and collect all revenue associated with stadium operations. And while the team pays operational costs on game day, Maryland pays for all general maintenance.

Do Stadiums Create Jobs and Bring In Tax Revenue?

But what about the long-term economic benefits of having a new stadium and a happy NFL team in your city or state? In looking at the impact of stadiums overall on local economies, the authors of the Kansas City Fed study looked at two measures in particular: job creation and tax revenue benefits. They found that, to accurately assess the impact of a professional sports franchise, you have to measure not just the number of jobs created but also the number of jobs lost.

"[T]he presence of a professional sports team also creates job losses, because individuals who spend money to attend sports events have less to spend at businesses elsewhere in the host metro area," the authors said. "Less spending results in job losses." The Kansas City Fed authors found that the net jobs created from hosting a professional sports team is "certainly less than a thousand and likely to be much closer to zero."

King Banaian, chairman of the economics department at St. Cloud State University in Minnesota, is an avid Boston Red Sox fan and reformed sports economist. He agrees that, in painting a rosy picture of the benefits of new stadium construction, proponents rarely discuss the associated opportunity costs. "You have to look at a piece of land and consider its uses now, for a stadium, or if you built a factory," Banaian said. "Is a stadium going to get you the best return? Is it the best use of that land? Usually not."

Banaian also points out that, when a stadium is plunked down in a neighborhood, it becomes the predominant attraction in that neighborhood. That's good on game days, but what about the rest of the year? "What kind of activity is there around the Metrodome on days when there are no games?" he asks. "You go into Hubert's, and there's 12 people in there. These places become black holes when there are no events."

Looking at the tax revenues generated by sports franchises, the greatest benefits come from nonresident spending. "Nonlocal sports fans visiting to attend games pay sales taxes on all local purchases before, during, and after games," the Kansas City Fed authors said. "Such spending 'imports' tax revenue, which in the absence of a professional sports team would have accrued to governments outside the host metro area."

The host city further benefits from spending by nonresidents, because the taxes they pay reduce the amount of taxes local residents need to pay. "The difficult part, of course, is estimating the number of visitors and how much they spend on average," the Kansas City Fed economists said. What matters is not the number of nonlocal residents who attend games but the number of nonlocal residents whose visits are explicitly motivated by the presence of a team. "The distinction is crucial," the authors said. "Nonlocal residents who attend games may be visiting the host metro area for non-game-related reasons such as business or family. If so, their spending at games most likely represents a shifting away from spending on other forms of local entertainment. . . ."

This conclusion would seem to challenge the results of another study, "Economic Impact of the New Orleans Saints," by Timothy P. Ryan of the University of New Orleans. He estimates visitor spending associated with the Saints at $51 million. While some of this—particularly for visiting teams and media covering the game—is justifiable, you have to wonder, as the Kansas City Fed authors do, just how much of that spending is attributable directly to the Saints, especially in New Orleans, which before Hurricane Katrina was a convention and tourism mecca. Ryan's study assumes "that 20 percent of visiting ticket holders spend an average of 1.5 days in New Orleans and spend $200 per day in the city." But how can Ryan be certain that even 20 percent of out-of-town ticket holders came to New Orleans just to see the Saints? The short answer is: He can't. If the Saints weren't in town, would these visitors have come anyway and spent the ticket money to see the Preservation Hall Jazz Band, have their palms read, or go on an airboat ride in the bayou?

No one knows. But you can bet that local advocates and politicians trying to convince taxpayers to build a new stadium for the local franchise won't care about the accuracy of the numbers in the impact studies they toss at taxpayers. Even more sadly, the findings of these studies largely go unchallenged—even by the local newspaper.

Net Benefits Fall Short of Promises

Meanwhile, our Kansas City Fed economists have figured that adding together net job creation, imported sales taxes, and increased income taxes results in an estimated economic benefit of $2.9 million per year for an NFL team. Of course, these benefits must be offset by the estimated cost of acquiring a sports franchise.

"Calculating the answer is straightforward," the authors said. "Assuming that metro areas can borrow (by issuing municipal bonds) at a 6 percent interest rate and that the proceeds are used to purchase an annual stream of benefits starting 1 year in the future and lasting for 30 years (a reasonable estimate for the life of a sports stadium), it follows that each $1 of annual benefits is worth $13.76 to the metro area."

As a result, on a net present value basis, the authors estimate that the value of the job and tax benefits from an NFL franchise is about $40.3 million a year. While that sounds like a pretty good multiplier, it falls far short of what most cities invest in stadiums.

"The average public outlay on new baseball and football stadiums completed between 1994 and 2000 was $188 million," the Kansas City Fed authors said. "Thus, for most sports stadium projects, costs exceeded the above estimated benefits by well over $100 million." Furthermore, these valuations likely overstate the benefits that a sports franchise brings to a community. As a result, the net present value of jobs and tax benefits from hosting an NFL franchise may be no more than $5 million, according to the Kansas City Fed study, which concluded, "Even using the upper-bound estimates from the analysis above suggests that the public outlays on current sports facility projects far exceed any associated jobs and tax benefits.

And the Kansas City Feds aren't alone. Economists Roger Noll and Andrew Zimbalist, writing in their 1997 book *Sports, Jobs, and Taxes: The Economic Impact of Sports Teams and Stadiums,* conclude, "The economic case for publicly financed stadiums cannot credibly rest on the benefits to local business, as measured by jobs, income, and investment."

The bottom line, then, is that the benefit to a host metro area from increased economic activity as measured by net job creation and increased tax revenues appears to fall far short of the public outlays typically needed to retain and attract professional sports teams.

TAXPAYERS FIGHT TO PICK UP THE TAB

As compelling as this evidence is, it hasn't kept most major American cities from continuing to pursue new sports franchises or build publicly financed stadiums. What's truly amazing is that some cities that lost NFL franchises paid even more to lure a new team than they offered the old one to stay.

For instance, the Cardinals left St. Louis in 1987 after the city refused to give them $120 million for a new stadium. Yet less than three years later, voters approved $280 million in public funds for a new football stadium—before they even had a team to play in it. Depending on how you crunch the numbers, the Rams contributed only about 20 percent of the total cost of relocating the team from Los Angeles to a new stadium in St. Louis, which some economists estimate cost taxpayers an aggregate $720 million. In exchange, the Rams get 100 percent of all concession revenues and 75 percent of advertising revenue (90 percent if it exceeds $6 million). Before the team even agreed to move, a local business group guaranteed that 85 percent of the suites and club seats would be sold and the Rams could keep all the revenue.

"There is the potential for the Rams to 'cover' the annual cost of their lease from the advertising they sell in the stadium built for them with taxpayers' funds," writes sports economist Mark Rosentraub in his book *Major League Losers*. In the end, the Rams may pony up zero dollars for their shiny new stadium—against the taxpayers' three-quarters of a billion dollar investment.

The Colts Bolt and Land in Clover

And then we turn to the courtship of the Colts. By the early 1980s, the city of Indianapolis had already poured $400 million into downtown office complexes and hotels. As a result, the $80 million price tag for the Hoosier Dome seemed like a bargain. The stadium was funded largely by a 1 percent countywide tax on food and beverages. But with construction under way in 1982, it looked unlikely that Indianapolis would get one of the NFL's expansion franchises. Panicked, mayor William Hudnut called an old friend, Baltimore Colts owner Robert Irsay.

Under threats that the team would move elsewhere, the city of Baltimore had given the Colts $25 million in 1979 to renovate Memorial Stadium. In 1984, it offered another $15 million and a city-backed guarantee on ticket sales, but the lure from Indianapolis was too great. On March 29, 1984, with armed guards standing by to keep angry fans at bay, the Colts packed up and moved to Indianapolis.

And who can blame them? Their new home offered them a low-rent lease on a 60,000-seat stadium with 99 luxury suites, and they didn't have to pay a dime. In 1999, the renamed RCA Dome underwent $20 million in renovations, adding 5,000 club seats, 5 super suites, and a renovation and expansion of the existing suites.

Looking at the Colts' income statement in Kagan's *The Business of Pro Football 2002*, the team took in $4.5 million in luxury suite revenue and another $1 million in naming rights alone—all for a facility it didn't spend a dime constructing. Still unsatisfied, the Colts convinced the taxpayers of Indianapolis to make up the difference if the team's revenues were below the NFL median.

If you think that was a sweet deal, just look at the agreement the Colts negotiated in August 2005 for a new stadium that the city hasn't even figured out how to pay for yet. The 30-year deal that will keep the Colts in Indianapolis through 2034 only charges the team $250,000 in annual rent. All the Colts have to do is play all home games in the new stadium. The new contract does, at least temporarily, buy the Colts' fidelity; the team is forbidden from even entering negotiations to relocate during the life of the contract and must keep its headquarters and training facility within the city. Also, the city will no longer be on the hook for ensuring that the team's revenues are in line with the NFL median.

What do the Colts get in return? They retain the rights to all football-related revenue in the new stadium as well as half of any nonfootball revenue up to $3.5 million a year. The Colts will also get all revenues from naming rights, signage, and sponsorships in the new stadium. The city's capital improvement board will take care of maintenance and even game-day expenses at the new stadium. The Colts, who announced the deal during an August 2005 preseason game, included the obligatory mumblings about jobs and economic development. According to the capital improvement board chair Fred Glass, the project "will pump thousands of jobs and billions of dollars into the city's economy."

But apparently that's not the most important part of the deal.

"The lease means the Colts will be here for a generation," Glass told the *Indianapolis Star*. "Folks can feel comfortable buying their grandkids a Colts T-shirt." I'm sure that comforting thought helps everyone in Indianapolis sleep better at night. What should disturb their slumber, however, is the reality that, based on current stadium cost projections, those same grandkids might have to help pay off that $500 million T-shirt bequeathed to them by their grandparents.

Baltimore Builds a Nest for the Ravens

So after being burned by the Colts, what did Baltimore do? The city gave away the farm to the Cleveland Browns and owner Art Modell, who was agitated because Cleveland was spending hundreds of millions of dollars renovating the city's waterfront, building new homes for the baseball Indians and basketball Cavaliers, and building the Rock and Roll Hall of Fame. Cleveland had refused to give any money to Modell, who had taken over Municipal Stadium in 1995 and agreed to make more than $100 million in renovations to the 65-year-old facility. So Baltimore, which had hesitated to pony up a measly $15 million to keep the Colts, gave him a deal he couldn't refuse.

The new lease guaranteed the team—to be called the Baltimore Ravens—30 years of free rent plus a $50 million cash relocation bonus. The team also would get a 10 percent management fee for concerts and other nonfootball events. A number of sports columnists thought it a sweetheart deal. They were right, of course.

In a 1996 Congressional Research Service study, economist Dennis Zimmer estimated that the rosy scenario presented by stadium advocates overestimated the impact of the new Ravens stadium by *236 percent*. Based upon public expenditures for the stadium, each job that was created cost the taxpayers about $127,000. By comparison, Maryland's Sunny Day Fund, an economic development program, creates jobs at a cost of about $6,000 each.

Zimmer also echoed the arguments of St. Cloud State economist King Banaian, stating that any economic assessment of stadiums has to look not just at what the taxpayers got for their money but what they didn't get. "If an alternative generates $2 million of benefits net of subsidy and the stadium generates $1.5 million net of subsidy, the stadium can be viewed as imposing a $0.5 million loss on taxpayers, not a $1.5 million benefit," he said.

Cleveland and Cincinnati Join the Stadium Follies

Cleveland, of course, was devastated by the loss of the Browns, the team with which the city identified more than any other. As Joanna Cagan and Neil deMause note in *Field of Schemes*, when the story was covered in the national press, it was "perhaps the only time the *New York Times* has ever run a photograph of a grown man wearing a dog mask, smoking a cigar, and weeping."

So what did Cleveland do after being burned by the Browns, who moved to Baltimore, which was reeling from being burned by the Colts? It vowed to tear down Municipal Stadium and build a brand-new, football-only stadium for $290 million, the majority of it financed by the city of Cleveland, the state of Ohio, Cuyahoga County, and the Regional Transit Authority. The team has a very generous 30-year lease, gets all stadium rentals, and pays for maintenance and operations, but it does not pay property taxes. Upon hearing the terms of the deal, Modell, happily ensconced in Baltimore, said, "If they gave me half of what they're doing now, I'd still be in Cleveland."

As we've seen in other examples, Cleveland ended up paying more for a new franchise than it would have paid to keep the old one. And it was willing to do so shortly after spending an estimated $350 million to $450 million—mostly from the taxpayers—to renovate the central downtown market and build Jacobs Field for the Indians and Gund Arena for the NBA Cavaliers.

But perhaps the sweetheart of all deals—and the one potentially with the most dire consequences—was hatched about three hours south of Lake Erie in Cincinnati. In 1996, Hamilton County voters approved a 5-cent sales tax that was supposed to raise more than $1 billion over 20 years. More than $450 million was earmarked to build the Bengals a new stadium, which team owner Mike Brown named after his father, legendary football coach Paul Brown. The 30-year lease for the 65,000-seat stadium that features 114 luxury suites and 7,620 club seats allows the Bengals to keep all revenues from ticket sales, suites, advertising, broadcasting rights, and concessions. The team also gets a share of revenue for non-Bengal events.

What was the Bengals' contribution? The team kicked in $25 million from the sale of personal seat licenses toward the cost of the stadium, which came in $50 million over budget. The Bengals also will pay $11.5 million in rent over 9 years of the 30-year lease. The team will continue to pay about $1 million in game-day operating expenses, but Hamilton County will begin reimbursing them in 2017.

That was the plan anyway. According to stories that began surfacing in August 2005, the fund that was earmarked for paying off the stadium debt and rolling back property taxes was expected to be about $8 million in the red by 2006. "The deficit could hit almost $300 million by 2032, when the debt is to be repaid," the *Cincinnati Inquirer* reported. The problem is that the county expected sales tax collections to grow by 3 percent a year. But from 2000 to 2005, receipts only grew by 1.3 percent. If the tax receipts continue to grow at a 2 percent rate, the deficit by 2032 will be an estimated $191.5 million. At 3 percent, the shortfall will drop to just about $81 million. Either way, the taxpayers will be on the hook for a lot of money.

Schools Lose Out, and No Lessons Are Learned

What's perhaps even more disturbing is that many of the cities we're talking about—Indianapolis, Cleveland, Cincinnati, Baltimore, and St. Louis—are not idylls of bucolic urban splendor. These cities have serious, deep-seated financial and social problems that make forking over several hundred million dollars for a sports stadium seem even more ridiculous.

Marge Misak, a longtime Cleveland community activist, was one of the few voices of dissent when mayor Michael White announced that Cleveland would build a new stadium and resur-rect the Browns. Her objections came at the same time that residents were starting to learn of the cost overruns associated with Jacobs Field and Gund Arena. Nonetheless, she was a lone voice in the wilderness. "It was kind of an astounding juxtaposi-tion," she said, "because you would think that there would be questions about 'Did we learn our lesson here?'"

Apparently not. The Cleveland city council voted 13–8 to fund the new stadium. And as Cagan and deMause note in *Field of Schemes*, the number of Clevelanders living in poverty rose from 17 percent in 1970 to 40 percent by the mid-1990s. The school system was in a shambles as well. Only about 40 percent of students graduated high school on time. The day before the new Browns stadium was approved, the school system an-nounced that it would cut $52 million from its budget, lay off more than 150 teachers, and end athletic programs. Schools su-perintendent Richard Boyd declared that Cleveland schools were "in the worst financial shape of any school district in the coun-try." Furthermore, in 1996, the Gateway Economic Development Corporation, which oversaw the construction of Jacobs Field and Gund Arena, agreed to pay $1.6 million—most of it to Cleveland schools—in back taxes.

That brings us back to Minnesota. Despite Rolnick's very sen-sible contention that Hubert's patio is the only net economic ben-efit to result from the construction of the Metrodome, stadium proposals for the Twins, Vikings, and University of Minnesota were very much alive and well in the halls of the Minnesota leg-islature during the 2006 legislative session.

In September 2005, new owner Zygi Wilf, a New Jersey real es-tate developer who bought the Vikings from Red McCombs for more than $600 million, floated a stadium proposal. The new sta-dium—with a price tag of $790 million—would be built in Blaine, a Minneapolis suburb that in 2005 was also the fastest-growing com-munity in Minnesota. The stadium would be part of a $1.7 billion complex of housing, shops, and offices that Wilf hopes to build on land he's already acquired.

Of the $790 million price tag, $280 million, or about 35 percent, would come from the Vikings. Part of that money—$92 million—would come from the NFL's G3 fund, which issues bonds from shared NFL ticket revenues and gives loans to teams for stadium construction. About $280 million would come from Anoka County in the form of a 0.75 percent sales tax hike that was approved in January 2004. Another $230 million would come from the state in the form of tax increment financing (a funding vehicle commonly used for public-private projects) and funding for road improvements. Any extra sales tax revenue from the project would go to the stadium, not into state coffers.

"This is an opportunity that comes once in a generation," said Wilf.

Probably not. As noted, Blaine was the fastest-growing community in Minnesota in 2005. The housing, shops, and restaurants will come—with or without a stadium. "This is TIF [tax increment financing] on steroids," said St. Cloud State economist King Banaian. "What is the value to Blaine of putting a stadium on a piece of property that will be developed anyway?"

Indeed, even stadium project manager Steve Novak admits that the highway improvements will eventually come—with or without a stadium. "We're just asking that they be accelerated," Novak told the St. Paul *Pioneer Press*.

"The Vikings stadium is a prime example of government projects that help the private sector," said Banaian. "It's easy to lobby for, but hard to develop grassroots support against." Ironically, given the fact that money was taken from the Cleveland schools to build that city's sports palaces, the *Pioneer Press* found a couple of teachers at lunch in Anoka the day the Wilf proposal was announced who seemed content with the stadium plan. "It's a penny," said Matt Jarolimek. "You could spend that on gas. I would rather spend it on a stadium."

But Art Rolnick has a better idea for economic development, and it focuses on education and early childhood development. "Around the country, billions of public dollars are spent each year to subsidize private companies so that they will either locate or expand their businesses in hometown markets," he and fellow Minneapolis Fed economist Rob Grunewald wrote in a May 2005 paper, "A Proposal for Achieving High Returns on Early Childhood Development." "Recent studies of this approach to economic development, however, make clear that the so-called economic bidding war among state and local governments is actually counterproductive. . . . One of the most productive investments that is rarely viewed as economic development is early childhood development (ECD). In a previous essay we found that, based on [several longitudinal ECD studies], the potential annual return from focused, high-quality ECD programs might be as high as 16 percent (inflation adjusted), of which the annual public return is 12 percent (inflation adjusted)."

Based on his studies, Rolnick is proposing that Minnesota give him the $230 million it would invest in a Vikings stadium to start a scholarship fund for poverty-stricken families with at-risk children. The endowments would be used to provide scholarships for children of families who couldn't afford high-quality early childhood educational programs, paying both tuition for the children and mentoring for the parents. And the awards would be outcome based, meaning that they "would include incentives for achieving significant progress toward the life and learning skills needed to succeed in school."

As we finished up our cheeseburgers on Hubert's patio, Rolnick noted that his proposal has already received about $30 million through a program called the Minnesota Early Learning Fund. But that's a pittance compared to the $500 million the Vikings have requested. Unfortunately, I think I know who'll get all their funding first.

Can Cities Get Off the Ride?

If the evidence that stadiums return a paltry sum to taxpayers is so overwhelming, why do cities keep playing this game? "You can't unilaterally withdraw," Rolnick said. "If Minneapolis doesn't build the Vikings or Twins a new stadium, someone else will. And it may be someone who's not in Minnesota."

And team owners aren't the only culprits. State and local governments constantly engage in bidding wars for private entities, be it the Minnesota Vikings or 3M. "Competition among states for specific businesses is commonplace and growing more costly," Rolnick and coauthor Melvin L. Burstein wrote in the January 1996 issue of *fedgazette*, the Minneapolis Fed's monthly publication. "Competition for sports franchises is a drop in a big bucket of public money spent to subsidize businesses."

So what's Rolnick's solution to stop the subsidy merry-go-round?

"Only Congress, under the commerce clause of the Constitution, has the power to enact legislation to prohibit the states from using subsidies and preferential taxes to compete with one another for businesses. Congress could enforce such a prohibition in a variety of ways. . . . [I]t could tax real and imputed income from public subsidies, deny tax-exempt status to any public debt used to compete for businesses (there is already a limitation on the tax-exempt status of certain kinds of state and local public debt), and impound federal funds payable to a state engaging in such competition."

Many economists argue that one of the reasons that sports franchises—and the NFL in particular—are so successful at lobbying for public funds is that they control supply and demand. There are only 16 NFL games per season and 32 teams. That's more than enough—or a little—to keep demand high.

"Professional sports leagues function as cartels," said a study from the American Society of Real Estate Counselors. "To enhance the financial performance of the member teams, leagues maintain an excess demand for franchises. Cities compete with one another for the limited supply of teams, and the winning city bid has included government financial assistance for the construction of sports infrastructure. Those cities that do not provide subsidies risk losing or not acquiring a franchise. If an investment in professional sport is not prudent, then it follows that, 'Bad money does chase out good money,' as a consequence of city competition for the limited number of teams."

Add to this the widely held belief that cities actually benefit from having an NFL franchise and fanatical fans who lobby politicians to keep their favorite team in town, and it's easy to see how these bidding wars escalate.

FORBES' 2005 NFL FRANCHISE RANKINGS

Every year, *Forbes* magazine ranks the 32 NFL franchises on a number of categories, including current value, operating income, and revenue. The team revenue ranking gives us some idea of how effectively the franchise is cashing in on club seating. Here, based on *Forbes'* 2005 rankings, are the five highest and five lowest revenue teams in the league.

Highest-Revenue Teams	Lowest-Revenue Teams
1. Washington Redskins	32. Arizona Cardinals
2. New England Patriots	31. Minnesota Vikings
3. Dallas Cowboys	30. San Diego Chargers
4. Philadelphia Eagles	29. Indianapolis Colts
5. Houston Texans	28. Atlanta Falcons

Source: *Special Report: The Business of Football*, Forbes.com, September 1, 2005

UNSHARED REVENUES FUEL THE STADIUM BOOM

In addition to a natural desire for a free place to play, NFL teams have huge economic incentives for desiring new or renovated stadiums. In 1994, nonshared revenue from stadiums accounted for about 12 percent of a team's total revenues. By 2003, that figure had grown to 22 percent and continues to grow, as teams keep building new stadiums heavily laden with club seats and suites. Some of this increased revenue can be attributed to the new stadiums themselves, but much of it is the direct result of higher ticket prices and increased concessions revenues from premium seating and exclusive clubs.

"No innovation can match the luxury box for sheer money-making power without improving either the quality of the game or the enjoyment of the average fan," said deMause in *Field of Schemes'* assessment of stadium financing. "Along with their cousins, the club seats, luxury boxes are about money, pure and simple."

That's because, in addition to the higher ticket prices for club seats, fans in higher-priced seating spend an estimated 25 percent to 50 percent more on concessions than those in the cheap seats. That's a function of personal income, higher-priced foods, and wait service, according to a study by Chris Bigelow, president of Bigelow Companies, a sports marketing firm. With regular ticket prices going up around the league and the advent of luxury seating and stadium clubs, the clientele at football games becomes more exclusive and upscale. As a result, fewer stadium amenities are priced for the average Joe.

The move toward creating luxury-focused stadiums is tied closely to the NFL's revenue-sharing model. More than 54 percent of total NFL revenue is shared, so if teams want to increase their individual profitability, they must grow that 46 percent of revenue that isn't shared. A good way to do that is through lucrative

IT'S A DIFFERENT BALLGAME FOR THE HAVES AND THE HAVE-NOTS

As stadiums increasingly cater to wealthier fans, the experience of attending a live game changes for everyone. Consider, for example, the availability and expense of parking. Often, parking close to the stadium is part of a season ticket package. You pay for a season-long parking pass—usually $200 or $300, depending on how close you want to be to the stadium. If you're just going to one game, you often have to park far away from the stadium and walk or take public transportation. Parking was my biggest headache during the 2005 season though, as credentialed media, it was easier for me than for the typical fan. I paid $40 in Denver for a parking spot fairly close to Invesco Field at Mile High; most other places I paid $20 or $25, primarily because I was arriving four hours before the start of the game and was able to get good spots.

In Washington, D.C., only years of journalistic experience and a business card allowed me to talk my way into the temporary parking lot near FedEx Field. After I got my credentials, I had to drive ten minutes to Landover Mall and take a shuttle bus back to the stadium. Given my experience, I can only imagine the expense and hassles facing nonmedia, non-club-member, non-season-ticket-holding fans looking for parking before the game. As the old saying goes, "The nicer the nice, the higher the price." But the higher prices at many of today's new or renovated stadiums don't always translate into improved niceties for everyone attending the games.

---

stadium deals, financed by taxpayers and including high-revenue club and suite seats.

The NFL, of course, understands all this. At the league's 1994 winter meetings, commissioner Paul Tagliabue gave a presentation entitled, "First-Class Stadiums: NFL Priority." He cited a survey by *Money* magazine that "reinforced our own priority on stadium matters. It is more important than ever that we as a league focus on our stadiums because of the high expectations of our fans."

At the league's 1999 winter meetings, the owners agreed to allow teams to qualify for NFL loans for up to 50 percent of the private contribution toward stadium construction projects. The program, called G3, takes a portion of the NFL's national television contract and invests it in bonds. The money is then used to fund loans to teams building or renovating stadiums.

"The NFL and other leagues have organized stadium committees whose function, in part, is to support the efforts of individual teams to convince their sometimes skeptical and financially strapped host cities to do their part to finance the NFL's efforts to uphold the ideal of league financial democracy," noted a December 1996 paper from the American Society of Real Estate Counselors that looked at stadium revenue and financing. "In addition, individual leagues recognize that entertainment dollars are scarce, and there exists interleague competition for consumer loyalty and spending. This financial contest has increasingly emphasized playing facilities; owners agree that fan-friendly structures are of significant strategic importance."

Club and premium seating can be very lucrative for NFL franchises. The Chicago Bears, one of the NFL's founding franchises, completed a $655 million renovation of Soldier Field in 2004, adding 8,500 extrawide, padded club seats, which cost fans about $250 per ticket compared with $65 for regular seats. The new seats earned the Bears almost $20 million in local revenue in 2005.

The Tampa Bay Buccaneers, another of the NFL's small-market franchises, had poor attendance for years. Then the team built Raymond James Stadium in 2000, complete with 12,000 club seats that sell for as much as $335 a game and earn the team about $20 million in annual revenues. Today, the team has a 110,000-person season ticket waiting list.

These are just a few examples of the trend toward upscale stadium offerings that's sweeping through large and small markets alike. And as luxury amenities become the norm at stadiums around the country, the experience of attending a live game is changing dramatically.

The Redskins Cash In at FedEx Field

As you read earlier in the chapter, the Atlanta Falcons have indeed done well in adding upscale amenities to their facility, the Georgia Dome, a nondescript, concrete behemoth with a Teflon dome originally built for college football. But the true master of upscale amenities is Daniel Snyder, owner of the Washington Redskins, the first NFL franchise to be valued at more than $1 billion. The Redskins play at 91,704-seat FedEx Field, built in 1997. Their fans choose from a smorgasbord of high-end ticket packages, nearly all of them sold out, in one of the few privately built NFL stadiums.

Starting at the bottom, fans can pony up $3,500 and buy what the Redskins call "Dream Seats," basically the first three rows of seats all the way around the lower level of the stadium. These 1,485 seats are padded—unlike the other 33,404 lower-level seats—and because it's such a hike to the concession stands, wait staff will bring you complimentary hot dogs, peanuts, and soda.

The next level up in opulence at FedEx Field is the club seats, which in 2005 were priced from $2,350 to $3,900. Club levels are the most common type of enhanced season ticket pricing in the NFL. Patrons pay premium prices for midlevel seats and access to better food, drinks, and amenities served in a club or barlike atmosphere. Club seats vary in price and amenities from stadium to stadium, but those at FedEx Field are clearly some of the best in the league. And Snyder, never one to rest on his laurels, has ongoing plans to make the club level even plusher.

The club level at FedEx Field held about 15,700 fans in 2005 and is like many other upscale clubs around the league—only more so. It is tastefully decorated in muted tones that remind patrons of the team's red, white, and gold colors but aren't nearly as loud. The lounges on the club level feature overstuffed tan leather chairs around simple black coffee tables amid soft lighting. Each table has a small numbered placard for wait service.

And there's the Macanudo Cigar Bar, the only indoor smoking lounge in the stadium. It's just what you'd expect: dark wood paneling, those overstuffed tan leather chairs again, and, in addition to a full-service bar and restaurant, a humidor where you can buy your favorite cigar—maybe a $20 Opus X or a $25 Davidoff. A bar runs the length of the back wall, while floor-to-ceiling smoked glass separates the front of the club from the walkway around the club level. There are big-screen plasma TVs everywhere and, about an hour before kickoff, a surprising number of women lighting up with their male companions, the sweet smell of good cigars hanging heavy in the air.

If you're not interested in cigars, the Tailgate Club might be your next stop. The Tailgate Club, which was sold out with 3,000 members for the 2005 season, carries a one-time initiation fee of $1,295 and a per-season fee of $490—neither fee covering the cost of the ticket you must purchase for the game. Upon entering the Tailgate Club area, members get a gift each week. (The week I was there, the gift was a faux leather CD case shaped like a football, complete with white strings, striping, and "The Washington Redskins" printed in white block letters.) For their fees, fans also get free food and soft drinks and pregame entertainment, such as a performance by the Redskins cheerleaders and autograph sessions with Redskins alumni. On the menu this week were hot dogs, hamburgers, BBQ ribs, chips, and a variety of desserts. Philips Seafood, a Washington-area restaurant, samples a different dish for Tailgate Clubbers each week; this week it was crab soup. Mixed drinks and beer can be purchased from one of the Red Bull–branded bars.

All of this is consumed in a segregated area on the stadium's main level, giving Tailgate Club members a large area to wander, mingle, and visit sponsor tents, like the one XM Satellite Radio had set up here. There also was a Canon booth where fans could put their head atop a mannequin in a Redskins uniform, have their picture taken, and get it printed out instantly. A video arcade features dozens of Xbox games, all set on free play. About two hours before the game, the arcade was filled with children and adults alike playing Tiger Woods Golf, Madden 2006, and NASCAR 2006. The Tailgate Club opens three hours before kickoff, reopens five minutes before the end of the first half, and closes at the end of the third quarter. Tailgate Club members also get access to the club level after the game, meaning that, if the Redskins play at 1:00 PM, fans can go up, hang out in the Macanudo Cigar Bar or any of the other club-level lounges, and watch the 4:00 PM NFL games.

If the Tailgate Club isn't rich enough for your blood, then you can try to join the exclusive Touchdown Club, which in 2005 had just 150 members, all of whom paid $7,500 a ticket with a two-ticket minimum. Touchdown Club members get a slightly more upscale pregame buffet and more elbow room. They also get greater access to the cheerleaders and former players, who don't hold autograph sessions but actually mingle with the club members during the pregame party. In addition to an upscale buffet in an even more exclusive area, Touchdown Club members get pre- and postgame access to the club level, field passes, and one away-game trip. The 2005 trip was to Tampa Bay and included airfare, hotel, dinner, breakfast on game day, and club-level seats. Touchdown Club members also are invited to a VIP party during the NFL draft and at the Redskins' training camp.

In between the Tailgate Club and the Touchdown Club (sort of) are the Loge seats, another large common club area that was carved out of the upper-level suites atop FedEx Field. The Loge has 2,500 premium seats that go for $3,900 each. While they are in the upper reaches of the stadium, they still afford a great view of the field, especially the new seats that were built on an overhang above the club level. Fans can order club-level food that is brought to their seats by wait staff or belly up to the Red Zone Morton's bar, which opened at the start of the 2005 season. It's a well-appointed bar featuring premium draft beers and top-shelf liquors, all surrounded by flat-screen TVs showing other NFL games (or the Skins game). While most of the Loge seats are your typical padded stadium seats, the last row of each section features a small, flat counter and bar stools with backs.

"Loge ticket holders either love them or hate them," said Seda Atam, the Redskins marketing manager who oversees premium seating and is responsible for much of the new amenities. "Some patrons ask for them, and others specifically say they don't want to sit in them."

Two tiers of suites ring the upper reaches of FedEx Field. Their tenants are the usual litany of corporate clients, heavily weighted by the industries that regularly lobby our national government in nearby Washington. But if you're an individual, you can purchase one of the Owner's Suites, which seat eight and start at $200,000. Like the Tailgate and Touchdown Clubs (and the Owner's Club in Atlanta), the Owner's Suites come with free food and a cash bar. If the suite is a little confining, you and your guests can hang out in the Owner's Club, a wood-paneled, tastefully appointed bar and lounge area that features those comfy, overstuffed leather chairs—again—and a billiards room.

If you've been keeping track, all of this premium-priced seating means big money for the Redskins—and every other NFL team trying to emulate them. In 2005, the Redskins earned $5.2 million from the Dream Seats, $2.25 million from the Touchdown Club, $3.9 million just from the initiation fees for the Tailgate Club, another $1.5 million from the per-season fee, and who knows how much more from game tickets scattered throughout the stadium. The Loge seats bring in another $9.7 million, and the 15,700 club seats—at an average price of $3,100—bring in a whopping $48.8 million. That's more than $71 million from premium seating alone, and who knows what the team earns from the regular suites and the Owner's Suites, but it's clearly a figure in the tens of millions of dollars. No wonder the Redskins lead the league in per-club revenue.

And they're not stopping. The Tailgate Club is in its third year, and the Touchdown Club is in its first. The Redskins doubled the size of the Tailgate Club after the first year and hope to do the same with the Touchdown Club in 2006. In short, every team in the NFL wishes it were the Washington Redskins—at least in terms of club and other premium-seating revenue. And a few are giving the Skins a run for their money.

Small-Market Teams, Premium Dreams

The size of a team's media market doesn't necessarily correspond to the luxury of its stadium. The New York Jets and Giants, for example, are in the largest media market in the country. Yet they come in at the bottom of the NFL's club-level revenue rankings, because there is no such seating in aging Giants Stadium. All of that will change—perhaps as soon as 2009—when the two teams build another stadium they will share near New Jersey's Meadowlands complex. Further, a large NFL media market clearly isn't a requirement to have a successful club level. A number of teams from smaller markets have cashed in on the luxury stadium movement.

In Charlotte, the club level at Bank of America Stadium is as luxurious as those at FedEx Field. Like many around the league, the Carolina Panthers club level isn't filled with cigar-smoking businessmen (it's a smoke-free facility) but with families and couples, reflecting the fact that today's NFL audience is nearly

50 percent female. The 11,000 club seat holders in Charlotte have 8 distinctive clubs to choose from over a 50,000-square-foot area. They sit at comfortable tables with wait service, listen to muted three-piece combos playing light jazz and easy rock, and eat nachos grande, paninis, soup, and salads.

Comfortable, spacious lounges, with names like the Red Zone, Panther's Den, and the Press Box, feature full bars with mixed drinks and attendants dressed in black button-up smocks with the Bank of America logo on the breast. There are flat-screen TVs everywhere, showing the week's NFL highlights and the pregame show. The walls are decorated in a sports theme, with an electronic scoreboard and black silhouettes of NFL officials explaining what the various penalties mean.

The Locker Room is an upscale convenience store on the club level at Bank of America Stadium that sells premade roast beef sandwiches, salads, chips, and sports drinks. The team shop on the club level is a little more upscale, too, selling Greg Norman brand golf shirts with subtle team logos and muted colors. This is a step up from the main concourse level, where, during my last visit, fans paid $3.50 for a hot dog and $4 for a souvenir soda, not outrageous prices by today's stadium standards. Fans on the concourse also can buy a Wendy's hamburger or Subway sandwich or opt for regional fare, such as a pulled-pork barbeque sandwich. Domestic draft beer is available along with imports such as New Castle, Bass Ale, and Stella Artois.

The Panthers stadium also offers Suite 87, a club within a club that's 7,800 square feet but only seats 124 fans. Membership includes a personalized locker as well as pregame hors d'oeuvres. Traditional football fare—barbeque sandwiches and chicken wings—is served by wait staff between kickoff and the end of the third quarter. And a private bar features beer, wine, and mixed drinks. Suite 87 patrons each get a seat in front of the floor-to-ceiling glass that looks out on the field. Also, a wall of flat-screen TVs show every other NFL game under way. If that's not your thing, then you can go into the billiards room and shoot a game of nine-ball.

What makes this luxury palatable for Carolinians is the fact that most of it was built with private money. Yes, the taxpayers donated the land and made about $15 million in infrastructure improvements—mostly off-ramps from Interstates 77 and 85. But nearly $150 million of the stadium's $250 million cost was financed by the sale of personal seat licenses, a fee fans pay for the right to buy tickets. And buying them they are. The price of PSLs for some of the club and luxury seating at Bank of America Stadium is five figures, as in $10,000 or more.

The United Club at Denver's Mile High Stadium is another example of a small-market team cashing in on the club-level trend. While Broncos games have been sellouts for 35 consecutive years, not until the team opened Invesco Field at Mile High in 2001 did they move up the ranks in terms of revenue. The team's 8,800 club seats generated $20 million in revenue and contributed almost half of the team's $43 million profit last year.

In addition to being luxurious, the United Club makes it hard to forget where you are. The club features crescent-shaped bars with flat-screen TVs, all abutting floor-to-ceiling glass that looks out on the Rocky Mountains to the west and the downtown Denver skyline to the east. Like many club levels, the one here is open and airy, with plenty of pregame seating to watch the teams warm up. There's also a sit-down buffet for $10 that features salad and a meat entrée (beef tenderloin the night I was here). And gelato and Belgian waffles are offered for dessert.

Red Zone and Gray Zone tickets, located at midfield, sold out at $3,625 and $3,350, respectively, for the 2005 season. Blue Zone seats, which are more toward the southern end zone, were $2,745. Orange Zone seats, furthest into the end zone but still affording a great view, sold out at $2,080. Each price includes a $500 per seat "performance deposit" that the team keeps until ticket holders fulfill their contract, which runs from three to seven years.

The club seats in Denver really aren't a bad deal, when you figure that midfield, lower-level reserved seats are $850 and there's a 21,000-person waiting list. For an extra $1,200, you get access to a luxurious club about halfway up the stadium that features some truly upscale amenities, such as a free pregame massage (tips welcome).

A YEAR-ROUND BOOST FOR UNSHARED REVENUES

But perhaps the best example of how a small-market team can cash in on club-level amenities comes from the team in the NFL's smallest market—the Green Bay Packers. The team was ninth in revenue in 1997, but as more modern stadiums came online the team started to plummet through the ranks. By 1999 the Packers were 16th, and if the team didn't do something about it, they were projected to be 25th out of 32 teams by 2003.

Faced with those economics, the Packers, the only publicly held NFL franchise, floated some more stock and completed a $200 million renovation of Lambeau Field. The team upgraded the stadium's suites and added 3,000 club seats priced at $200 a game that sold out almost as soon as they went on sale. That earned the team more than $8 million in new revenue alone.

But the addition that caught everyone's eye was a new atrium that's home to the team offices, the Packers Hall of Fame, a team store, and a year-round sports bar and restaurant called Curly's, named after team founder Earl "Curly" Lambeau. Curly's is divided into three sections: a sit-down restaurant that offers walleye sandwiches and burgers, a traditional sports bar serving drinks and finger food, and a Packers-themed arcade. The latter has video games as well as games of skill, such as a football toss to a plywood Packer with a hole in his stomach. Curly's fills up as soon as the gates open, and a wait forms almost instantaneously for seating in the restaurant. The souvenir shop does a healthy business year-round.

But where the atrium really pays off for the team is when the Packers aren't playing at Lambeau Field. The atrium has become a year-round destination, and not just for Packers fanatics. In renovating Lambeau Field, the team specifically designed the club and suite levels so that they could be configured to hold annual meetings and corporate seminars.

The atrium, which can seat up to 1,000, also hosts hundreds of wedding receptions every year—and not just because the space is at Lambeau Field. The space draws weddings, dinners, and corporate events because it offers some of the finest catering and facilities in the Green Bay area.

"We now have 1,600 special events a year," said Steve Klegon, the Packers director of business development. "We have at least one wedding reception every Saturday."

Stadium and Hall of Fame tours bring more than 200,000 people to Lambeau Field on nongame days. Curly's serves countless meals before, during, and after games. The Packers even use the atrium to hold their annual tent sale, which features the previous year's Packers merchandise at huge discounts.

"The growing importance of deriving revenue from non-shared sources made it imperative that the Packers renovate Lambeau Field to increase its revenue-generating capacity," said Kevin M. Bahr, a University of Wisconsin economist and author of a 2000 study that looked at NFL revenue sharing and its impact on small-market teams. "The Packers estimate that a renovated Lambeau Field should provide an additional $20 million of annual revenue and place the Packers in the top half of the NFL in annual revenue. The renovation to Lambeau Field, combined with the NFL's revenue sharing and salary cap, should allow the Packers the opportunity to compete on a relatively level financial playing field."

"The atrium is the smartest business decision we ever made," Klegon said.

It was so smart that other NFL teams are looking to copy it, partly to improve their own revenue streams but also to allay growing concerns from taxpayers who've been tapped too long to pay for lavish facilities that are only used eight or ten weeks a year. By making stadiums year-round, some teams are making the community feel as though it has more ownership of the place—that the stadium is somewhere they can go and enjoy, even if they're not season ticket holders.

Atlanta, which is not only growing revenue but doing it within the confines of the Georgia Dome, a place that wasn't built for today's NFL, is thinking about an atrium-type addition. Not only would it include year-round restaurants and other entertainment venues, but Falcons president Dick Sullivan said he thinks the team could build a hotel as well. The Houston Texans, one of the top revenue teams in the league, also are thinking about copying the Packers atrium model by adding a year-round restaurant or other entertainment venues. The model would work particularly well for the Texans, because Reliant Stadium is just one of four facilities in Reliant Park, a complex of arenas and stadiums that's also home to the annual Houston Livestock Show and Rodeo.

NFL owners are increasingly seeing suites, club levels, and atriums as venues that allow them to increase revenue not only during games but all year. And such amenities fit in nicely with a growing marketing strategy within the NFL that tries to make the connection between the fan and the team more than a four-month affair. Teams are increasingly looking for ways to maintain—and tap into—fan loyalty well beyond the regular season. Some teams do this with off-season cruises, dinners, draft-day events, and expanded training camps. "Today, marketing to the NFL fan is all about maintaining a year-round connection," said Reid Sigmon, director of stadium development and event operations for the Cleveland Browns.

Unfortunately, despite all this economic data to the contrary, taxpayers don't seem to be wising up. State legislators and governors are increasingly pressured by active and influential fan groups to fund public sports stadiums. Taxpayers who are so willing to pay for teams and stadiums put added pressure on politicians to fund new ballparks to keep teams where they are.

Regardless of the debate surrounding the public financing of stadiums, it would appear that the NFL's 2006 revenue-sharing agreement, with the top 15 teams in revenue handing over almost $900 million to be divided among the remaining 17 clubs, did much to quell concerns about the NFL becoming a league of haves and have-nots. Nevertheless, there's certain to be debate—especially among the teams at the bottom of the NFL revenue chart—that it's not enough. But at least for now, the NFL has done what it can to ensure that the finances remain balanced in the NFL. As we explore further in the next chapter, most analysts agree that much of the NFL's success is directly linked to just this competitive and economic balance.

CHAPTER TEN

DOWN TO THE WIRE

INSIDE THE 2006 NEGOTIATIONS

After having looked at all the economic factors outlined in the previous chapters of this book, many folks might still be asking themselves: Why did these billionaire owners, many of whom made their money in some of the toughest, most competitive industries on the planet, agree to abide by the NFL's decades-old, quasicollectivist revenue-sharing system? Although the model has obvious benefits for Charlotte, Jacksonville, Cincinnati, and other small-market teams, how could ruthless capitalists and big-market team owners like Dan Snyder, Jerry Jones, and Bob McNair accede to giving some of their hard-earned cash to support less-successful—some would say less entrepreneurial—franchises?

Perhaps the *Wall Street Journal* editorial page, that bastion of free-market intellectual capital, said it best in a March 10, 2006, editorial in response to the NFL collective bargaining and revenue-sharing agreements. "Once again, NFL owners and players have determined that they have a mutual interest in keeping a good thing going . . . ," the *Journal* editors wrote. "Contrast that with what's happened in pro hockey, where an entire season was missed last year because of the players' rapacious stupidity. Or to baseball, whose richest owners want to dominate every year. The performance gap between teams that can afford the best, most expensive players and the poorer ones that cannot becomes more obvious—and the season more boring—every year."

It's hard to argue with the resounding financial and competitive success of the NFL. After all, even with the minor adjustment to revenue sharing in the 2006 labor deal, we shouldn't forget that the league will still generate more than $6 billion a year when all's said and done. Not bad, even if you are among those who think the NFL owners group is a bunch of Marxists. But while many have described the NFL's revenue sharing as a form of socialism, the *Wall Street Journal*'s editors were quick to counter: "The truth is that in the NFL, while owners and players compete on the field, off the field they are business partners whose real competition is with other forms of entertainment. By sharing revenues, they all get richer. That isn't socialism . . . it's just good capitalist sense."

We know now that the owners opted to tweak the system in March 2006, retaining the business model that has served them so well for so long. But what arguments led up to the talks and eventual settlement? How close did the league come to throwing it all away in the name of individual greed? What does the business model portend for the future? Did the big-market owners make a tactical error and allow the proverbial camel's nose under the tent in agreeing to share some of their riches with the smaller-market teams? Or was the tweaking of the system just that, a minor adjustment that did more to keep the peace than to alter the way the business model fundamentally works?

This chapter looks at the "capitalist sense" behind the NFL's 2006 contract settlement. More specifically, it explores how the bedrock theories of the NFL's economic model—the reverse draft, revenue sharing, the salary cap—have played out in the real world and what lessons we can learn from the successes and failures of America's other "big" professional sports league, Major League Baseball. Finally, we'll take an inside look at the 2006 NFL contract negotiations, where the league's owners, in a nerve-wracking, last-minute decision, voted to preserve the NFL's economic system. "Collectivism," "socialism," "a welfare state for billionaires"—call it what you will; in the end, these owners salvaged an economic model that has distinguished the league among all others and has helped NFL football to become the most beloved game in America.

IS SHARING ESSENTIAL? NFL OWNERS EYE THE LESSONS OF MAJOR LEAGUE BASEBALL

As many of you sports junkies know, commentators are always quick to compare the NFL and Major League Baseball (MLB). They really are the big leagues in America, with the NBA and NHL playing relatively minor roles. At the heart of any "NFL versus MLB" debate is the issue of which league has the more successful economic model. In other words, do salary caps and unshared revenues create a superior professional sports league?

The "which league is better" debate, of course, is one of the great barroom discussions of all time, and it will likely go on as long as there are Yankees and Red Sox and Packers and Jaguars. But fans and commentators aren't the only ones making those comparisons. Following the stadium-building boom of the 1990s, as the impact of escalating unshared revenues began to become apparent in NFL finances, a few scholarly studies offered compelling support for the solid financial benefits of the NFL's level playing field. Without question, the NFL owners were well aware of those studies' findings as they entered the 2006 contract negotiations.

Kevin M. Bahr, professor in the Division of Business and Economics at the University of Wisconsin at Stevens Point, analyzed and compared the financial and on-field performance of the

NFL's Green Bay Packers and Major League Baseball's Milwaukee Brewers to compare the success of small-market teams within
the economic models of the NFL and Major League Baseball. He
found that the big difference between the two leagues—and the
subsequent success or failure of small-market teams like the
Packers and Brewers—is the NFL's revenue sharing. While NFL
teams share about 54 percent of league revenues, less than 20 percent of Major League Baseball revenues are shared. Further, Major League Baseball players have no salary cap.

From 1996 through 1999, Major League Baseball local revenue constituted about 79 percent of total industry revenue, and
the disparity in local revenue from team to team is huge. Bahr
found that the 1999 Montreal Expos were at the bottom of the local revenue hierarchy with $12 million, while the New York Yan-
kees were (and always have been) at the top with $176 million—
quite a difference. Of course, the Yankees distanced themselves
even further from the rest of the league when they created the
YES Network, a cable television network that broadcasts games
as well as Yankee talk shows, historic game replays, and the like.
In 2005, the Yankees earned more than $225 million in local reve-
nue from the YES Network alone.

The economic setup doesn't guarantee that the Yankees are
the best team every year, but in a league with no salary cap, a
team's individual wealth is certainly a bigger factor than in the
salary-capped NFL. While the NFL's most affluent team might
have a payroll almost double that of the least affluent, in the Major League Baseball the difference can be much larger. Bahr found
that in 2000, for example, "The New York Yankees' payroll of
$112 million was nearly eight times that of the Minnesota Twins."
Bahr goes on to note that, ". . . the ability to generate superior revenues provides the capacity to pay superior salaries." And, Bahr
found, there is a significant performance disparity between the
Major League Baseball teams that pay big salaries and the teams
that don't. Since 1994, for example, only 3 of the 48 possible post-

season spots were taken by Major League Baseball teams in the bottom half of the industry's payroll. And of 189 postseason games, only 2 were won by these low-payroll teams.

A 1999 blue-ribbon panel asked to look at baseball's finances came to a similar conclusion. The panel, headed up by former Senator George Mitchell, former Fed chair Paul Volcker, and syndicated columnist and baseball fanatic George Will, found that the large and growing revenue and payroll disparities in Major League Baseball are leading to a "chronic competitive imbalance." Furthermore, modest revenue-sharing enhancements that were part of baseball's 1996 collective bargaining agreement "did not moderate payroll disparities or improve competitive balance."

Bahr isn't alone in his assessment of the superior success of the NFL among professional sports leagues. Karl W. Einolf of Mount Saint Mary's College did a study that compared the franchise payroll efficiency of the NFL from 1981 to 2000 with that of Major League Baseball from 1985 to 2001. Einolf found a substantial difference in franchise efficiency between the two organizations, and he attributed it to differences in their financial structures. "Major League Baseball franchises, with little revenue sharing and no salary cap, tend to be less efficient than NFL franchises," Einolf said. "Big spending and inefficient Major League Baseball franchises tend to come from large media markets, although this is not the case in the NFL."

Between 1995 and 1999, for example, ten different teams played in the Super Bowl, with only the Packers and the Denver Broncos making repeat appearances. This trend has continued over subsequent years, as well. True, the New England Patriots won three of four Super Bowls starting in 2002, but they played different opponents each time (and, let's not forget, they were also lauded for doing it with one of the lowest payrolls in the NFL). And in 2003, when the Patriots didn't make the big game, the Tampa Bay Buccaneers and Oakland Raiders went to the Super Bowl. The Bucs hadn't been to the Super Bowl since their founding in 1976, and the Raiders hadn't been to the big game since they won Super Bowl XV in 1981, beating the Philadelphia Eagles, 27–10. The Eagles wouldn't make it to another Super Bowl until 2005, when the Patriots beat them 24–21.

We also should note that the Redskins had the highest payroll in the NFL, but—until they made the playoffs in 2005—consistently brought up the rear of the NFC East. By contrast, the New England Patriots had one of the lowest payrolls in the NFL and won three out of four Super Bowls. All of these statistics support Bahr in his assessment of the NFL's success, which he summed up by saying, "Revenue sharing, combined with a salary cap and free agency, has leveled the financial playing field and allowed teams to effectively compete."

The NFL owners clearly understand this. "We have the system that everyone wants," said Bob Harlan, president and chief executive officer of the Green Bay Packers. "[Baseball commissioner] Bud Selig sits on the board, and he has told me on more than one occasion that Major League Baseball would love to have the NFL revenue system. Because he knows that it's absolutely vital to the survival of the Green Bay Packers and other small-market teams."

"Have we kept the league, which is viable financially, competitive with 32 teams?" New York Giants general manager Ernie Accorsi asked in a February 2006 interview. "I think the NFL is night and day on that subject. That's what drives everything. It drives the competitiveness, the quality, the motivation of the teams. It drives fan interest. . . . Nothing is more at the root of the league's competitiveness than the real chance to rise and fall, win and lose."

ANY GIVEN SUNDAY

So how are Bert Bell's reverse-draft system and the NFL's broad revenue-sharing model holding up after 70 years? I think the chart below illustrates that both systems work quite well. Here, you can see that NFL teams can have a horrible season, then bounce back the next—even winning the Super Bowl. Of course, it works the other way around, too. Owners can assemble a good team, but even a few years at the back of the draft line take their toll.

1996

New England Patriots from 6–10 to 11–5
Detroit Lions from 10–6 to 5–11

1997

New York Jets from 1–15 to 9–7
Buffalo Bills from 10–6 to 6–10
New York Giants from 6–10 to 10–6

1998

Buffalo Bills from 6–10 to 10–6
Dallas Cowboys from 6–10 to 10–6
Atlanta Falcons from 7–9 to 14–2

1999

Indianapolis Colts from 3–13 to 13–3
Washington Redskins from 6–10 to 10–6
St. Louis Rams from 4–12 to 13–3
Atlanta Falcons from 14–2 to 5–11

2000

Denver Broncos from 6–10 to 11–5
Philadelphia Eagles from 5–11 to 11–5
New Orleans Saints from 3–13 to 10–6

2001

New England Patriots from 5–11 to 11–5
Chicago Bears from 5–11 to 13–3
Minnesota Vikings from 11–5 to 5–11
San Francisco 49ers from 6–10 to 12–4

2002

Indianapolis Colts from 6–10 to 10–6
Chicago Bears from 13–3 to 4–12

2003

Pittsburgh Steelers from 10–5 to 6–10
Oakland Raiders from 11–5 to 4–12
Dallas Cowboys from 5–11 to 10–6
Carolina Panthers from 7–9 to 11–5

2004

Pittsburgh Steelers from 6–10 to 5–1
Tennessee Titans from 12–4 to 5–11
San Diego Chargers from 4–12 to 12–4

2005

Cincinnati Bengals from 8–8 to 11–5
New York Giants from 6–10 to 11–5
Chicago Bears from 5–11 to 11–5
Philadelphia Eagles from 13–3 to 6–10

Source: Author research

MARCH 2006: HAMMERING OUT THE FUTURE OF THE NFL

Big-market teams versus small-market teams and teams with newer, high-revenue-generating stadiums versus those with less profitable stadiums: these were just some of the factors that divided NFL owners as the 2005 season began without a new collective bargaining or revenue-sharing agreement. While the players and owners were trying to keep the focus on the expiration of the collective bargaining agreement, fundamentally, the debate leading up to the 2006 negotiations was about locally generated revenues and how to share them. It pitted big-market, high-revenue franchises like the Dallas Cowboys and Washington Redskins against small-market, low-revenue franchises such as the Buffalo Bills and Cincinnati Bengals.

New stadiums played a monumental role in deciding which camp individual owners were in, as these stadiums generated significant local (unshared) revenue, creating economic disparities even among teams from the same size markets. The Green Bay Packers, for example, have long argued in favor of broad revenue sharing, because they're in the smallest market in the NFL. But with their $300 million renovation of Lambeau Field, the Packers also benefited significantly from locally generated stadium revenue. By contrast, Cincinnati Bengals owner Mike Brown, another small-market owner, was one of the most vocal advocates for broader revenue sharing. Brown's position particularly galled owners like Jones and Snyder, because Brown not only had most of his new stadium paid for by the taxpayers of Hamilton County, Ohio, but he chose to forego at least $100 million in stadium-naming rights fees by naming the stadium after his father, legendary coach Paul Brown, rather than a paying sponsor.

And, of course, there's a third party here: the players. They were determined to leverage the potential for an uncapped salary year to encourage the owners to part with more of their newly enhanced revenues. The owners were divided as to how the labor talks should proceed, with some claiming that revenue sharing was separate and apart from the collective bargaining agreement (CBA) negotiations and a matter to be resolved among the owners. Gene Upshaw, executive director of the NFL Players Association (NFLPA) saw it differently. The NFLPA knew that stadium-generated revenues had lined the pockets of owners over the past decade. Until the owners decided how much revenue they were going to share among themselves, Upshaw and the players were loathe to give them the labor peace that they so desired.

"The two, in my mind, from my perspective, aren't connected," said Jones during Cowboys training camp. "I think if we ultimately see something that is doable between labor and the league, then you can have it without any additional revenue sharing."

Trying to maintain some decorum during this sometimes-ugly battle were some of the oldest owners in the league, like Wellington Mara of the New York Giants and Dan Rooney of the Pittsburgh Steelers. They remembered how tough it was when the league didn't have a lucrative national television contract and how tough it was to go it alone, living off hot dog sales and advertising on local radio and television stations that didn't pay nearly as much as ABC and Fox.

Pragmatists like the Philadelphia Eagles general manager Joe Banner also understood historically what made the league work financially and competitively. "The NFL came through a period where virtually every stadium was built 100 percent with public money," he said. "When that was true for the whole league, there wasn't a big difference in terms of profitability. It was a very narrow band." That all changed, Banner said, when there began to be disparities in public financing of stadiums and the revenues that new stadiums generated. "As a result, you had some cases where you had high-revenue teams that were turning a modest profit, because they were servicing a lot of debt, and low-revenue teams that were making a significant profit," Banner said. "That's what changed the terms of revenue sharing going forward."

The Players and Owners Square Off

As early as 2004, Gene Upshaw told NFL owners he believed that eight powerful franchises have obtained an unfair economic advantage over the rest of the league. "When we started this process, there were 14 teams above the [league revenue] average and 14 below it, and everyone was close enough to keep things fair," Upshaw said. "Now we have 8 haves and 24 have-nots, and the haves are getting a discount on everything."

Upshaw also noted that the biggest disparity was in unshared revenues, primarily due to the stadium building boom that had begun in the mid-1990s. "The money that isn't shared has gone from 30 percent (of total revenues) in 1994 to 37 percent today, and with revenues at almost $6 billion, that's a significant amount of money," he said. "We've had a good deal for ten years now, and we want that to go forward, but the model has to change."

That may be, but owners like the Houston Texans' Bob McNair argued that their entire financial structure for the team was based upon the old revenue-sharing model. Furthermore, some owners were servicing significant debt based upon keeping much of the revenue they generated from their new stadiums. "The union is using published information on gross revenues, and we are looking at net income," McNair said. "The high-revenue teams are also the ones that have invested heavily in their franchises, so when you look at what money we have at the end of the day, the disparity isn't of the significance that some people would have you believe."

McNair also made the point that no correlation exists between high-revenue teams and winning percentage. "There's no correlation between salaries paid and winning percentage," Mc-Nair said. "We have a good balance in the NFL, and a number of teams in the highest payroll quartile are located in the lowest quartile of revenue teams."

But small-market team owners, like the Buffalo Bills' Ralph Wilson, didn't see it that way. He said in no uncertain terms that more revenue sharing was needed just for teams like his to survive. Like Cincinnati's Mike Brown, Ralph Wilson's pleas often fell on deaf ears, because he, too, had foregone tens of millions of dollars in stadium naming rights. (He named the field after himself.) Nevertheless, he held firm in his position: "They want to knock us down and have us get up at the count of nine, so they can have another fight and knock us down again," Wilson said in a pointed interview in the *Buffalo News*. "There's about eight or ten of the high-revenue clubs that seem to be united in a block. They are united. They want to keep the disparity."

If Wilson was right about anything, it was that there's disparity in the league. As Bahr's study highlighted, the top revenue-producing team in the league, the Washington Redskins, took in $300 million in revenue in 2005, more than double what some of the lowest-revenue teams in the league, like the Arizona Cardinals, Indianapolis Colts, and Buffalo Bills earn. "We just want to have enough revenue under the new collective bargaining agreement to give us a chance to field a competitive team," Wilson said. "If we don't get that, then along the line, the league is going to be totally unbalanced. It's not going to be the league it used to be."

Throughout this long-running debate, the NFL tried to mediate the discussion and keep the league running. But even the league was skeptical that the owners and players could reach an agreement. "In my view, this is a matter of Gene [Upshaw] wanting more money for the players and coming up with this idea as a way to do that," said Harold Henderson, the league's executive vice president for labor relations. "I think their expectations are excessive and probably are going to be difficult to reach, but that's what a negotiation is all about."

"We should be clear about one thing," commissioner Paul Tagliabue told the owners. "Our own recent history tells us that a failure to come together now and agree upon solutions—both internally and with the players' association—will produce alternatives that are far more negative for all clubs, all players, the league, and the players' association than the cost of a solution will be to any one club, group of clubs, player, or category of players."

The Wisdom of the Past Prevails

In the end, the participants in the 2006 NFL contract negotiations—players and owners, small-market and big-market teams, teams with new stadiums and teams with old stadiums—seem to have reached an agreement that the wealth of the league as a whole mattered more than the individual success of any individual team. As a result, the new NFL economic model looks a lot like the old one.

Under the terms of the collective bargaining agreement that took effect with the 2006 season, the players get a bigger piece of the NFL revenue pie than ever. From 2006 to 2011, the players will get a whopping 59.5 percent of *total* revenues, compared with about 56 percent of what had previously been called Gross Designated Revenues (which only included TV money, merchandising revenue, and away-game ticket sales). The new collective bargaining agreement also enhanced some of the player benefits. "There is a health care-IRA-type element set aside that the players will get funded in proportion to the length of their career," said Paul Tagliabue. Further, the agreement includes expanded postcareer medical coverage for players. "It's quite a significant improvement in benefits," Tagliabue added. On revenue sharing, the owners agreed that the top 15 teams would contribute about

$900 million into a pool over the life of the contract. That pool would be divided among the 17 lower-revenue teams.

"It was really a tremendous effort by owners across the entire spectrum of the league, no matter how you define the spectrum —whether it's in terms of longevity, whether it's in terms of big market, small market or high revenue, low revenue," said Tagliabue, in his announcement of the agreement. "Everyone came together after these two full days of discussions and reached a consensus not only on the collective bargaining agreement but on some major new revenue-sharing features to support the ability of all teams to function well under the collective bargaining agreement. . . . We ended up with one single resolution that brought all of the different ideas together."

According to Tagliabue, a compromise proposal was first presented during the final day of deliberations by Woody Johnson, owner of the New York Jets, and Jonathan Kraft, president of the New England Patriots, who was representing his father, Robert Kraft, the team's owner. That plan was modified by Dan Rooney, owner of the Super Bowl XL champion Pittsburgh Steelers, and Dick Cass, president of the Baltimore Ravens. It was then given one last revision by New York Giants president John Mara, Carolina Panthers owner Jerry Richardson, and Denver Broncos owner Pat Bowlen. Arthur Blank, cofounder of Home Depot and the owner of the Atlanta Falcons, as well as Dallas Cowboys owner Jerry Jones, also contributed to the final resolution that was presented to the owners. It was approved on the first vote, 30–2, with Buffalo Bills owner Ralph Wilson and Cincinnati Bengals owner Mike Brown casting the only no votes.

"It was a good compromise," said Indianapolis Colts owner Jim Irsay.

"We're delighted with the new CBA and that a salary cap system was preserved," said Packers president Bob Harlan. "Continuation of the salary cap was our number-one goal, because without it, the long-term viability of the Packers would be in doubt."

"I think all of us feel good that we got something done," New York Jets owner Woody Johnson said.

"The NFL has been the premier sports league in North America for decades," said Tampa Bay Buccaneers general manager Bruce Allen, after the agreement was announced. "This deal should allow us to continue with our unprecedented growth."

Oakland Raiders owner Al Davis attended the meeting in spite of poor health, because he felt it was too important to miss. He said he could have imagined some teams leaving the NFL after the 2007 season and starting their own league if a new collective bargaining agreement had not been reached. "There would have been anarchy," said Davis, who once sued the NFL over the right to move his team. "I came because I wanted labor peace. They don't particularly love me, because I'm going to go my own way and do what I think is right," he said of the other owners. "I've fought them, but I also love the league and what's best for football, for the players, and the owners. This needed to get done."

Even Jerry Jones and Daniel Snyder, the two owners who argued most vehemently to preserve the old revenue-sharing structure and wanted teams to rely more on entrepreneurship than collective well-being, praised the deal. "We couldn't walk out of this building and not have a deal," said Jones. "I expected to come out of this without having my Christmas list intact, and I met my expectation." Said Snyder, "Some of us had to give and take a little more than others, but things have a way of working out. We just wanted to get this done for the sake of the league."

A Less-Than-Perfect Solution?

For all of the upbeat, blue-sky comments coming out of the settlement, you can rest assured that we haven't heard the last of this debate. I'm sure that owners Jerry Jones and Dan Snyder were less than happy to give up even a sliver of the revenue stream they've worked so hard to build, just as small-market owners Ralph Wilson and Mike Brown weren't happy with the relatively meager bone the high-revenue owners threw to them. "This is a bad deal for the NFL for the next six years," Ralph Wilson said a day after the new agreement was signed. "It's too much money," said the 87-year-old owner, noting the agreement to give players 59.5 percent of revenue. "And it's particularly a bad deal for medium- and small-market clubs."

In fact, Wilson argued, not only do the players get too much of the league's $6 billion of annual revenue, but the agreement does not address the fundamental problem of economic inequality between big- and small-market teams. "The deal is just about the same," Wilson said. "Maybe the high-revenue clubs are picking up a slight increase in money. But it's still not good." Wilson was also critical of how the owners were asked to vote on the deal at the 11th hour. "Most of the owners didn't understand any of this stuff, including me," Wilson said. "I got a sense in the room that these fellows were just afraid of any work stoppage. They were afraid of the union. They were going to accept anything."

Cincinnati's Mike Brown was equally critical of the agreement. "The deal is tremendously costly," Brown said. "The high-revenue teams, although they were willing to shift money to low-revenue teams, weren't prepared to shift money in proportion to the amount they put costs on us." Brown said he thought the deal was too lucrative for the players and that high-revenue teams didn't put enough into the pot. Like others, Brown argued that, while the league will take in $47 billion over the six years of the CBA, less than $1 billion will be shared. "The highest-revenue teams export $45 to $50 million of cost onto other teams," Brown said, arguing that by driving up revenues and salaries, high-revenue teams raise costs for the whole league. As a result, the Redskins, the highest-revenue team in the league, with an estimated $287 million in annual receipts, will share just 1 percent of its revenue. Added Brown, "They are prepared to revenue share in the range of $6 million. It's a good deal for the top teams." The Bengals, who had an estimated $171 million in revenue, will spend about 70 percent on salaries. By contrast, the Redskins will only spend 42 percent of their revenue on salaries. "In our system, the lower-revenue teams are taxed at a higher rate than the high-revenue teams," Brown said. "We don't think that's working well."

But other owners argue that the NFL revenue disparities are cyclical and eventually work themselves out. "I do think this thing is cyclical, and so there are always going to be teams who are on the lower revenue side and will have different opportunities to move into the upper-revenue areas," said San Francisco 49ers owner John York.

The NFL owners very much echoed that sentiment in their comments following the settlement. "As far as the agreement, it is a tough, expensive agreement, but I think we will be fine," said Steelers owner Dan Rooney. "I think we will have to watch our expenses and things like that and be fiscally responsible, but it is a great thing. This gives us labor peace for a while, which I think is what has separated the National Football League from other sports. I think it will be good for the league."

But maybe not so good for the Steelers. Had there been no agreement, the salary cap for 2006 would have been $94.5 million, putting a lot of teams into a cash crunch and thereby restricting them from going after some of the Steelers' marquee, unrestricted free-agent players. "In some regards, we would have been better off [without an extension] because the other people wouldn't be able to go after our players, because they wouldn't have any money," said Rooney. "But basically, I think that this was the best system."

THE FINAL SCORE: EXCELLING ON AN EVEN PLAYING FIELD

The successful negotiation of the 2006 NFL contract was a moment of personal triumph for Paul Tagliabue. At 65, this was expected to be his last CBA negotiation, and indeed, on March 20, 2006, Tagliabue announced that he would resign his post as NFL commissioner in July. While many observers like to point out that Tagliabue is a lawyer and that's somehow indicative of the kind of person you need running the league these days, the settlement that he negotiated was very much in the spirit of Bert Bell and Pete Rozelle. In years to come, it will be seen as one of the defining moments in the history of a very successful NFL commissioner. The agreement ultimately demanded that the teams put aside their individual best interests and do what was in the best interest of the league.

In an online exchange following the settlement, Vic Ketchman, senior editor of *Jaguars.com*, the official site of the Jacksonville Jaguars, noted that the league's latest agreement was, ultimately, a continuation of the NFL's time-tested model. Ketchman wrote, "Pooling the revenue is best for the league. It's a philosophy of 'leaguethink,' and 40 years later, it's still working. That's what the league's owners did on Wednesday night. They confirmed that 'leaguethink' still exists."

And in a sentimental nod, the settlement was a good way to conclude the first NFL negotiations to come after the death of Wellington Mara, one of the patriarchs of the league. "I think he would have been proud of the way the process worked," said his son, John. Ironically, the Giants may be hurt by this deal until they get a new stadium. But as Mara—father and son—made clear, the NFL is about more than one team. "At the end of the day, the overriding issue was: What is in the best interest of the league; what can we get 24 people to vote for?" said John Mara. "And I think the deal that we got is not perfect. It is going to hurt some people in the short term. It will hurt some other people in the long term. But overall, without question, it is in the best interest of the league, principally because we have labor peace."

In the wake of the 2006 negotiations, many fans, economists, players, and even NFL team owners would agree with Philadelphia Eagles owner, Jeff Lurie, who said, "If you can create a sport where every single market has an equal chance to win, you are going to have a very popular game. That's what football is all about. Whether you're a big market or small, there's equal opportunity."

To be sure, the NFL *has* maintained the even playing field by providing equal opportunity for all its members. But that's not to say that every team can expect to enjoy equal revenues. As you'll learn in the next chapter, in spite of the expanded revenue-sharing agreement of 2006, some owners have figured out how to maximize performance, maximize revenues, and take the NFL business model to a whole new level. I call the franchises owned by these entrepreneurial masterminds the "super teams" and I predict that their ventures and business successes will vie with the league's traditions to determine the future of professional football in this country.

CHAPTER ELEVEN

SUPER TEAMS, SAVVY OWNERS, AND THE FUTURE OF THE NFL

A handful of entrepreneurial gentlemen epitomize the 21st-century NFL team owner. Some of them, like the Dallas Cowboys' Jerry Jones, the New England Patriots' Bob Kraft, and the Washington Redskins' Daniel Snyder are well known. And, although Atlanta Falcons owner Arthur Blank, the Houston Texans' Bob McNair, and the Denver Broncos' Pat Bowlen might fly under the radar screen, these owners, too, are accomplishing truly remarkable and significant things in their approach to the business of the NFL.

Each new, brash, young owner that enters the league brings a new dimension to the battle for the heart and soul of the NFL economic model. Rooted in generational and cultural differences, the outcome of this struggle will define the league as it moves through the coming years. For that reason, I take special interest in the NFL team owners—rookies and veterans alike—who demonstrate a vibrant entrepreneurial spirit in the management of their teams. And that's why I've chosen to close this book with a few brief profiles of these giants of the NFL and the franchises they own. By understanding where these business leaders are taking their teams, you're also getting a glimpse of what well may be the future direction of the NFL.

JERRY JONES AND THE DALLAS COWBOYS

While Jerry Jones has owned the Dallas Cowboys since 1989, he is truly a 21st-century owner. That's because he, perhaps better than anyone else, epitomizes the entrepreneurial spirit that must partner with the league's revenue-sharing model to ensure that the NFL continues to be a financial success. In the realm of local marketing, advertising, and sponsorship, perhaps no one outshines Jerry Jones. While Dan Snyder is an impressive marketer for his Washington Redskins, Jones is equally talented in generating local revenue, and he does it in a 30-year-old facility.

Texas Stadium is a marvel of modern marketing. Jones was among the first to understand the possibilities of marketing sponsorships within the stadium—a revenue generator that has become standard operating procedure at most NFL stadiums. But it is during the game that Jones really distinguishes himself and his ability to turn anything and everything into a marketing event, generating revenue that he doesn't have to share with the rest of the league.

During the pregame show, the scoreboard reads, "Welcome referees," with the message sponsored by a local eye clinic. While other teams run onto the field through an oversized inflatable helmet, the Cowboys run onto the field through a purple, inflatable tunnel sponsored by Levitra, one of the new drugs for erectile dysfunction. During the 2005 season, commercials for HBO's *Curb Your Enthusiasm* played on the Jumbotron during TV time-outs, while another promo for HBO gave fans a quote and asked them to guess if it was said by Cowboys coach Bill Parcells or Tony Soprano. The replays on the Pepsi-sponsored scoreboard were courtesy of Miller Lite, a kids' quiz was sponsored by CVS, and a local radio station sponsored the "Hit of the Game."

Off the field, Jones doesn't miss a trick, either. His Cowboy Club Golf Course charges $160 for a round on the weekends, and Texans are more than happy to pay for the privilege of changing clothes in a replica of the Cowboys locker room. The lockers feature player names and numbers, such as Hall of Fame quarterback Roger Staubach. The Dallas Cowboys cheerleaders, the first squad to garner national attention, pose for catalog shoots and appear at local events. In fact, the Dallas Cowboys make so much money from off-field promotions and events, they don't participate in the NFL's revenue-sharing program for merchandise—and they're the only team that doesn't do so.

Of course, Jones' entrepreneurship, his ability to make a buck on almost anything, has earned him the ire of some of his fellow owners. And while his brash, Texas style may rub some people the wrong way, it's hard to argue with his success. The Cowboys won the Super Bowl in 1992, 1993, and 1995, making Jones the first owner in NFL history to win three Super Bowls within seven years of buying a team. And before the New England Patriots won Super Bowl XXXIX, Dallas was the only team in the NFL ever to have won three Super Bowls in four seasons. And with five victories, the team has tied the NFL record for most Super Bowl wins. In the past three decades, 26 new owners have come into the NFL, and only Jerry Jones and New England's Bob Kraft have won more than two Super Bowls.

BOB KRAFT'S NEW ENGLAND PATRIOTS

While Jones and Kraft share the honor of Super Bowl records, the comparisons pretty much stop there. In 1994, Kraft, who purchased and built up his father-in-law's paper-packaging business to acquire a huge personal fortune, paid $172 million for the Patriots at a time when the team was bleeding red ink and had won just 19 of their previous 80 games.

"I knew, sitting in the stands back in the 1970s, that I wanted to one day own the team," Kraft said in a March 2006 interview. In the span of a decade, he turned the Patriots from perennial cellar dwellers into the first NFL dynasty of the 21st century. In 2005, the Patriots joined the Cowboys and Redskins as the only NFL teams to be valued at more than $1 billion in *Forbes* magazine's annual survey. The team that once lost money and barely ever sold out its games now brings in about $236 million a year in revenue, netting about $50 million.

In a theme that will repeat itself throughout this chapter, Kraft said he turned the Patriots around by treating it like any other business and by applying the principles that had proven to be successful in his other business dealings. "I think some people come into the NFL and start doing things differently because of the glamour of the business," Kraft said, "but in the end, you have to run the NFL business the same as you run your other businesses."

Kraft, a Harvard Business School graduate, hires good people and says there's no room in his organization for big egos. In the end, Kraft says, success is about getting good people that you can trust. "I have three rules," he said. "One is integrity, character, and loyalty; two is work ethic; and three is brains. If you don't have one, then two and three don't mean anything."

Kraft also understood early on that not only owning the team was valuable, but so was owning the stadium and land around it as well. It was a hard lesson he learned when he owned the Boston Lobsters, a professional tennis team that played at Boston University's Walter Brown Arena. Kraft saw firsthand the money he sacrificed to the university in parking and concession revenues. So when he decided to go after the Patriots, the first thing he did was start buying up the land around the stadium.

"In 1985, I took a 10-year lease on 330 acres around the stadium," he said. "My banker thought I was nuts because I was just getting parking revenue."

Thanks to some financing troubles for the Sullivan family, who had owned the Patriots and the stadium, by 1988, Kraft had the land, the stadium, and $2 million a year in concessions and other stadium-related revenue. In 1994, after the team had changed hands twice, he finally bought the team itself from James Busch Orthwein for $172 million—50 percent more than his investment bankers told him the team was worth.

"They offered me $75 million to get out of the lease," Kraft said. "Instead, I bought the team for the highest price ever paid for any team in any sport in the world. I turned down $75 million and paid $172 million. That was a nearly $250 million swing."

With that purchase, Kraft spent a record sum for one of the worst teams in the NFL. The Patriots were last in revenue and last in payroll. The team had the worst record in football, winning only 14 games while posting 50 losses in their previous 4 seasons (1990–1993).

"In the 34 years that the team had existed, they had never sold out the season," Kraft said, "so we went around and made 70 speeches in 90 days."

The grassroots approach to spreading excitement about the Patriots worked, and before the start of his first season as the new owner, the team announced that the regular season was a complete sellout. It was the first time the franchise had ever sold out all of their home games before the start of the season. Since then, every game has been a sellout and there is a 50,000-person season ticket waiting list.

"We were local people, and fans identified with us and supported us," Kraft said. "They have ever since."

Parcells took the Patriots to the Super Bowl in 1996 (they lost), before leaving the team for the interdivision rival New York Jets. After three seasons of diminishing returns under head coach Pete Carroll, Kraft brought in Bill Belichick. Belichick is analytical and doesn't have the monster ego that comes with many NFL coaches. By any measure, it's a partnership that works.

"We knew we had to put a quality product on the field and make people feel a sense of pride in the Patriots' brand," Kraft said. "What fans wanted was a team that could play in the post-season. We went to the Super Bowl in 1996 in our third year of ownership and won a championship game at home. It was a terrific thrill."

While Belichick and his staff were busy building a team, Kraft set out to build a new stadium. The old stadium was out of date and had only 34 suites, hardly the kind of NFL venue that could compete with the new stadiums being built at that time by other teams around the country. More importantly, despite the fact that Kraft owned the stadium and controlled the parking and concessions, those revenues barely serviced his debt.

"I realized that, if we didn't have a stadium worthy of NFL competition, we wouldn't be able to stay in the league and compete in the league," Kraft said.

He built a privately financed $350 million palace, selling its naming rights to Gillette. Gillette Stadium has 87 suites, more than twice the number in the old stadium. The stadium also has over 6,000 club seats and two 60,000-square-foot Fidelity Investment Clubhouses that are utilized by premium seat members year-round for corporate or social functions. For all that, Kraft rakes in almost $50 million a year in earnings or $236 million in revenue (according to Forbes estimates). It's also important to note that Gillette Stadium is one of the few NFL stadiums that are privately owned and the only one built completely with private money.

"We decided to bite the bullet and take the risk ourselves," said Kraft. "That put us in control of our own destiny and allowed us to be able to compete with anyone."

And while the Patriots were one of the teams that helped cobble together the March 2006 collective bargaining agreement (CBA) and revenue-sharing agreement, the deal would not appear to be in the best interest of the Patriots, a high-revenue team.

"In some ways, it would have been better for the Patriots if there were no deal," Kraft said. "But we understood that the owners who came before us always put the league first. And we feel strongly that the strength of the NFL is that every team should be able to compete."

And while the labor peace that came with the 2006 agreement is welcome, like any good businessperson, Kraft said you always have to plan for the bad days.

"You always have to run a business for the tough times," he said. "We knew that when we were looking at the prospect of financing the construction of a new stadium, if we didn't have a labor agreement, we would have difficulty competing with the teams that had new stadiums and high revenues."

And one day the tough times will arrive. Kraft said, "It could have happened this time, and we were preparing for that," in case there wasn't a labor settlement. "But we've always felt that New England was a great market. If we gave people a great venue, in the end it's about allowing us to compete."

So much so that in the past Kraft contributed his own money to meet the salary cap and make the team competitive.

"Now with the new stadium, the revenue model supports that," he said. "It was a huge risk—$350 million of debt. But we believed."

And for all the success that Kraft has had in and out of the NFL, he still sees himself as merely a custodian of the Patriots. "Our family is very privileged," he said. "If you do a good job running the team, you can have a good impact philanthropically in the community. But I have always viewed the Patriots as a community asset."

Kraft also offered one last bit of advice: Have fun.

"This is the most fun business in the world," Kraft said. "No one should buy a team and run it to make money. There are other ways to make money. The bottom line in the NFL is wins and losses. Make decisions and do everything you can to make your team win. The P&L [profit and loss] will come along. That's the difference in this business: You're generating all your efforts to put your team in the best possible position to win."

DAN SNYDER AND THE WASHINGTON REDSKINS

Which brings us to Mr. Snyder, perhaps the most reviled owner in the NFL. His accomplishments were more than adequately detailed in Chapter 8, so I'll be brief here. In 2005, Snyder moved to take over Six Flags, Inc., the theme park operator. In Securities and Exchange Commission (SEC) filings associated with that bid, Snyder revealed that, since taking over the Redskins in 1999, he has increased sponsorship revenue from $4 million to $48 million. Snyder was able to boost those revenues through a number of canny marketing maneuvers. He sold the stadium's concession equipment to an independent distribution company and earned the proceeds to reduce the franchise's debt, even as he unloaded responsibility for maintaining or running the equipment. In addition, the filing noted, "Mr. Snyder, through his venue pricing management, has created a special events business line at FedEx Field Stadium, generating over $2 million of earnings from a single venue. Since his acquisition of the Redskins in 1999, he has transformed the franchise into the most valuable franchise in U.S. sports (according to *Forbes* magazine) at over $1.1 billion, increasing annual revenues from $162 million to $300 million."

That is indeed impressive. As noted in a previous chapter, the SEC filing also highlighted the dramatic financial success of the "tap and go" payment system instituted by Snyder for all concessions at FedEx Field. The system is simple: Season ticket holders give the Redskins a credit card number in exchange for a Redskins-branded debit card. Instead of paying with cash or credit card, "tap and go" customers go to a special line, order their food and beverages, and merely pass their debit card over a scanner.

"I love it," said Randy Williams, Jr., a Redskins season ticket holder. "It's so quick and easy. Before, I didn't like to go to the concession stand during the game because I was afraid I'd miss some of the action, even with TVs at the stand. Now, tap and go is so quick and easy to use that you can go get food and be back in your seat without missing a play."

The system is just one example of how the Washington Redskins cater to their customers like no other team. It's also a perfect demonstration of the business acumen Snyder brings to his role as an NFL team owner.

"Dan Snyder has received a lot of criticism," said Atlanta Falcon's owner Arthur Blank. "I will tell you this, though. In terms of marketing and promotions, he has done a fabulous job in extending and building the Redskins brand. While some people may find him personally abrasive, I can't imagine there's an owner in the league that doesn't appreciate what he's done with that team."

ARTHUR BLANK AND THE ATLANTA FALCONS

Arthur Blank's done quite a bit for the Falcons. Blank—cofounder of Home Depot—has successfully transformed Atlanta's Georgia Dome, adding numerous upscale amenities, including the exclusive Falcon's Owners Club.

"When I first came into the NFL, Bob Kraft told me that people would say this is 'a different business.' But his advice to me was to use the same business principles that were successful for me when I was at Home Depot and apply them here.

"He was absolutely right," Blank said. "The general business principles are almost the same. This is a customer service–driven business that's dependent upon the quality of associates within the building, finance, etc. It all drives the quality of decisions and results."

As for Bob Kraft, a key component of Blank's business philosophy has been to focus on hiring the very best people. "Some people are not just right for the job I have for them now," Blank said, "but have the capacity to grow with the business. At Home Depot, as the organization grew, we didn't want to have to replace people who couldn't meet the changing demands."

Another key to Blank's business success has been listening to his customers. That was a lesson he learned at Home Depot, which first opened its doors in 1979. "We weren't doing very well," Blank said. "We lost half of our start-up money in the first nine months. We could have sat back and said this is what the market needs, the customers don't understand it, they'll figure it out."

Instead, Blank and his partners accepted what the market was telling them and adjusted their business model to satisfy customer demands. "What ultimately led to our success," said Blank, "was the fact that we kept asking our customers—time and again—what we did right and what we did wrong."

Blank found out that much of the customer feedback had to do with Home Depot's service, hours, and a variety of other factors. "We kept changing the model—not our values and principles," Blank said. "That's an important distinction and what ultimately made Home Depot succeed."

So when he came to the Atlanta Falcons, he followed the same model. "We inherited a franchise that had the second-lowest stadium utilization in the league," Blank said. "In 40 years, the Falcons had never had a waiting list for tickets."

Blank went to work. The Owners Club and other stadium amenities would come later. First Blank had to reprice the tickets. When he arrived in 2001, there were typically 20,000 empty seats at every game.

"We found that there was no price differentiation in the tickets," said Dick Sullivan, the Falcons executive vice president in charge of sales and marketing and one of Blank's old hands from Home Depot. "We asked how much tickets cost in the last row of the stadium and how much they cost on the 50-yard line, and the answer was the same."

It may sound counterintuitive, but raising the price on something actually raises its perceived value. And that's what the Falcons did; by making the lower-level seats more expensive, they made them seem more desirable. At the same time, the team worked to improve the on-field product. As a result, the overall value and demand for Falcons tickets went up. Today, the Falcons are one of the hottest tickets in the NFL and have a 40,000-person season ticket waiting list.

Another complaint from fans was about parking, which was almost nonexistent. So the team began buying up lots around the stadium that could be used on game days. And for those lots that it couldn't buy, the franchise worked out leasing arrangements for the football season. Today, fans have access to 20,000 parking spaces, 10,000 more are in the works, and some lots are reserved specifically for tailgating.

The Falcons also worked closely with MARTA, Atlanta's rapid transit system, to figure out how to move fans more efficiently and increase ridership. And the team created Falcons Landing, a tailgate-style experience that features live music, food, and games (much like Jerry Jones' Corral outside Texas Stadium). The team also revamped its Web site, making it one of the most popular in the NFL among fans and fantasy players.

The net result? Under Arthur Blank's leadership, the team has posted double-digit gains in compound annual growth. And there are plans to make the Georgia Dome a year-round facility, possibly with a Lambeau Field–style atrium featuring restaurants, museums, and retail space. There's even talk of a Falcons hotel at the Georgia Dome.

How did Blank do it?

"A lot of people say much of our success is tied to [star quarterback] Michael Vick, and it is," Blanks said. "But before we signed Michael Vick, we sold out the entire building, and we did it by asking the fans in the community why they didn't come to games."

That's important, Blank said, because he knew that the fans that were coming to the games were diehard and would come no matter what. "We spoke to the other 4.5 million people in the market who weren't coming to our games."

What he found is that the fans wanted to feel as though they were part of the team, that they had an ownership stake. "They wanted an organization that had an attachment to the community," Blank said. "I think that's a great part of the organization of this league and team," he added. "It is understanding that this club is really owned, if you will, by this community. It's a community asset. They don't make player and coaching decisions, but we need to understand that they are the real stakeholders here. If they don't feel like that, then they're not going to turn on the TV, fill the Georgia Dome every week, and we won't be able to sell the sponsorships."

Indeed, they're all tied together, Blank said. "The NFL has a game, but it has a brand and business, too."

And in today's NFL, you have to sell not just a game but an experience, an experience and emotional connection that NFL teams are increasingly trying to extend beyond the 16 weeks of the season. And with that strategy, Blank was a perfect fit for today's NFL. "At Home Depot, we would tell our associates that this business is not about selling a hammer, it's about building a relationship with the customer," Blank said. "Yes, you have to sell products, but the relationship is more important."

Blank also understands that the NFL is not only competing against other entertainment venues and options but has to appeal to a very diverse audience to succeed. "On Sundays, everyone has things to do, whether you're worth a billion dollars or two dollars," he said. "We're asking our fans to give us six hours. That's a big block of their time. They're giving us much more than the value of the ticket. We have to give them back an experience that reflects and honors the amount of time they're giving us.

"I think the responsibility is on us to create a value, win or lose, that they feel like they've had a good day," he said. "You do that by creating a good atmosphere, making the experience better. It doesn't just happen because you win games. We don't take that attitude, because we can't assume we're going to win all our games, go to the playoffs every year. We have to build that loyalty."

And best of all, Blank said, the NFL is full of smart creative people who are trying to do exactly that every week of the season.

"When I would see something good in a Lowe's store, I would never call my counterpart at Lowe's and ask how they're doing this, how is it working so well?" Blank said with a chuckle. "But in the NFL, I have 31 other partners to talk to about what works and what doesn't. If you understand the notion of best practices and keep your ego in check, you can learn from all of them to understand why they're successful."

BOB MCNAIR AND THAT OTHER TEXAS TEAM

"O-4 Crying Out Loud"

That was the headline in the *Houston Chronicle* the day after the Houston Texans lost to the Tennessee Titans, 34–20, to post the worst record (0–4) in the league in 2005. If many were grumbling that the Houston Texans were among the worst-performing teams in the league during the 2005 season, few would question the team's business success as an NFL franchise. And most of the credit for that success goes to the entrepreneurial spirit of Bob McNair, the man who owns the team.

In a matter of just a few years, the former energy industry entrepreneur and his management team brought an NFL expansion franchise to Houston and convinced local politicians and voters to get behind the new team and one of the most expensive sports stadiums in the country. Today, the Houston Texans, in spite of their poor performance on the field, are at the top of the league in terms of revenue and continue to draw sellout crowds week after week. Making this all the more unlikely is the fact that Bob Mc-Nair is one of the most down-to-earth, honest, likable guys in a league where the egos of the players are dwarfed only by those of some owners.

"I worked my tail off for more than 20 years and then was suddenly declared 'an overnight success,'" McNair said, with a hearty and genuine laugh.

Indeed, it wasn't always happy times for this North Carolina native. McNair grew up in a mostly poor family in Forest City, a tiny community of about 7,500 in the foothills of the Carolina Blue Ridge, about halfway between Charlotte and Asheville.

"I'd sometimes hitchhike to town and was often picked up by these moon shiners," McNair recalled in an October 2005 interview. "They'd have a load of hooch in the back seat and say, 'Hey kid, sit on those boxes,' hoping police wouldn't be inclined to look inside if they were pulled over."

He went to public school, then to the University of South Carolina. Eager to make something of himself, he started out working in sales, selling an advertising program to soft drink bottlers. Then in 1959, he got into what was then an industry in its infancy, leasing cars. "The biggest challenge was the fact that most people didn't know what it was," McNair said. "Back then, people didn't lease cars; they bought 'em."

Over the following years, McNair struggled to grow his business of leasing cars, trucks, and heavy equipment. In the process, he learned much about finance as he combated the economic perils of late-1970s stagflation and deregulation. Eventually, he sold the business and spent the next four years paying down his accumulated debt.

In the meantime, he got into long-distance telephone service and electrical power cogeneration, a process that generates electrical and thermal power at the same time. It was through the cogeneration business, Cogen Technologies, that McNair started working with and befriended an entrepreneurial guy at General Electric by the name of Jack Welch.

In the wake of the 1970s energy crisis, Congress passed a number of initiatives to encourage conservation, including tax incentives for cogeneration. Armed with a mandate from Congress, McNair's cogeneration plants began cranking out cheap electricity. To help him run his plants most efficiently, McNair relied heavily on General Electric. He used GE financing, engineering expertise, and equipment to build his plants. He hired GE engineers as consultants. All of this resulted in several billion dollars of business between Cogen Technologies and GE.

"When I first met Jack Welch and we got to know each other, he asked me what my goals were," McNair recalled. "I told him I wanted my company to have a market value of $1 billion and employ 50 people."

That may sound like a small number of employees for a $1 billion company, but McNair understood the benefits of outsourcing long before it made the cover of *Business Week* or became Lou Dobb's nightly whipping boy. By the time McNair cashed out of Cogen Technologies in 1999, it was the largest privately held cogeneration company in the world with 1,400 megawatts of aggregate capacity. Moreover, he had his 50 employees and net worth of $1.5 billion, 50 percent above the goal he'd set for himself.

He also had started to think about a sports franchise.

He initially looked at an NHL franchise, but that didn't work out. The NFL talked with him about possibly purchasing the Miami Dolphins after Joe Robbie died.

"I considered it," McNair said, "but it wasn't in Houston."

He also looked at taking over a partnership seeking an NFL franchise in St. Louis, but, again, it wasn't in Houston. Having been in Houston almost 40 years, McNair and his wife, Janice, now truly call it home.

Being so well connected in the community, he understood the citywide devastation of losing the Houston Oilers. Perhaps more importantly, he saw it as a civic obligation to step forward and bring the NFL back to Houston. "I had the finances, the political capital, and the time," he said. "I really thought I was in the best position in the community to bring an expansion franchise here."

But before he even started lobbying the NFL for a franchise, he realized he needed to get Houston on his side. "When the Oilers were here, they were 'Bud Adams' team, not Houston's team," McNair said. "Any new team needed to be 'our team,' not 'my team.'"

The first step was to overcome strong community opposition to building a new stadium. Many people looked at the Astrodome or Rice Stadium and said, "What's wrong with them?" McNair's first task was to explain to the community the economics of modern NFL stadiums, which, as we've seen in previous chapters, call for upscale club level seats, suites, and private clubs to enhance local revenue. So McNair hired an engineering firm to figure out how much it would cost to upgrade the Astrodome or Rice Stadium.

"They told us that it would cost as much to renovate either of those stadiums as it would to build a new one," McNair said. Once he explained this to the fans and the business community, he started to gain support for a new franchise and a new stadium.

McNair also proposed an innovative partnership. Instead of building a standalone NFL stadium that would be used only eight or ten days a year, he convinced Harris County and the Houston Livestock Show and Rodeo to build a multiuse complex. The rodeo alone draws more than two million spectators a year over a three-week period. The complex could also be used for conventions and trade shows.

With the fans on his side and his sterling reputation in Houston's business and social circles, McNair convinced the community to adopt his plan. Harris County agreed to increase hotel and rental car taxes to pay for most of the stadium, and Reliant Energy paid $300 million for 30 years' naming rights for Reliant Park, which includes Reliant Stadium, Reliant Astrodome, Reliant Hall, Reliant Center, and Reliant Arena.

When Houston was formally awarded an expansion franchise in 1992, McNair had already done a lot of the preliminary legwork. He'd spent $10 million of his own money on development costs and stadium design. Because he already had the design plans in hand and the NFL had put the city on a tight schedule to get the franchise up and running in a state-of-the-art stadium, McNair had a leg up.

"With a project like this, everyone wants to dip their oar in the water, if you know what I mean," McNair said in his folksy Carolina way. "Because we planned ahead, we had the [stadium] design before we had the franchise."

That allowed McNair to put his personal stamp on the new stadium. He wanted it to be family friendly. That's important to McNair, who went on to tell a story about taking his family to a University of Texas game, where people were drunk in the stands, acting out, and using foul language. McNair thought that one guy sitting near him and his wife was going to hit his girlfriend.

"And if he hit her, I'd have to hit him," McNair said.

So Bob McNair made it clear from the first game that there would be no tolerance for such behavior in Reliant Stadium. "We don't put up with obscene language, drunks."

Indeed, walking through the stadium before the October 9, 2005, game against the Tennessee Titans (the team that used to be the Houston Oilers), the scoreboards and other electronic billboards often displayed customer service messages. One told fans to alert ushers to any unruly behavior; another encouraged fans to contact the Texans with any suggestions on how to improve customer service.

As for the suites and club level, McNair said that he understood from the very beginning that they had to be special. Not just because that's the standard for today's NFL stadium, but because of the heavy debt he has to service for the team and the stadium. McNair paid $700 million for the expansion franchise, in addition to his share of the stadium costs. While the taxpayers picked up the majority of the cost, McNair came up with $75 million from the sale of personal seat licenses and $25 million from the team; he also pays $8 million a year in rent and day-of-game expenses.

"They had to generate a lot of money," McNair said of the club seats and suites.

To guarantee that the premium seating would produce the necessary revenue, he applied the core business principle of nearly every successful NFL franchise owner—hire the best people. For instance, the Texans hired Walt Disney Company to train their service personnel.

"If a fan's only personal interaction with the team on game day is the parking lot attendant and the usher, then we want them to be the best," McNair said.

And it shows. The hosts and hostesses on the club and suite levels are all dressed in khaki slacks, white shirts, and red blazers. Everyone greets you with "Hello," "Good morning," and "How are you today?" The bartenders on the club level also dress uniformly, wearing white shirts, dark vests, ties, and slacks. In addition to being well dressed, they're also well groomed. No nose piercings or visible tattoos here.

And he changed a long-standing Houston Oilers policy that prohibited tailgating. "The Oilers didn't allow tailgating at the Astrodome, and that angered a lot of people," McNair said. While changing that policy may not seem like a major move, it is. That's because tailgating truly "enhances the fan experience," one of the NFL's most oft-stated industry buzz phrases. Tailgating helps to transform what could be "just a game" into an event around which many people plan four or five months of their year. Tailgating is now an integral activity at Reliant Stadium.

For those who don't want to do their own cooking, there's the Budweiser Plaza, a pregame party area that features live music and food and can accommodate up to 5,000 fans. McNair also insisted that the team have a band. "Bob very much believed that a marching band was one of the things that differentiated football from other sports," said Jamey Rootes, president of business operations for the Texans.

Along the way, McNair had become one of the most familiar faces in Houston's business and philanthropic community. He has been on the boards of Rice University, Houston Grand Opera, the Free Enterprise Institute, and the Federal Reserve Banks of Dallas and Houston. He's enshrined in the Texas Business Hall of Fame and has received the Antidefamation League's Torch of Liberty Award, among many other honors.

So what are the primary lessons he learned on his road to unassailable success?

One of the most important is the idea that a business needs to be properly capitalized. "When I first started out, I thought that if you were smart and worked hard you'd succeed," McNair said. "That's not true. You also need capital."

He also learned to focus on character. "Just because someone's smart doesn't necessarily mean they'll be a good team player," said McNair, who admitted that over the years, he has hired some people who came up short on character.

"I learned—sometimes the hard way—that you can pretty much guarantee that, if someone's not doing the right things in their personal life, they're not going to do the right things in their business dealings," he said. "Knowing what I know now, I would never hire people like that. Eventually, they're a liability."

If McNair were to sum up all these experiences into one core business philosophy, it would be this: never look to make money, but add value. "If you add value, the money will follow," McNair said.

PAT BOWLEN SEES THE NFL LOOKING IN NEW DIRECTIONS

Pat Bowlen of the Denver Broncos, one of the owners with the longest tenure in the league, sits on the NFL's all-important television committee and fully understands the important balance between shared and nonshared revenues. Indeed, he was one of the owners who had a hand in reaching the March 2006 CBA and revenue-sharing agreement. But ask Bowlen what the key is to the Broncos success and, like many of the smarter owners around the league, he'll echo the words of Bob Kraft and Arthur Blank by telling you it's all about hiring the right people.

"I've always put a premium on talent," he said in a September 2005 interview. "Coaches, players, staff. The most important thing you can do, I think, is get the best people. Don't look at the bottom line."

But he also understands that in today's NFL revenue climate, it helps if you have a good stadium. "It's really the most important thing for a football operation," Bowlen said. "When I started in the league, it was all about football. Now it's a completely different business."

Having been in the league for more than 20 years, Bowlen clearly understands the economics and operations of today's stadiums. "In some ways, the stadium boom has created a disparity for some teams," he said. "It has continued since then, and nearly every team in the league has either built or is building a new stadium. It's key if you're going to generate the kind of local revenues you need today."

Although Bowlen understands the economic power of stadium revenues, he was a firm believer in the NFL's broad revenue-sharing model long before the 2006 CBA and revenue negotiations. When asked about the renewal of the NFL Trust, the agreement by which the league shares revenues, he said, "I think it's very important to the ongoing business of the NFL that we have a Trust, share those revenues—at least a large part of those revenues—and it doesn't matter whether they're the Denver Broncos or Indianapolis Colts. Everybody's sharing in that revenue, and I think that that's the underpinning of our league and very important."

He also believes that, as much as free agency controls player movement, it's still about choosing the right people. "In many ways, I think free agency has been around long enough now that we've all made our big mistakes and signed the wrong people and, in some cases, signed the right people," Bowlen said. "It's all about getting the right guys and making them work within the salary cap."

But Bowlen was also one of the calmer owners going into the 2006 CBA and revenue-sharing negotiations. He didn't think the NFL economic model was fundamentally broken. "I think you can always overreact to slight changes, and I think there are always going to be slight changes in the NFL business model," he said. "Furthermore, I don't think they're going to significantly impact small-market teams."

As Bowlen considers the future, he seems to feel assured of the stability of the NFL and its willingness to continue to support teams such as the Broncos. "We're basically a small-market team," he adds, "and I feel fairly comfortable that we'll do all right."

SOME FINAL THOUGHTS ON THE GREATEST SHOW ON EARTH

And what about my own perspective on the future of the NFL? After having delved into the history of the league and spending months interviewing the owners, managers, players, and fans, I've come to a few conclusions of my own about the NFL's past—and about what lies ahead.

The NFL was catapulted to its current success through smart management and marketing. By leveraging the newly emerging technology of television, the league was able to supplant Major League Baseball as the American spectator sport of choice. Landing a prime-time broadcasting slot propelled the league further into the consciousness of America's cultural mainstream—even to the point that citizens around the country are more than willing to subsidize the business of football in their own cities. Today, the NFL continues to develop innovative ways to exploit new media and thus further build its worldwide presence and credibility—and its profits. Through it all, the NFL has managed to capitalize on the individual successes of its teams to enrich the league as a whole. Given its astounding history of savvy management, I have little reason to doubt that even more profitability and competitive success await the NFL in the future.

I hope that you, too, are coming away from this story with a better understanding of the league, how much it struggled in the early years, and how it ultimately succeeded. And I hope you've enjoyed hearing from just a few of the millions of people who are touched by the NFL—from commissioner Paul Tagliabue and vice president of consumer apparel Susan Rothman, team owners like Bob Kraft and Arthur Blank, Minneapolis economist Art Rolnick, the Cleveland Browns' Bone Lady, and even the ultimate sports bar regular, Randy Williams, Sr., of Morton, Illinois. I learned a lot about the world of professional football through my conversations with these folks, and I hope I've passed their ideas, enthusiasm, and insights along to you.

I also hope I've been able to help you understand the sometimes convoluted and confusing economic workings of the league and the importance of the issues that owners and players grappled with as they went into the 2006 labor and revenue-sharing negotiations. And, ultimately, I hope this book has helped you understand why the NFL works. The owners who locked themselves into that ballroom in Dallas for two days in March 2006 certainly did. Like the players, owners, and commissioners who came before them, these members of the NFL understood that, by sharing more money with the players and by dispersing just a bit more of the larger-market teams' riches to the smaller-market teams, the league will continue to build, as the saying goes, "a rising tide that lifts all boats." After all, that's what makes the NFL the most successful sports league in history.

Resources

- "Super Tube: The Rise of Television Sports," by Ron Powers (1984, Coward-McCann)
- "Field of Schemes: How the Great Stadium Swindle Turns Public Money into Private Profit," by Joanna Cagan and Neil deMause (1998, Common Courage Press)
- "Sports, Jobs, and Taxes: The Economic Impact of Sports Teams and Stadiums," edited by Roger G. Noll and Andrew Zimbalist (1997, Brookings)
- "Major League Losers: The Real Cost of Sports and Who's Paying for It," by Mark S. Rosentraub (1999, Basic Books)
- "Fifty Years of College Football," by Bob Boyles and Paul Guido (2005, Sideline Communications)
- 2005 NFL Record and Fact Book
- NFL.com press release archives
- Pro Football Hall of Fame Archives, Canton, Ohio
- "What Are the Benefits of Hosting a Major League Sports Franchise," by John Rappaport and Chad Wilkerson (First Quarter 2001, Kansas City Federal Reserve Bank Economic Review)
- "What Is the Economic Impact of Hosting the Super Bowl?" by Craig Depken and Dennis Wilson (January 2003, Texas Labor Market Review)
- "Super Bowl or Super (Hyper)Bole? Assessing the Economic Impact of America's Premier Sports Event," by Robert A. Baade and Victor A. Matheson (2003, Williams College)

- "Mega-Sports Events as Municipal Investments," by Phil Porter, economist, University of South Florida (1999, Sports Economics)
- "Professional Sports Facilities, Franchises, and Urban Economic Development," by Dennis Coates and Brad R. Humphreys (2003, University of Maryland, Baltimore County)
- "The Effects of Professional Sports on Earnings and Employment in the Retail and Services Sector of U.S. Cities," by Dennis Coates and Brad R. Humphreys (2003, Regional Science and Urban Economics)
- "The Impact of Stadiums and Professional Sports on Metropolitan Area Development," by Robert A. Baade and Richard F. Dye, (1990, Growth and Change)
- "Economic Impact of the New Orleans Saints," by Timothy P. Ryan (2002, University of New Orleans)
- "The Employment Effect of Teams and Sports Facilities," by Robert A. Baade and Allen R. Sanderson (1999, "Sports, Jobs, and Taxes")
- "The Business of Sports and Small-Market Viability: The Green Bay Packers and the Milwaukee Brewers," by Kevin M. Bahr (2001, Central Wisconsin Economic Research Bureau)
- "NFL Players to Attend Wharton Executive Education Program," press release, Wharton School, University of Pennsylvania
- "Beer 21, Dot-Coms 0," by Jerry Della Femina, Jan. 21, 2001, The Wall Street Journal
- Red Zone Inc. SEC Filing Re: Six Flags Inc. (NYSE: PKS), August 2005
- Forbes Magazine's 2005 NFL Franchise Value Rankings
- Green Bay Packers 2005 Annual Report
- Author interviews and research

Index

Atlanta Falcons Owner's Club, 168-69
Atrium, 200-201
Attendance, 58-59
Away team sales, 5

A

AAFC. *See* All-American Football Conference
ABC, 68, 73, 77, 79, 84-88, 90, 92-93, 162, 209
    Sports crew, 91-92
Academy Awards, 84, 158
Accenture, 160
Accorsi, Ernie, 75, 76, 208
Adams, Bud, 71, 236
Adams, Sam, 24, 42
Adidas, 128
Admiral Television, 67
Advertisers, 154-57
Advertising
    super stars, 159-60
AFL-NFL merger, 77, 85
Airborne, 162
Akron Pros, 51
Al's Bar Fantasy Football League, 117
Alexander, Shaun, 43
Ali, Muhammed, 164
All-American Football Conference (AAFC),
    57, 58-60, 72
Allen, Bruce, 216
All in the Family, 86
Alltell Stadium, 143
America Online, 108, 110, 116, 118, 157
America's Game, 59
American Express, 155
American Football Conference, 77, 85
    (2005) championship, 49
    championship game, xii
    South, 22
American Football League, 1, 71, 72- 73
American Professional Football Association
    (APFA), 51
American Society of Real Estate Counselors,
    187, 191
Anderson, Mike, 24
Anheuser-Busch, 125, 157
Antidefamation League, Torch of Liberty
    Award, 239
APFA. *See* American Professional Football
    Association
Apple Macintosh, 155, 159
Apprentice, The, 69
Arizona Cardinals, 13, 213
Arledge, Roone, 87-88, 90-91
Armed Forces Radio, 104
Arrington, LaVar, 50
Associated Press, 45, 64
    2004 NFL Most Valuable Player, 22
Astrodome, 236
AT&T, 77
Atam, Seda, 195
Atlanta Braves, 111
Atlanta Falcons, 8, 13
    CBA 2006, 215
    merchandising, 140
    Monday Night Football, 84
    new media, markets, 102
    playing in NFL, 40
    stadium, 192, 201
    Super Bowl, 165-66
    super team, 221, 229-33

B

Baade, Robert A., 144, 149-52, 174
Bahr, Kevin M., 200, 206-7, 213
Bally's, 125
Baltimore Colts, 17, 60, 63
    Monday Night Football, 88
    stadium, 179
    Super Bowl, 155
    television, 65-66, 68-70, 73-74, 76
Baltimore Ravens, 13, 133, 174, 181, 215
Banaian, King, 154, 175, 181, 185
Bank of America Stadium, 7, 196
Banner, Joe, 32-33, 211
Barry Sanders Rule, 41
Base salary, 27
Bass Ale, 197
Belichick, Bill, 225-26
Bell, Bert, xii, 17, 48, 53-64, 68, 69-70, 211, 219
Bell, John Cromwell, 53
Best Buy, xvi
Bettis, Jerome, xi, xii
Bidwill, Charlie, 53, 58
Bigelow, Chris, 189
Bigelow Companies, 189
Bird, Larry, 156
Birk, Matt, 35-36, 37-40, 42
Biro, Ladd, 113-14, 119
Black Bear, Peter, 52
Blank, Arthur, 84, 165, 215, 221, 229-233, 240,
    242
Bledsoe, Drew, 40, 42
Blue Zone tickets, 198
Bodenheimer, George, 81
Bolton, Lisa, 163
Bone Lady, 83-84, 242
Bonuses, 16, 34-35
Bostic, Jeff, 121
Boston Braves, 53
Boston Lobsters, 224
Boston Patriots, 12
Boston Red Sox, 11, 175, 205
Boston University, Walter Brown Arena, 224
Bowlen, Pat, 19, 215, 221, 240-41
Brady, Tom, 40
Brand
    awareness, 120
    building, xvi
    birth of, 123-24
    NFL look, 128-30
    official, 124-25
Brees, Drew, 44
Brown, Mike, 11, 182, 210, 213, 215-218
Brown, Paul, 11, 57, 59, 182, 210
Brunell, Mark, 23
Buckner, Brentson, 24
Bud Light, 156
Budweiser, 159, 165
Budweiser Plaza, 239
Buffalo All-Americans, 52
Buffalo Bills, 1, 10-11, 22, 24, 42, 44
    CBA 2006, 211, 212-14, 215-16
    merchandising, 133
    new media, markets, 107-8
Bugel, Joe, 121
Bugs Bunny, 156

Burstein, Melvin L., 187
Business managers, 43-46
Business of Pro Football 2002, The, 179

C

Cable, 98-99, 105-6
Cagan, Joanna, 182, 184
Canon, 194
Canton Bulldogs, 51, 52
Capanomics 101, 133
Carling Beer, 71
Carlisle Indian Industrial School, 51
Carolina Panthers, 7, 13, 24, 33, 49, 61, 132, 197-98, 204
Carr, Joe, 57
Carroll, Pete, 225
Carson, Johnny, 87
Carvey, Dana, 156
Cass, Dick, 215
Cassel, Dr. Mitchell, 133
Caterpillar Corporation, 104
Catoe, Paul, 139
CBS, xiii, 71, 73, 77-78, 85-88, 90, 92-93, 95-96, 155-56, 163
    contract, 65
    Sportsline, 116
Cell phones, 18
Champion, 128
Champs, 126
Charles, Ray, 157
Cheerleaders, 222-23
Chicago Bears, 6, 17
    even playing field, 51-58
    merchandising, 123
    Monday Night Football, 105
    stadium, 191
    television, 66, 68, 76
Chicago Cardinals, 52, 58
Chicago Tigers, 52
Chicago White Sox, 167
Cialis, 161
Cincinnati Bengals,11, 49-50,106, 182-83, 210, 211, 216-217
Cincinnati Reds, 61
Cleveland Browns, 11, 13, 43
    even playing field, 57, 58-59, 63
    Monday Night Football, 83
    new media, markets, 103-4, 105-106, 108
    stadium, 181, 182, 201-2
    super team, 242-43
    television, 67-68, 70-71, 73
Cleveland Cavaliers, 181, 182
Cleveland Indians, 51, 181, 182
Cleveland Rams, 58
Cleveland Tigers, 52
Club, 201-2
    fees, 168-69
    seating, 191, 192, 198-99
Club-level ticket sales, 5, 6-7
Coates, Dennis, 148-49, 174
Coca-Cola, 9
Cogen Technologies, 235
Cohen, Jerry, 136-37
Collective bargaining agreement (CBA), xv, 2-3, 11, 14-15, 22-23, 203-5
    1993, 26
    2006, 27-29
    past wisdom, 214-15
    settlement disagreements, 216-218
    Tagliabue's legacy, 219-20
Collective TV contract, 74-75

Collins, Kerry, 23, 50
Columbus Panhandles, 52
Concessions, 5, 228-29
Condon, Tom, 30-32, 38
Conference championship, 26
Congressional Research Service study (1996), 181
Connie Mack Stadium, 64
Conzelman, Jimmy, 59
Coopervision, 133
Coors, 124-25
Coppola, Shane, 111
Cowboy Club Golf Course, 223
Credit cards, 161
Crockett, Zack, 24
Culpepper, Duante, 40
Curly's, 199, 200
Curtis, Todd, 104-5
Customer-based business, 230-33
Customer service messages, 237
CVS, 222

D

D'Ermilio, Lou, 61, 162
Dallas Cowboys, xiv, 2, 8, 14
    CBA 2006, 209, 210, 215
    Merchandising, 128, 137
    Monday Night Football, 95
    super team, 221, 222-23
Dallas Texans, 60
Dancer Fitzgerald Sample, 68
Darnall, Debra, 83-84
Davis, Al, xv, 216
Davis, Kathleen, 146
Davis, Stephen, 24
Dawg Pound, 106
Day, Chiat, 159
Dayton Triangles, 51
Dead cap space, 29
Decator Staleys, 51
Defined gross revenues (DGR), 26
Della Femina, Jerry, 159, 161, 164
deMause, Neil, 182, 183-84, 189
Denver Broncos, xii, 7, 14, 19, 24
    CBA 2006, 208, 215
    even playing field, 49
    Monday Night Football, 88-90, 95
    Stadium, 198-99
    super team, 221, 239-41
Depken, Craig, 144-46, 151-52, 153-154
Desperate Housewives, 162
Detroit Heralds, 52
Detroit Lions, 36-37, 62-63, 103, 171-172
Detroit Rescue Mission, 153
Detroit Tigers, 171
DGR. *See* Defined gross revenues
Dick's, 126
Diet Pepsi, 156
DiGisi, Robert, 97, 158
Digital video recorder (DVR), 112
DirecTV, 78, 97, 98, 112, 113-14, 119
Disney (Walt) Company, 95-96, 238
Ditka, Mike, 123
Divisional playoffs, 27
Dolman, J.P., 98
Dot-coms, 163-64
Double dipping, 9
Downwind, Xavier, 52
Dr. Pepper, 161
Drafted player contracts, 29

Dream Seats, 192, 195
Duluth Kelleys, 53
DuMont television network, 68-69
Dungy, Tony, 132

E

EA Sports, 134, 135
Economic model, 203-5
    Major League Baseball lessons, 205-8
Einolf, Karl W., 207
Eisen, Rick, 135
Eisner Communications, 162
"Employment Effect of Teams and Sports
    Facilities, The," 174
Entrepreneurial owners, 8-10
Epidemic.com, 164
ESPN, 81, 93, 96, 97
Estadio Azteca stadium, 18

F

Falcons Landing, 231
Falstaff Beer, 68
Fang, Red, 52
Fantasy football, 18, 101-2, 112-14
    coming of age, 115-19
    friendly NFL, 114-15
Fantasy players, 100
Favre, Brett, 32, 40, 105
FedEx Field, 6-7, 9, 190, 192-96, 228
Field of Schemes, 170, 182, 183-84, 189
Fiesta Bowl, 38
Fifty Years of College Football, 91
Filchock, Frank, 60
First-round draft choices, 25
Floating cap, 30
Forbes, 226, 228
    2005 NFL franchise rankings, 189
Ford, 98
Forte, Chet, 90, 92
Fortune 500, xvi, 42
Fox, 78, 97, 98, 159-60, 162, 209
Fox Sports, 61
Franchise, xvi-xvii
    efficiency, 207
    rankings, 189
Franchise player, 25, 31
    exclusive, 25-26
Frankford Yellowjackets, 54
Free agency, 2, 15, 22
    knots in, 25-26
    market, 34
FUBU, 126
Future direction, 210, 211, 241-43

G

G3 fund, 184, 191
Gambling, 60-61
Ganis, Marc, 109
Gateway, 98
Gateway Economic Development
    Corporation, 184
Gatorade, 135
General Electric, 235
General Motors, xvi
Georgia Dome, 8, 168, 192, 201-2, 229, 231-32
Giambi, Jason, 45-46
Giants Stadium, 196
Gibbs, Joe, 23, 109
Gibson, Derrick, 23

Gillette Stadium, 226
Glass, Fred, 180
GoDaddy.com, 163
Google, 109
Grant, Bud, 123
Gray Zone tickets, 198
Green, Ahman, 44
Green Bay Packers, xiii, 6-8, 12, 13
    CBA 2006, 205-6, 208, 210, 215-216
    even playing field, 53, 54, 57, 61
    merchandising, 103, 104-5, 107, 132
    Monday Night Football, 95
    playing in NFL, 29, 32, 33, 35, 36, 43-44
    stadium, 199-200
    Super Bowl, 140, 141
    television, 67-68, 73, 75, 76
Greenspan, Alan, 7
Greg Norman brand, 197
Grim, Allan K., 68, 74
Grimm, Russ, 121
Gross Designated Revenues, 214
Groza, Lou, 67
Grunewald, Rob, 186
Guaranteed money, 15-16, 35-43
    costs of, 40-43
    who gets, 38-41
Guido, Paul, 91
Guinness, 165
Gund Arena, 182, 183, 184
Guyon, Joe, 51-52

H

Halas, George, 53, 55, 58, 60-61, 76
Hamilton, Bruce, 174
Hammond Pros, 51
Hapes, Merle, 60
Harlan, Bob, 208, 215-216
Harris County (Texas), 236-37
Harris Poll (2004), 84
Harrison, Marvin, 22
Harvard Business School, 43-44
Harwell, Ernie, 171
Haynes, Michael, 45
HBO, 222
Healey, Ed, 52
Heisman Trophy, 39
Henderson, Harold, 213-14
Hilfiger, Tommy, 126
Hilton, Barron, 71
"Hit of the Game," 222
Hogs, 121-22
Holiday Inn, 146, 162
Hologram program, 136
Home Depot, xvi, 84, 165, 215, 230-31, 232
Home ticket sales, 5
Hoosier Dome, 179-80
Hornung, Paul, 61
Host committee events, 164
Houston Livestock Show and Rodeo, 8, 201,
    236-37
Houston Oilers, 236, 237, 238-39
Houston Texans, xv, xvii, 8, 12, 103, 130
    CBA 2006, 212-13
    stadium, 201
    super team, 221, 233-40
Hubert's (restaurant), 167, 171-72, 175, 184, 186
Hughes, Howard, 88
Hughes Sports Network, 88
Huizenga, Wayne, xiv, 137
Humphrey (Hubert H.) Metrodome, 167

Humphreys, Brad, 174
Hunt, H.L, 71
Hunt, Lamar, 71-73

I

Indianapolis Colts, xi, xii, 4
    CBA 2006, 213, 216
    even playing field, 49
    merchandising, 130, 132-33
    new media, markets, 103-4
    playing in NFL, 21, 30-32, 40-41
    stadium, 179-80
    super team, 241
    television, 67
International markets, 17-19
Internet, 18, 107-110
Invesco Field, 7, 190, 198
Iorio, Pam, 139
Ironhorse Marketing, 158
Irsay, Jim, 4, 215

J

J. Peterman Company, 126
Jackson, Janet, 156, 163
Jackson, Joe, 30
Jacksonville Jaguars, 205, 219
Jacksonville Regional Chamber of Commerce, 147
Jacobs Field, 182, 183, 184
Jacoby, Joe, 121
James, Edgerrin, 43
Jansen, Jon, 23
JCPenney, 158
Joel, Billy, 155
Johnson, Woody, 215, 216
Jones, Dhani, 44
Jones, Jerry, xiv, 8-9, 11
    CBA 2006, 203, 209, 210, 215-16, 217
    merchandising, 127-28, 137
    super team of, 221, 222-23, 231
Jones, John, 141
Jordan, Michael, 156
Journal of Advertising Research, 154

K

Kagan World Media, 79, 179-80
Kahn, Peter, 74
Kansas City Chiefs, 21, 89
Kansas City Federal Reserve Bank *Economic Review*, 173-78
Karras, Alex, 61
Kayser, Dennis, 124
Kelly, Jim, 22
Kemp, Jack, 7, 134
Kennedys, 75
Kent, Larry, 124
Kentucky Derby, 155
Ketchman, Vic, 219
Kintner, Bob, 68
Klegon, Steve, 8, 200
Kmart, 126
Kraft, Jonathan, 215
Kraft, Robert, 12, 19, 215, 221
Kremer, Ken, 38

L

Labor
    issues, 14-15
    model, xv

Lackner, Al, 33-35, 41-43
Lambeau, Earl "Curly", 53, 199
Lambeau Field, 6-8, 199-200, 210
Landry, Tom, 124
Lange, Lisa, 163
Lass, Nick, 52
LastMinuteTravel.com, 164
Layden, Elmer, 56
Leaf, Ryan, 41-42
League economics, 11
LeBas, James, 149
Levitra, 161, 222
Lewis, Marvin, 49
Lifeminders.com, 164
Likely to be earned (LTBE) bonus, 34, 35
Lingo, Walter, 51-52
Locally generated revenues, 210
Locker Room, 197
Lodish, Len, 158, 159, 163
Loge seats, 194-95
Logo, 126-28
Lombardi, Vince, 74
Lone Wolf, Ted, 52
Los Angeles Dodgers, 66
Los Angeles Dons, 57
Los Angeles Rams, 21, 58, 64, 66-67, 70, 122-123, 178-79
Losman, J.P., 42
Louis Harris sports survey, xiii
Lovitz, Jon, 155
Lowe's, 233
LTBE. *See* Likely to be earned bonus
Lurie, Jeff, 220

M

Macanudo Cigar Bar, 193
MacCambridge, Mike, 59
MacPhail, Bill, 85-86
Madden, John, 134
Madden 2006, 18, 194
Madison, Sam, 24
Major League Baseball, 11-12, 65-66, 69, 72, 79-81, 84, 94, 97, 110-11, 205-6
Major League Losers, 170, 179
Mallot, Jerry, 147
Manning, Eli, 16, 30, 37, 38
Manning, Peyton, xi-xii, 21-22, 30-32, 37-41, 49, 67, 132, 141
Mara, Jack, 3, 74
Mara, John, xiv, 3, 215, 219-20
Mara, Tim, 52, 55, 76
Mara, Wellington, xiv, 3-4, 74, 76, 209, 219-20
Marino, Dan, 22
Marketing, 17-19
Marshall, George Preston, 52, 58, 60
MARTA, 231
Maryland Stadium Authority, 174
Maryland Sunny Day Fund, 181
Matheson, Victor, 149-52
May, Mark, 121, 132
McCarthy, Brian, 61
McCartney, Paul, 156
McClintock, Dana, 163
McCombs, Red, 184-85
McDowell, Rider, 162
McIntosh, Damion, 24
McKay, Rich, 140
McNabb, Donovan, 40
McNair, Bob, xvii, 12, 203, 212, 221, 233-40

McNair, Steve, 21
Meatloaf, 113-14
Media, 17-19
Media Metrix, 108
Medical coverage, postcareer, 47
Merchandising, 17-19, 121-22
    birth of NFL brand, 123-24
    licensing fees, 4
    logo wars, 126-27
    marketplace clean up, 135-37
    NFL takes control, 122-23
    rewards of, 137-38
    video games, other, 133-35
    women's apparel, 130-33
Met Life, 160-61
Miami Dolphins, xiv, 24, 122, 137, 235-36
Michael, Larry, 109-10
Microsoft, 98
Midway Games, Inc., 134
Mile High Stadium, 198
Miller Brewing, 124, 165
Miller Lite, 222
Milloy, Lawyer, 42
Milwaukee Brewers, 204
Minimum team salary (MTS), 28
Minimum threshold, 31
Minneapolis Federal Reserve Bank, 167
Minnesota Early Learning Fund, 186
Minnesota Twins, 167, 170-71
Minnesota Vikings, 15
    merchandising, 123, 134
    new media, markets, 103, 104-5, 117
    playing for NFL, 34-37, 39-40
    stadium, 167, 170-71, 184-85, 186-87
Misak, Marge, 183
Mitchell, Andrea, 7
Mitchell, Freddie, 44
Mitchell, George, 205
Modell, Art, 181
Monday Night Football, xiii, 18, 61, 81, 83-85,
    132, 134
    ESPN move, 95-96
    NFL network, 99-100
    playing to camera, 90-92
    prime time tv, 85-88
    ratings, 92-93, 94
    revenue stream, 96-99
    star qualities of, 88-90
Money survey, 190-91
Montreal Expos, 206
Morgan Stanley Dean Witter, 98
Moss, Randy, 15
Moulds, Eric, 42
Mount Saint Mary's College, 207
MoveOn.org, 162-63
MTS. *See* Minimum team salary
Multiyear contracts, 25-26, 29
Muncie Flyers, 52
Murphy, Tom, 112
Mutscheller, Jim, 69

N

Namath, Joe, 61, 88, 155
NASCAR, 84, 97, 194
Nasdaq, 164
National Basketball Association, 47, 80, 84, 97
National Economic Research Associates, Inc., 96
National Football Conference, 85
    (2005) championship, 49
National Football League (NFL)

101 Workshops for Women, 84
2005 playoffs, xi
    architect of, 53-56
    Blitz, 134-35
    building, 57-58
    Business Ventures, 127
    Championship games, 68-69
    Combine, 109
    Crazy Lenses, 134
    Europe, 106-7, 156
    financial ground, 62-64
    formation of, 50-51
    Offensive Player of the Year, 22
    Network, 99-100, 106-7
    Properties, 123, 126-27, 132-33
    success formula, xii-xv
    Sunday Ticket games, 112, 113-114, 118
    Total Access interview, 135
    Trust, 135
National Football League Players Association,
    xiv, 2, 3, 14, 15-16
    CBA 2006 negotiations, 210-12
    merchandising, 124, 133-34
    playing in NFL, 29, 32-33, 37, 43, 44
    at work, 46-48
National Hockey League, 48, 79, 80, 124, 205
Nautica, 125
NBC, xiii, 70, 78, 85-86, 90, 93, 82, 95-96, 155
NCAA
    basketball tournament, 96-97, 157
    Football 6, 135
Nelson, Lindsay, 91
Network negotiations, 75-79
New Castle, 197
New England Patriots, 10, 19, 40
    CBA 2006, 207-8, 215
    super team, 221, 223-28
New York Giants, xii-xiii, xiv, 3, 4, 17
    CBA 2006, 207-8, 209, 215
    even playing field, 52-53, 54-55, 60, 63
    merchandising, 123-24, 129, 133-134
    playing for, 30, 38
    stadium, 196
    television and, 65, 68-69, 70, 73-75
New York Jets, 15
    CBA 2006, 215-16
    merchandising, 123-24
    Monday Night Football and, 85, 88
    stadium, 196
    Super Bowl, 155
    Super team, 226
New York Mets, 111
New York Yankees, 11-12, 45, 57, 205, 206-7
NFL Experience, The, 164
NFL Record and Fact Book, 58
NFL.com, 108, 115
NFLPA. *See* National Football League Players
    Association
Nike, 128
NLTBE. *See* Not likely to be earned bonus
Noll, Roger, 149, 178
North American Sports Network (NASN), 106
Not likely to be earned (NLTBE) bonus, 34
Novak, Steve, 185

O

O'Malley, Walter, 66
Oakland Raiders, xv, 23-24, 37, 50, 216
Official Beer of the NFL Players, 124
Official products, 165

Official sponsors, 165
Off-season workouts, 27
Oil companies, 61
Olympics, 146
    (1996), 125
    summer, 97
Online, 107-8
Oorang Indians, 51-52
Orange Bowl, 88
Orange Zone tickets, 198
Orthwein, James Busch, 225
OurBeginning.com, 164
Outsourcing, 235
Owens, Terrell, 15, 35
Owner's Seats, 195-96
Owners Club, 196, 229, 230

P

Palmer, Carson, 49
Panther's Den, 197
Parcells, Bill, 123, 222, 225
Paris, Sidney, 60
Parking, 5
Payless Sports Memorabilia, 136-37
Pay-per-view, 99
PDAs, 18
Penn, Schoen, and Berland, 157
Pension payments, 47
People for the Ethical Treatment of Animals
    (PETA), 163
Peppers, Julius, 132
Pepsi, 9, 136, 154, 156, 222
Pepsi Punt, Pass and Kick competition, 84
Performance bonus, 21
Personal seat license, 6
PGA Tour, 97
Philadelphia Eagles, 15-16, 17, 32-33, 35, 44
    CBA 2006, 207, 209, 219
    even playing field, 53, 54, 56, 58, 59, 64
    merchandising, 131-32, 133-34
    Monday Night Football, 67
    Super Bowl, 161-62
Philips Seafood, 193
Pittsburgh Steelers, xi, xii, xiv, xv, 11-12, 19
    CBA 2006, 209, 215, 218
    even playing field, 49, 50, 53, 64
    merchandising, 130
    Monday Night Football, 108-9
    playing, 33
    television, 71, 73, 74, 94
Pitt Stadium, 91
Plaut, Tamara, 148-49
Players, training as business managers, 43-46
Players, Inc., 124-25
Playing field, 49-50
Playing time, 47
Playoff bonuses, 141
Polo, 125
Porter, Phil, 142-43, 144, 147, 149
Postseason payments, 27
Pottsville Maroons, 53
Powers, Ron, 68-69, 90, 91, 92
Practice squad salary, 27
Premium food, alcohol, 169
Premium seating licenses, 5-8, 9, 12, 169, 189-
    96, 238
Preseason compensation, 27
Press Box, 197
Prime time, 85-88
Pro Bowl, 24, 36, 50, 106, 111

    (2005), 137
    MVP, 22
Pro Football Hall of Fame, 45, 51-52, 61
"Proposal for Achieving High Returns in Early
    Childhood Development, A," 186
Providence Steam Rollers, 52
Pryce, Trevor, 23
Puma, 128
Putzier, Jeb, 24

R

Racine Cardinals, 51
Racine Tornadoes, 53
Rappaport, John, 173
Raymond James Stadium, 191
RCA Dome, 179
Reality TV, 68-69
Red Bull bars, 193
Red Zone, 197
    channel, 111, 119
    Morton's bar, 194
    tickets, 198
Redner, Joe, 139
Reebok, 128, 129-30, 132
Reed, Andre, 22
Reeves, Dan, 57
Reliant Energy, 237
Reliant Stadium, 8, 148, 201, 237, 239
Restricted free agent, 26
Revenues, 1-2
    player's piece of, 214-15
    shared. See Shared revenues
    stadium dispute, 5-14
Revenue stream, 5-6, 114
Reverse-order draft, xiii, 2-3, 17
Reynolds, Jamal, 29
Rice Stadium, 236
Richardson, Jerry, 215
Richey, Charles R., 121, 122
Rickey, Branch, 72
Robbie, Joe, 236
Rochester Jeffersons, 52
Rock and Roll Hall of Fame, 181
Rock Island Independents, 53
Rodriguez, Alex, 47-48
Roethlisberger, Ben, xi
Rolnick, Art, 145, 167-68, 170-73, 184-88, 242
Rookie
    contract, 30-31
    phenoms, 39
Rookie Symposium, 45
Rooney, Art, 52, 56, 62
Rooney, Dan, 11-12, 215, 218
Rooneys, xiv, 74
Rootes, Jamey, 239
Rose, Pete, 61
Rosenbloom, Carroll, 60, 74-75
Rosenhaus, Drew, 36
Rosentraub, Mark, 145, 178-79
Rothman, Susan, 85, 126, 130-33, 134, 242
Roy Rogers, Inc., 123
Royalty, xv
Rozelle, Alvin Ray "Pete," xii-xiii, 3, 17
    CBA 2006 and, 219
    Merchandising, 122-23
    Monday Night Football, 83, 85, 88, 92-93,
        97, 99
    NFL players, 61, 64
    Super Bowl, 155
    television, 70-79

S

Salary
    minimum, 27
    one star's, 30-32
Salary cap, xii, 4, 14, 22, 27-35, 206, 215-216
    cutting players and, 23-24
    stretching, 28-30
Salary floors, 28
Sam Adams, 165
San Diego Chargers, 41-42, 43, 136, 167
San Diego Wigs & Beauty Supply, 136
Sanderson, Allen R., 140, 174
San Francisco 49ers, 38, 56, 60, 140, 218
Satellite radio, 110-12
Satellite television, 103-7
Saturday Night Live, 155
Schedules, 61-62
Scherick, Ed, 68
Schmittlein, 158
Schramm, Ted, 70
Scott, Ridley, 155
Season stats, 209
Seattle Seahawks, xii, 18-19, 33, 49, 94
Securities Exchange Commission, 228
Selig, Bud, 208
Sellouts, 225-26
Shared revenue, 11, 14, 18-19
    CBA 2006, 203, 205-8, 212
    model, xiii, xiv-xv, xvi, 5-6, 10-11, 22
    television and, 71, 75
Sharper, Darren, 29, 37
Sherer, Susan, 152
Sigmon, Reid, 201
Signing bonus, 21, 29, 32
Sirius Satellite Radio, 110-11, 114
Six Flags, Inc., 9, 228
Smaller markets, 10-12, 196-202
Smart, Rod, 24
Smith, Alex, 16, 30
Smith, Alex, 38-39
Smith, Red, 64
Snyder, Daniel, xiv-xv, xvii, 2, 3-4, 7, 9, 11, 34
    CBA 2006, 203, 208, 216-17
    merchandising, 137
    new media, markets, 109
    stadium, 192
    super teams, 221, 228-29
Soldier Field, 6, 192
Soprano, Tony, 222
Sponsorship revenue sharing, 125
Sporting Goods Manufacturers Association, 132
Sports Broadcasting bill, 75
Sports Illustrated, 157
Sports, Jobs and Taxes, 178
SportsLine, 108
Sports Management Research Institute, 146
Sports Network, 71
Sprint, 112
St. Cloud State University, 154, 175, 181, 185
St. Louis Browns, 66, 72
St. Louis Cardinals, 178
St. Louis Rams, 133, 140, 178-79
Stadiums, 166, 167-69, 210, 222
    affect on schools, 183-86
    Baltimore Ravens, 181
    building, xiii, 13-14, 213, 226
    Cleveland, Cincinnati, 182-83
    costs, benefits, 172-74

Indianapolis Colts, 178-80
    jobs, revenue creation by, 174-77
    net benefits of, 177-78
    revenue generation, 210
    revenues dispute, 5-14
    small-markets, 196-202
    sports economists on, 172-73
    taxpayer-funded, 169-72
    taxpayers and, 177-78
    unshared revenues and, 187-92, 199-202
    Washington Redskins, 192-96
Starke, George, 121
Starter, 128
State Island Stapletons, 52
Staubach, Roger, 222
Stella Artois, 197
Stichweh, Rollie, 91
Stone, Ron, 23
"Story of Professional Football, The," 62
Strayhorn, Carole Keeton, 147
Suite 87, 197-98
Suite-level ticket sales, 5, 7
Suites, 202
Sullivan family, 225
Sullivan, Billy, 72
Sullivan, Dick, 165-66, 200, 231
Sunday Ticket package, 77
Super Bowl, 6, 11, 17, 136-37, 139-43, 223
    ads that don't work, 161-64
    advertisers and, 154-64
    broadcast rights, 93-94
    business of, 164-66
    creating of, 155
    Detroit's experience, 151-54
    economic numbers, 142-45, 146-49
    employment impact, 151-52
    indirect benefits, 145-46
    loser, 27
    new media, markets, 107
    questioning NFL numbers, 150-51
    ratings, 94
    sellout, xiii
    television, 81, 84, 98
    winner, 27
Super Bowl (1996), 225-26
Super Bowl (2005), 98
Super Bowl I, 155
Super Bowl III, 88, 155
Super Bowl XV, 208
Super Bowl XVI, 94
Super Bowl, XVII, 121
Super Bowl XXIII, 155
Super Bowl XXXIII, 142-43, 150, 151
Super Bowl XXXVIII, 143, 148-49
Super Bowl XXXIX, 143, 147, 223
Super Bowl XL, xii, xv, xvi, 19, 32-33, 137-38, 152-54, 156, 215
"Super Bowl or Super (Hyper)Bole?," 150
Super Hogs, Inc., 122
Super teams, 220, 221
    Atlanta Falcons, 229-33
    Dallas Cowboys, 222-23
    Denver Broncos, 240-41
    Houston Texans, 233-40
    New England Patriots, 223-28
    Washington Redskins, 228-29
Super Tube: The Rise of Television Sports, 68, 90, 91
Syracuse University, 99

T

Tagliabue, Paul, xiv, 29, 38, 45-47
    CBA 2006, 214-15, 219-20
    merchandising, 135-37
    Monday Night Football, 99
    stadiums, 190-91
    super teams, 242
Tailgate Club, 193-94, 195, 196
Tailgating, 239
Tampa Bay Buccaneers, 14, 33, 191, 208, 216
Tampa Bay Convention and Visitors Center,
    139
Tap and go payment system, 228-29
Target, 159
Tax increment financing, 186
Tax revenues, 175-77
Taylor, Lawrence, 134
Team
    apparel, 123
    performance incentives, 35
    store merchandise sales, 5
Television, 17, 18-19, 63, 65-66
    first experiments with, 66-67
    game format, xvi
    ratings, 92-94, 95
    rights, 5, 71, 73, 74-75
    Rozelle and, 70-71
    sports broadcasting, 69-70
    today, 79-81
Tennessee Titans, 21, 134, 233, 237
Texas Business Hall of Fame, 239
Texas Labor Market Review, 144
Texas Stadium, 8, 9
Theisman, Joe, 134
Thomas, Randy, 23
Thompson, Robert, 99
Thorpe, Jim, 51-52
3M, 187
Thunder, Baptiste, 51
Tiger Woods Golf, 194
TNT's Sports Bar and Grill, 103, 104
Tomkovick, Charles, 142, 154-55, 157, 160-161,
    165-66
Topping, Dan, 57
Touchdown Club, 7, 194-95, 196
Transition players, 25-26
Travel days, 27
Two for the Money, 61

U

Unitas, Johnny, 17, 70
United Airlines, 7
United Club, 198
University of Pennsylvania, 43, 97
    Franklin Field, 64
Unrestricted free agent, 26
Unshared revenue, xiv, 5, 199-202, 205
Upshaw, Gene, 4, 15, 29, 37-38, 46, 209, 211-212
Upton, Frances, 54

V

Van Buren, Steve, 59
Van Meek, Sandra, 84
Vanderjagt, Mike, xi
Veeck, Bill, 66, 72
Veterans, 39

Viacom, 108
Vick, Michael, 40, 232
Video arcade, 193
Vincent, Troy, 44
Visa, xvi, 155
Volcker, Paul, 207

W

Walker, Denard, 23
Walker, Javon, 35, 36-37
Wal-Mart, 126, 129, 132
Walton, Joe, 123
Washington Redskins, xiv-xv, xvii, 2, 6-7, 9, 17
    CBA 2006, 208, 210, 213, 217-18
    even playing field, 50-51, 52-53, 55-56,
        57, 58, 59-60
    merchandising, 121-22, 133-34, 137
    new media, markets, 102, 104-5, 109-10
    playing for, 22-23, 34
    stadium, 192-96
    as super team, 221, 228-29
Washington, Ted, 23
WBKB, 68
WebMD, 164
Welch, Jack, 235
Westwood One Radio, 109, 111
Wharton Executive Education, 44
Wharton School, 43, 44, 97-98
Wharton Sports Business Initiative, 44
"What Is the Economic Impact of Hosting a
    Super Bowl," 144
White, Eddie, 132
White, Michael, 184
Wild card, 27
    division winner, 27
Wild Card Super Bowl XL, 50
Wilf, Zygi, 184-85
Wilkerson, Chad, 173
Will, George, 207
Williams, Gregg, 109
Wilson, Dennis, 144-46, 151-52, 153-54
Wilson, Ralph, 1, 3, 6, 11, 213-217
Winslow II, Kellen, 43
Wireless broadcasts, 110-12
WLS (Chicago), 68
Women fans, 83-85
Wood, Robert D., 92
Workout bonus, 28
World Series, 47

X-Y

XM Satellite Radio, 110-11, 193
Yahoo!, 116, 117, 118
Yankee Stadium, 65, 72
Yelkur, Rama, 154-55, 161, 166
YES Network, 206
York, John, 218
Young, Steve, 22

Z

Zenith TransOceanic Radio, 104
Zimbalist, Andrew, 178
Zimmer, Dennis, 181
Zona, Chuck, 126-30, 133, 136
Zucker, Dave, 135